Exploring Teachers' Thinking

Edited by
James Calderhead

CASSELL

Cassell Educational Limited:
Artillery House
Artillery Row
London SW1P 1RT

British Library Cataloguing in Publication Data

Calderhead, James
  Exploring teachers' thinking
  1. Educational psychology
  I. Title
  371.1'02'019   LB1051

ISBN 0–304–31383–1

Phototypeset by Activity Ltd., Salisbury, Wiltshire.
Printed and bound in Great Britain by Mackays of Chatham Ltd

Last digit is print no: 9 8 7 6 5 4 3 2 1

CONTENTS

List of Contributors   vi

Introduction
    James Calderhead   1

1   Individual, Institutional, and Cultural Influences on the Development of Teachers' Craft Knowledge
    Kenneth M. Zeichner, B. Robert Tabachnick and Kathleen Densmore   21

2   Ways of Thinking About Students and Classrooms by More and Less Experienced Teachers
    David C. Berliner   60

3   Teacher Planning
    Christopher M. Clark and Robert J. Yinger   84

4   '150 Different Ways' of Knowing: Representations of Knowledge in Teaching
    Suzanne M. Wilson, Lee S. Shulman and Anna E. Richert   104

5   Teachers' Assessments of Students' Difficulties and Progress in Understanding in the Classroom
    Rainer Bromme   125

6   Teachers' Knowledge Structures and Comprehension Processes
    Kathy Carter and Walter Doyle   147

7   'Knots' in Teachers' Thinking
    Angelika C. Wagner   161

8   Curriculum Change and the Classroom Order
    John K. Olson and Sandra Eaton   179

9   Teacher Responses to Curriculum Policy: Beyond the 'Delivery' Metaphor
    John Reynolds and Murray Saunders   195

NAME INDEX   215

SUBJECT INDEX   217

LIST OF CONTRIBUTORS

David C. Berliner is Professor of Educational Psychology in the College of Education, University of Arizona, USA.

Rainer Bromme is Senior Research Fellow at the Institut für Didaktik der Mathematik of the University of Bielefeld, West Germany.

James Calderhead is Lecturer in the Department of Educational Research, University of Lancaster, England.

Kathy Carter is Assistant Professor in the College of Education, University of Arizona, USA.

Christopher M. Clark is Professor of Education at Michigan State University, USA.

Kathleen Densmore is an educational consultant, and formerly Assistant Professor of Educational Studies, at the University of Utah, Salt Lake City, USA.

Walter Doyle is Professor in the College of Education, University of Arizona, USA.

Sandra Eaton is Communications Instructor at the Grande Prairie Regional College, University of Alberta, and was formerly a research officer at Queen's University, Kingston, Ontario, Canada.

John K. Olson is Professor of Education at Queen's University, Kingston, Ontario, Canada.

John Reynolds is Lecturer in the Department of Educational Research, University of Lancaster, England.

Anna E. Richert is Co-ordinator of Research and Development for the Teacher Education Program at Stanford University, USA.

Murray Saunders is Senior Research Fellow in the Department of Educational Research, University of Lancaster, England.

Lee S. Shulman is Professor of Education, and affiliated Professor of Psychology, at Stanford University, USA.

B. Robert Tabachnick is Professor in the Department of Curriculum and Instruction, University of Wisconsin-Madison, USA.

Angelika C. Wagner is Professor of Education at the University of Hamburg, West Germany.

Suzanne M. Wilson is Director of the Teacher Assessment Project at Stanford University, USA.

Robert J. Yinger is Associate Professor of Education at the University of Cincinnati, USA.

Kenneth M. Zeichner is Professor in the Department of Curriculum and Instruction, University of Wisconsin-Madison, USA.

INTRODUCTION

James Calderhead

TEACHING AS A 'PROFESSIONAL', THINKING ACTIVITY

Teaching is a complex process that can be conceptualized in many different ways, using alternative models, metaphors, and analogies. One metaphor that acknowledges the intentional, problem-solving aspects of teachers' work is that of teaching as a reflective, thinking activity. This highlights several key characteristics of teaching, which it shares with many other professions such as medicine, law, architecture, and business management. Consequently, the metaphor sometimes used is that of teaching as a professional activity.

According to this metaphor, teachers possess a body of specialized knowledge acquired through training and experience. Just as a doctor possesses formal knowledge of physiology and pathology, together with knowledge acquired from experience about patient behaviour and the various combinations of symptoms that complicate the task of diagnosis, the teacher has acquired knowledge about the curriculum, teaching methods, subject matter, and child behaviour together with a wealth of other particular information resulting from the experience of working with children in numerous contexts and with different materials. Like other professionals, teachers rely upon this specialist knowledge in their daily work.

A second feature of professional activity is its goal-orientation in relation to its clients. Doctors aim to cure their patients, lawyers to defend their clients' interests, architects to design buildings to suit their clients' specifications. In the case of teaching, who the clients are is a little more ambiguous. Although much of teachers' activity may be oriented to the education of their pupils, teachers, more so than many professionals, are also answerable to a number of others, including parents, administrators, advisers, inspectors, employers, curriculum development agencies, and politicians. These individuals and agencies are in a position to influence what teachers do by controlling the provision of materials, curriculum guidelines, and finance, and in the determination of the conditions in which teachers work. Influence might also be exerted at an

1

ideological level through the perpetuation of beliefs and ideologies of good classroom practice. There is rarely any consensus amongst teachers' 'clients' on what constitutes good practice. Consequently, teachers may encounter numerous expectations that can be in conflict with each other as well as with the beliefs of the individual teacher. The fact that there are no agreed goals for education and that there are several interest groups to whom teachers may be held accountable frequently results in teachers facing impossible dilemmas. Consider, for instance, the recently popular call for the school curriculum to return to basics, coupled with the equally popular demand for schools to prepare children for a future, technological, computer-oriented society!

A third characteristic is that the problems professionals deal with are often complex and ambiguous, and professionals must use their expert knowledge to analyse and interpret them, making judgements and decisions as they formulate a course of action intended to benefit their client. A lawyer, for instance, may encounter an array of conflicting evidence. His knowledge of court practice and legal procedures, together with his previous experience and knowledge of how witnesses and juries typically respond, enable him to make judgements about the plausibility of alternative lines of argument. He can decide how best to interpret and present evidence in court, which features to emphasize, and when doubts might be implied about particular points of fact in order to advantage his client.

Teachers similarly face complex situations, and this is well described by Doyle (1986), who concisely summarizes the complexity of the classroom environment in terms of six general features: *multidimensionality, simultaneity, immediacy, unpredictability, publicness,* and *history*. Classrooms are busy places. At any one time, teachers may be faced with a series of incidents to manage – keeping the class working quietly, for instance, while dealing with one particular child's difficulty and postponing or redirecting other children's requests for attention. As a result, teachers face competing demands and often teaching decisions are a compromise amongst multiple costs and benefits. For instance, in deciding whether to carry out a particular activity in groups or as a class, teachers may have to weigh the possible benefits of encouraging co-operative work and perhaps obtaining greater pupil satisfaction against the costs of more preparation, the risk of some pupils opting out and leaving others to do the work, and greater demands on teachers' managerial skill. The pace of teachers' activity in the classroom is necessarily rapid. There is also considerable uncertainty in the teachers' world. Unexpected events, distractions, and interruptions threaten to disturb the normal course of events. Lessons don't always go as expected, and children's behaviour is sometimes unpredictable. In addition, teachers, for much of the day, are 'on show'. How they are seen to cope with classroom situations can influence how individual children assess them and respond to them in the future. And as a result of classroom interactions, particularly those occurring early in the year when teachers and children are first assessing one another, each class develops its own norms, its own ethos, its own work routines, a history that shapes the ways in which it copes and responds to activities in the present.

Given this complexity of the teaching task, it indeed seems a remarkable achievement that teaching and learning occur in schools at all! The school and classroom environment clearly place a heavy burden upon teachers to attend to and process a large volume of information and continually to juggle conflicting and competing interests. Teachers must use their knowledge to cope with a constant barrage of complex situations.

In classroom teaching, however, there is often little opportunity to reflect upon problems and to bring one's knowledge to bear upon their analysis and interpretation. Teachers must often respond immediately and intuitively. This relates to a fourth feature of professional activity, namely that it involves skilful action that is adapted to its context. Through repeated practice and reflection on practice, the professional has developed various specialist and 'knowledgeable' skills. The lawyer, for instance, in his skills of cross-examination demonstrates a keen knowledge of human behaviour in a legal context and an awareness of alternative questioning strategies. The professionals' expert knowledge enables them to perceive significant features in their work and to respond to them. Teachers have extensive knowledge about children, curriculum materials, classroom organization, and approaches to instruction. This knowledge helps them to establish relationships with children, manage the class, decide how best to teach a particular topic, maintain the children's interest, and instruct them. The teachers' knowledge and experience of children in a classroom context has in some cases become so closely tied to their practice that they can, for instance, notice a child's inattention to work and readily identify it as a case of difficulty in understanding, attention-seeking, lack of interest, tiredness, or the child having an 'off-day', and respond appropriately, when to an outsider the same cues may be lost in a blur of classroom noise and activity.

Schon (1983) uses the term 'knowledge-in-action' to describe the knowledge that is embedded in the skilled action of the professional. Knowledge-in-action is sometimes inaccessible directly to professionals themselves in the sense that, although they can demonstrate it in action, they are unable to disclose it verbally. Just as expert tennis players, who might return shots in rapid succession, intuitively calculated to land at particular spots on the court, often cannot describe the knowledge of ball control that lies in their skilled performance, neither can lawyers in their skills of cross-examination or teachers in their classroom interaction.

In some respects, teaching sits uneasily alongside professions such as medicine, law, or architecture. Teachers, for instance, are not self-employed, in most countries they do not have their own professional association that oversees a standard of good practice, nor generally do they have high status or high salaries. In fact, it has sometimes been suggested that teachers' claims to professionalism can be viewed as status-enhancing strategies or as a means of defending competence, autonomy, and individualism from outside interference (Hargreaves 1981; Lortie 1975). Nevertheless, in terms of the types of activities in which professionals engage, there seem to be some enlightening similarities, and the metaphor may be a valuable one in helping us to conceptualize and explore further the nature of teachers' practice. Such a metaphor illuminates crucial aspects of teaching by guiding us towards an exploration of the nature of teachers' knowledge and the influences on its formation, how it is applied to the analysis of teaching situations, and how it has come to be embedded in teachers' actions. The object of this book is to draw together research from several perspectives that has begun to undertake this exploration of the professional aspects of teachers' work, and to consider its implications for the improvement of quality in classroom teaching.

THE PRACTICAL CONTRIBUTION OF RESEARCH ON TEACHERS' THINKING

The way in which we conceptualize teaching influences how we attempt to train teachers, or improve or support what teachers do. Often, attempts to improve the quality of teaching are based, implicitly at least, on fairly naive conceptions of teaching processes. The idea that educational innovation can be brought about by presenting teachers with a new list of objectives has been implicit in many curriculum innovations, for instance, yet clearly leaves out of account the real-life planning processes of teachers and how objectives might or might not figure within them. To take another example, there has been concern in Britain recently about the quality of maths teaching in primary schools, and a number of proposals have been suggested to solve the problem, including the recommendation that more maths graduates be recruited into the profession, and that a maths co-ordinator be appointed in each school to construct and advise on the curriculum. Such initiatives, however, presume a simple relationship between acquiring subject matter knowledge and teaching it and the subsequent learning of the pupils. These ideas also fail to acknowledge the complex processes by which teachers' practice is assembled and the difficulties of changing it once it has become established, routine, and adapted to its context. They also underestimate the difficulties of establishing a new role, such as 'curriculum co-ordinator', within the school and of carrying out the tasks this role might require, in a school situation and in addition to normal class teaching. Whatever efforts are made to change and improve classroom processes—whether taking the form of innovations in teachers' professional training, new curriculum initiatives, or policies for improved management of schools—assumptions are made about the nature of classroom practice. An important role of research is to provide more realistic models of teaching that help us conceptualize the nature of this practice more clearly, enabling supportive efforts, including training and policy-making, to be more constructive.

Furthermore, teachers themselves need a language and concepts that realistically represent their classroom practice, and that acknowledge the complexity of their classroom work. Such a language enables them to analyse and discuss teaching issues, and even, on occasions, to defend the integrity of their practice against the many interpretations and accusations that are made by those outside the profession who feel competent to devise their own, often ill-informed, understanding of educational processes. Research on teachers' thinking can help provide teachers with this language.

THE ORIGIN AND DEVELOPMENT OF RESEARCH ON TEACHERS' THINKING

The term 'teachers' thinking' has tended to be used fairly loosely by researchers to refer to various processes such as perception, reflection, problem-solving, the manipulation of ideas, etc. However, the term has come to unite a body of research which, although starting from a variety of different backgrounds and focusing on diverse educational issues, has a common concern with the ways in which knowledge is actively acquired and used by teachers and the circumstances that affect its acquisition and employment. The growth of this research over the past decade can be traced in a number of ways.

In the psychology of education, the early 1970s witnessed a dissatisfaction with essentially behaviourist approaches to the study of teaching. Criticisms were levelled on methodological, theoretical, and ideological grounds. At a methodological level, research instruments such as systematic observation schedules were viewed as narrow and selective in their focus on counting the frequency and sequence of a few discrete categories of teaching behaviour. The frequency with which teachers asked questions or praised pupils seemed to provide only crude statements about the nature of teachers' practice, neglecting for instance the different intentions and the different functions they served in the classroom. The fact that praise could be a routine gesture or an important motivator, or that teacher-directed questions could be a way of structuring pupils' thinking or a way of keeping the class involved in a lesson was left out of account. The growth of interest in cognitive psychology, acknowledging the active, 'meaning-making' of teachers and children, and the development of self-report methods such as protocol analysis and stimulated recall (in which teachers provide commentaries on their thinking while planning or while viewing a videotape of their own teaching), supplied a framework and a methodology to examine previously hidden aspects of teachers' work. In the United States, research in this area was given further impetus by the national review of research on teaching (NIE 1975) whose panel 6 advocated the setting up of a large-scale programme of research on the professional information-processing skills of teachers, following lines of research similar to those already established in the field of medical diagnosis.

Ideologically, viewing teachers as active agents in the development of their own practice, as decision-makers using their specialist knowledge to guide their actions in particular situations, underlined the autonomous, responsible aspects of teachers' work, and provided an appealing rationale for considering teaching as a worthy, complex, demanding profession, especially when contrasted with the previously dominant view of teaching as the mastery of a series of effective teaching behaviours.

At the same time, sociologists of education were becoming increasingly interested in the processes by which societal pressures come to influence classroom processes. Whereas sociologists in education had tended in the past to focus either on the functioning of schools within society (the role of schools in perpetuating the class system, for instance) or on the social processes of the classroom (such as the labelling of deviant children), a new concern emerged with how these two areas of enquiry interconnected. How do societal systems coupled with particular educational ideologies and beliefs influence classroom practice? How are individual teachers' beliefs, commitments and practices shaped and perpetuated? The brief for educational sociologists became much wider, and the mid 1970s brought several experiments with ethnography in an attempt to both illuminate the nature of classroom practice and situate this understanding within a matrix of societal influences and constraints.

During the 1970s, curriculum studies was also acquiring its own identity accompanied by a growth in the volume of empirical research. Despite widespread attempts to develop new curricula and associated materials for use in schools, curriculum development organizations seemed to be having minimal impact on classroom teaching. Several researchers directed their attention to the role of the teacher and the classroom context in the processes of curriculum change, and to examining the nature of the practical activity of teaching. How teachers thought about the curriculum and the various interactions that occurred in the process of implementing a new curriculum became a new focus of attention.

In addition to these evolving concerns in major fields of research, other researchers from the disciplines of philosophy, anthropology, and linguistics also developed interests in teachers' thinking and decision-making and in the verbal reports of teachers about their work. Consequently, the situation in the mid-1980s is that research on teachers' thinking is becoming characterized by considerable diversity in approach.

EXPLORING TEACHERS' THINKING—AN OVERVIEW

Given the alternative approaches to researching teachers' thinking, together with the current lack of knowledge about teaching itself, it seems appropriate that we view research in this area as exploratory. It is exploring new ways of conceptualizing teaching, of understanding issues concerning practice, and of directing us towards particular solutions to educational problems. Different research approaches may be offering us slightly different images of the teaching process, but by looking across these images and through their critical appraisal we may develop new insights into teaching, and discover new solutions to practical problems.

The chapters in this book are loosely structured into three inter-related sections. The first two chapters deal with the nature of teachers' professional knowledge, its growth and influences upon it, the next section contains four chapters concerning the ways in which knowledge is used in the task of teaching, and the final section has three chapters focusing on the role of teachers' thought and knowledge in the processes of educational change.

Zeichner, Tabachnick, and Densmore first of all review different conceptualizations of teachers' 'professional' or 'craft' knowledge, and review research concerning the influences on its development. They indicate how early research describing craft knowledge in terms of consistent belief systems (e.g. progressive/traditional) has been replaced more recently by research that recognizes the complexity and inconsistency of teachers' knowledge, viewing it as an interpretive framework, or series of 'implicit theories' by which teachers attach meaning to their environment and guide their actions within it. Their own research, which adopts a symbolic interactionist approach, uses the notion of 'perspective', defined as the way in which people interpret and define their environment (attach meaning to symbols) and use such interpretations to guide their actions. Using interviews and observations of lessons, they followed a group of student teachers through their year-long professional training and their first year of teaching. One might expect that student teachers' personal values and beliefs, and how they think about teaching, would be changed and modified through professional education and experience in the classroom. Zeichner, Tabachnick, and Densmore, however, challenge this view, suggesting that student teachers' perspectives are elaborated rather than radically changed by professional training. They found that students tended to select from their experiences whatever suited their own particular perspectives. For instance, they describe one student who viewed the task of teaching in terms of making the work interesting for pupils, involving them in active learning, and aiming for the children to become intrinsically motivated to learn. The student persisted with this view even after an extremely difficult teaching placement in which teachers were found to fulfil highly authoritarian roles, dispensing teacher-directed assignments that allowed for no experiment, discussion, or creativity.

The major constraints upon students' teaching appeared to come through the nature of the teachers' work and how the job was defined within the school in which they taught. For instance, whether the school had detailed curriculum plans for teachers to follow or whether it was customary for teachers to plan their own class's work within broad school guidelines presented different constraints and opportunities for the beginning teacher. Zeichner, Tabachnick, and Densmore, however, found that, even when a school had formal policies on classroom practice, teachers were not held rigidly accountable for their implementation, and its teachers generally also perpetuated a number of different informal perspectives on school practice. Schools in fact were generally characterized by various diverse 'cultures'. Hence it was usually possible for a beginning teacher who found him/herself in a school whose official culture and practices differed from their own to obtain support from some members of staff for their own particular beliefs and practices, and as long as they possessed the appropriate 'political skills' they could successfully negotiate their own approach to teaching within the school.

Berliner adopts an alternative approach to identifying the professional expertise of teachers, by examining the differences between novice and expert teachers in the way in which knowledge is held and used. Berliner emphasizes that what distinguishes the expert in any area of human activity is their ability to learn from reflection on experience, and it is as a result of this ˙earning that experts become more discriminating in their perception and more resourceful in their action. Berliner describes a series of simulated teaching tasks carried out with three groups of teachers: a group of experienced teachers who were also judged to be 'expert', a group of novice teachers in their pre-service training course or their first year of teaching, and a group of 'postulants', intending teachers who had high levels of subject matter knowledge but no experience of classroom teaching. The tasks involved such activities as planning a lesson for a class, for which they were given information about the children provided by a previous teacher, together with examples of the children's work and their test performances. Another task involved viewing slides of lessons in progress and describing what was happening. As expected, the greatest differences were found between the experts and the postulants. In planning a lesson, experts were much more selective in their use of information. They attended only to information that had some managerial or instructional significance, such as the size of the class and how it was used to being organized. The experts could also call upon a wealth of typificatory knowledge about children—they knew what children of this age were like and the kinds of difficulties they would commonly experience. The expert teachers also had a repertoire of routines on which they could call to organize the class and get it down to work. The postulants, on the other hand, were more concerned with fitting in with the past teacher's way of working, they memorized the previous teacher's comments on the children, and more readily accepted their validity. Postulants were also very much more dependent on the textbook, identifying where the children had 'left off', whereas the experts were more concerned with identifying what the children knew and understood. The beginning teachers were found to vary in these respects, generally coming somewhere between the experts and the postulants.

Berliner interprets these findings in a cognitive psychological framework of expertise, suggesting that experts have more elaborate *schema* (networks of knowledge for understanding practice), and a repertoire of *scripts* (knowledge that guides routine responses), which have been developed over years of experience and practice. The development of expertise in teaching is normally a time-consuming process (it is estimated, for instance, that the basic skills of classroom management usually require five years to master), but it is intriguing that some teachers learn more quickly and more easily than others. Equally, for some teachers, the adage that 'twenty years' experience is one year repeated nineteen times' is not far off the mark.

Berliner's research emphasizes the importance of the pedagogical knowledge base of teaching, and its significance for competent teaching. There are many implications of such findings for both policy and practice in teacher education. Berliner explores these and considers how the processes of professional learning can be enhanced and supported, examining the potential role of 'pedagogical laboratories'.

The second section of the book is concerned with the ways in which professional knowledge is applied in the day-to-day work of teaching. How do teachers think about their work? How do they use their knowledge to guide their teaching behaviour and to solve particular classroom problems?

Jackson (1968) distinguished two different phases of teaching—the *pre-active*, which occurs before the teacher enters the classroom, and the *interactive* in which the teacher works with the children. Based on his study of American primary school teachers, he suggested that each phase is characterized by a distinctive type of intellectual activity. Before the day starts or after the children have gone home, teachers are reflective about their teaching, and they engage in processes that resemble formal problem-solving. But in face-to-face interaction in the classroom, teachers are more intuitive and spontaneous.

In Chapter 3, Clark and Yinger review research on the pre-active, planning phase of teaching, focusing on its nature, functions and effects. Much of this research has been pursued from a cognitive psychological perspective. It suggests that planning can occur at different levels that are nested within one another—yearly, termly, unit, weekly, and daily, for instance. Teachers may possess different styles of planning, and the act of planning may serve different functions for teachers on different occasions. Basically, however, the process of planning is characterized as a mental rehearsal of ideas and knowledge about pupils, the school, and the curriculum that gradually intermesh, ideas becoming elaborated to form a mental plan or 'image' that acts as a guide to classroom action.

The contribution of this research, in Clark and Yinger's view, is to provide us with ways of thinking about teaching. In particular, they suggest that research on teacher planning has illuminated those aspects of teaching that it has in common with the design professions, such as architecture and town planning. Teachers have to identify, or 'frame', problems. For instance, deciding which topics will be covered in the social studies curriculum this year may involve successive framings and reframings of the problem, as knowledge about the availability of materials, school guidelines, the children, and the timetable is introduced into teachers' thinking. This can be viewed as analogous to the architect who toys with alternative basic designs as he considers the lie of the land, the context of the building, the planning regulations, etc., eventually elaborating his ideas into a finished plan. Teachers, they suggest, have to use their professional knowledge to analyse and solve unique classroom problems, and their skills lie in applying their knowledge in the process of problem formulation, or framing, and mentally experimenting with alternative frames and thinking through an eventual solution. Consequently, Clark and Yinger suggest that teachers' expertise is distinguished not only by knowledge-in-action, but also by their ability to reflect-in-action, using their knowledge to identify and analyse unique situations.

In Chapter 4, Wilson, Shulman and Richert begin to explore these reflective processes with particular emphasis on one aspect of teachers' knowledge that they feel has been neglected in research on teaching, namely knowledge of subject matter. Early attempts to correlate teachers' subject matter knowledge with pupils' learning led to inconsistent findings. However, as Wilson, Shulman and Richert point out, this is probably due to the crudeness of the paper-and-pencil tests used in the studies. Clearly, teachers must have some understanding of the subject matter before being able to teach it, and that knowledge seems likely to influence their classroom practice and their pupils' learning. However, the transference of subject matter knowledge from the mind of the teacher to the mind of the pupil is not a simple, or straightforward process. Consider, for instance, the well-stereotyped examples of the academically well-qualified teacher in the infant classroom who has difficulty getting down to the children's level, or the university professor who does brilliant research but is incomprehensible to his undergraduates.

Wilson, Shulman and Richert follow a group of beginning teachers through their professional training and into their first year of teaching to examine how their subject matter knowledge is translated into classroom practice. They found that, in planning school work, their teachers drew upon different kinds of knowledge about pupils, subject matter, school context, and educational aims to generate a new category of knowledge, which Wilson, Shulman and Richert term 'pedagogical content knowledge'. This refers to knowledge relating to the teaching of particular subject matter, including analogies, explanations, and examples that assist in communicating the subject matter, the aspects of the subject matter that pupils find easy or difficult, and the preconceptions that pupils may bring to the learning situation. They regard this as a special understanding of the subject matter for the purposes of teaching and describe the process by which it is generated as 'pedagogical reasoning'. Based on their research, Wilson, Shulman, and Richert outline an interesting six-stage model of pedagogical reasoning that emphasizes the role of evaluation in teaching, reflecting on classroom experiences, and a series of strategies for transforming subject matter knowledge into content and procedures for future teaching. Central to teachers' acquisition of pedagogical content knowledge is their own critical reflection on practice.

As Wilson, Shulman and Richert point out, one of the major difficulties in communicating subject matter is being able to allow for the prior knowledge, understandings, interests, and experiences of the pupils. This aspect of teachers' work is also taken up in Bromme's chapter on teachers' assessments of students' difficulties and progress in understanding.

Much of the early research on teachers' thinking and decision-making was based on an analogy between teachers' diagnosis and medical diagnosis. Like the doctor who diagnoses a patient's illness and prescribes a particular treatment, it was imagined that teachers diagnose the children's difficulties and state of progress and match appropriate tasks to them. While this may be an appropriate description in a few contexts (e.g. remedial teaching), Bromme suggests that it is a poor analogy for much of teachers' everyday assessment. In his study of the teaching of statistics in German secondary schools, he finds that teachers have an image in mind of the lesson they are about to teach, which includes an awareness of the new knowledge that is to be introduced, and the preconceptions that children might have. Teachers' thoughts during the lesson appear to be more focused on the 'instructional flow' and on implementing the lesson than on the difficulties of individual pupils, but when a pupil's understanding or lack of understanding signals that new knowledge has been understood or that old conceptions are preventing it being understood, these are noted by the teacher. At the end of a lesson, Bromme found that teachers had very poor recall of the achievements or difficulties of individual children, but had excellent recall for those events that had 'strategic' significance. Teachers, in fact, seemed to build up a mental picture of the typical problems, difficulties, and progress of the class, which helped in directing the course of a lesson. Lessons that teachers had tightly structured resulted in more recall of students' difficulties and understandings, as more strategic events occurred. More tightly structured lessons did not, however, lead to greater pupil learning in this study.

Bromme accounts for these processes in terms of the context of classroom instruction. Faced with having to teach a whole class, and given that each child may approach the understanding of new concepts and skills from a different perspective or knowledge base, teachers cannot feasibly monitor the knowledge growth of individual children. Consequently, as a constructive adaptation to this situation, they become vigilant of the crucial signals that indicate whether or not the required understanding is in general being achieved.

Bromme argues that an awareness of the processes that teachers employ in monitoring the progress of the class enables us to make these processes more effective (helping teachers become attuned to typical misconceptions, for instance), rather than encouraging teachers to develop new strategies (such as individual diagnosis and remediation) that may be impossible for them to use effectively on a large scale in the normal classroom.

Chapter 6 also examines how the processes of instruction are frequently constrained in real-life classrooms. Carter and Doyle suggest that teaching consists of two main tasks: achieving social order and managing academic work. They have researched how teachers understand these tasks, modelling teachers' interpretations on the basis of lengthy observations of teachers in action. They point out that managerial and instructional concerns constantly intermesh and that the former often appear to dominate teachers' thinking. They argue that teachers' decisions about the content and nature of classroom work are frequently based upon the logic of classroom management rather than the logic of the content, work being sequenced, for instance, in order to maintain children's interest rather than to enhance concept development.

Managerial concerns are particularly prominent when teachers present activities that the children find complex or difficult or unfamiliar. Such activities are accompanied by a greater threat of disorder and disruption. Carter and Doyle found that, with complex activities, teachers typically responded to this dilemma by renegotiating the work with the children, by breaking it down into simpler units, or by changing the reward system so that it was easier for the children to obtain high marks and appear to do well (e.g. by giving marks for effort or neatness). Teachers also tended to hold on to familiar routines for carrying out class work rather than introduce novel or uncertain procedures.

Although teachers typically strive to attain well-managed, orderly, productive classes, these features may be at the expense of the most useful learning experiences for children. Carter and Doyle suggest that teachers' concern with the managerial aspects of their work might often result in classroom experiences where children are learning to get 'right answers' without developing their understanding of the curriculum. Teachers may avoid situations in which children struggle with meaning, or grapple with challenging issues. Consequently, moves towards a curriculum that is truly demanding of children's intellect may require us to change our conceptions of the teacher's task and to change the criteria by which we commonly assess teachers' work.

The third section of the book concerns research on teachers' thinking and educational change. What happens to teachers' thinking during the process of change that either facilitates or impedes innovation? Each of the three chapters focuses on a different aspect of educational change: the first on impediments to professional development that exist in teachers' own mental processing, the second on the processes that teachers engage in when adapting and integrating an innovation into their classroom practice, and the third on the school processes, and particularly accountability processes, that appear to influence how teachers think about and cope with curriculum development.

As earlier chapters well demonstrate, teachers frequently encounter dilemmas to be resolved in their daily professional lives. This is not surprising given the unpredictable nature of teachers' work and the lack of agreement on the purposes of teaching itself. In addition, schools typically are fairly authoritarian institutions with many rules and expectations (concerning curriculum, behaviour, organization and display of work, etc.) that may conflict with individual teachers' own beliefs. We might therefore expect teachers' thinking to be occasionally prone to confusion. In fact, as Wagner observes, teachers' reports of their thinking are frequently not the tidy, rational accounts of behaviour that research sometimes leads us to believe. Indeed, they are often full of emotions, anxieties, and inconsistencies. In particular, Wagner is interested in the self-imperatives that teachers use to describe their thinking ('I must do ...' or 'I ought not ...'). Wagner suggests that teachers sometimes experience self-imperatives that conflict—for instance, 'I must finish this lesson on time' and 'I must let all the children contribute to this discussion'. This conflict often results in anxiety and confused thinking, and prevents teachers from finding a practical solution to the difficulties they face. Wagner terms these conflicts 'knots' in teachers' thinking and suggests that they are the source of a great deal of anxiety and inability to cope.

Wagner's approach to studying teachers' thinking is influenced by both psychoanalytic theory and cognitive psychology. Although psychoanalytic theory has had much to say about human thinking in general, it occurs surprisingly rarely in research on teachers' thinking. It has sometimes been criticized for its imprecision and apparent mystique, but here it is used to understand an area of teachers' thought and action that is difficult to explore and is often left out of account.

In her analysis of teachers' knots, Wagner points out that these frequently arise from teachers' fears (about their own personal effectiveness or a fear of violence). She suggests that 'knots' often have some association with childhood experience or an unpleasant past event, which must be confronted and 'thought through' for the 'knot' to be resolved. Once it is resolved, she argues, then teachers' thinking is freed to find solutions to the problems they face.

Wagner's solutions to the 'knots' in teachers' thinking emphasize identifying and confronting the core anxieties of teachers, rather than rationalizing teachers' fears away. However, it is frequently the case that teachers attempt to reduce their anxieties through some form of 'theory' or rationalization. Student teachers, for instance, sometimes dismiss their college tutors' critical comments on their teaching by telling themselves that their tutors only observed a few minutes of their teaching, don't really know what it's like in the school, and probably haven't taught in a school themselves for years! Similarly, experienced teachers have frequently been heard to 'explain away' some boring, unimaginative lessons in terms of the lack of facilities in the school, the class size, or the type of children. Such explanations may contain a hint of truth, but may also be convenient ways of avoiding facing up to the fact that one's teaching performance is poor. The theories that teachers construct to protect themselves in this way may well become obstructions to teachers' improvement of their own practice, and might also influence how they perceive and respond to attempts to innovate. There are occasions when teachers also have some unreal images of themselves that they wish to present to outsiders, and these too can influence the process of curriculum innovation, as indicated in the other chapters in this section.

Olson and Eaton consider how the process of curriculum change might be best understood and, in particular, focus on the role of the teacher in this process. Their own research study follows a group of primary school teachers attempting to incorporate computers into the curriculum.

Olson and Eaton found many uncertainties amongst the teachers of what this new area of the curriculum would be like. Teachers felt 'hands on' experience to be important, yet they were aware that this presented many organizational problems when there might only be one computer for the whole class. They thought that computers would aid children's problem-solving, though their conceptions of how this might occur were vague. They also thought that an important aspect of including computers in the curriculum was simply to enable children to become familiar with computers and how to use them, a feature that they summed up as 'computer awareness' or 'computer literacy'.

These concerns commonly resulted in a 'teach yourself' approach to incorporating computers in the classroom. Children were left to interact with computers on their own, or with the help of another pupil, using software that was easy to use and likely to make few demands on the teacher who would be teaching the rest of the class. One of the consequences of this approach was that software tended to be selected by teachers on the grounds of convenience rather than the skills or knowledge that might be developed through its use. Over time, teachers became aware that their ideas about the value of computers in the primary school were not being met in reality, and this caused them to rethink exactly what they wished to obtain from computer use and also led them to examine their own existing classroom practice more closely.

From this series of case studies, Olson and Eaton develop a model of curriculum change as 'a reflexive process', involving critical reflection on one's own practice. Teachers develop ideas, often crude ones, about an innovation. For instance, the teachers in this study appeared to have little understanding of what 'problem-solving' meant in the context of the primary school curriculum, or of how computers might facilitate it, or of how this might be dealt with in terms of classroom activities. Nevertheless, teachers attempt to implement the innovation, testing out their ideas as they go. An innovation contains both routine and novel aspects. The routine ones can readily be accommodated within the classroom context (e.g. drill and practice software), but novel aspects require teachers to think through their implications for classroom practice and perhaps to develop new ways of working (e.g. how to develop 'problem-solving skills'). However, teachers' decisions about how the innovation is to be incorporated into the classroom are not taken purely in terms of whether they seem likely to meet the claimed objectives for pupils' learning. Teachers also have concerns with how others perceive them. Some aspects of computer innovation, for example, enabled teachers to demonstrate to pupils, colleagues, and parents that they were 'modern' teachers, keeping up to date, catering for their children's needs and interests, etc. In deciding how to incorporate an innovation into their normal practice, teachers are also concerned with the issue of control. They attach high priority to being in command of classroom processes and being able to demonstrate their worth as teachers, and are consequently reluctant to change those aspects of their practice that help them achieve this.

Consequently, the process of implementation is accompanied by much thinking, not only about the innovation itself, but about teachers' existing practice, features of which are frequently highlighted as a result of the implementation. The interaction between these two areas of thought result in an improved understanding both of the innovation and their own teaching, and in a gradual accommodation of the two.

Olson and Eaton, however, point out that this reflexive process could, in reality, be more thorough and productive. Teachers are often not strong in self-criticism, or constructive and imaginative in their grasp of innovatory ideas and their implications, and support may be needed to make the reflexive process of change create the impact that is needed for curriculum developments of the future.

Olson and Eaton describe a curriculum innovation process in which the initiative and motivation to change comes largely from the teachers themselves. Reynolds and Saunders, in contrast, describe the possibly more common situation where the decision to innovate is taken by others and the innovation is foisted upon teachers to implement. While some of the processes identified by Reynolds and Saunders have much in common with those noted by Olson and Eaton, they also identify an alternative level at which teachers and head teachers operate during the process of innovation; this serves to maintain accountability to those involved or concerned with the innovation, and interacts with the process of implementation itself.

Reynolds and Saunders studied a series of primary schools at a time when the local education authority, in accordance with central government recommendations, had formulated guidelines for the primary school curriculum aimed to help newly established subject co-ordinators to review and update teaching practices within their individual schools. Much of the 'public' discussion surrounding this process—developing the guidelines, schools reacting to the guidelines and establishing their own curriculum plans—focused upon aims and objectives and concerned the development of formal curriculum policy documents. Although teachers and head teachers took part in these discussions, rarely were concerns about what the new curriculum might involve in terms of practice discussed.

This is in sharp contrast to the actual work of the subject co-ordinators, whose talk with other teachers dwelt on the kinds of activities that would be presented to children, how they could be managed, and which materials would be used. Co-ordinators, in fact, engaged in quite a complex process of adapting and translating aims to suit the context of their particular school, teachers and children, bearing in mind both long-term and short-term interests. Their impact on school practice occurred largely through frequent informal discussions of planning with colleagues, demonstrations of new ideas in their own classrooms, and providing teachers with content and materials, often to the extent of searching out and 'packaging' resources ready for use. Support from the head teacher, in terms of approval, finance and organization, was also found to influence the co-ordinator's impact upon other teachers.

The researchers explain this disjunction between the 'public' and 'private' processes of curriculum development in terms of the different demands of accountability and classroom practice. In practice, teachers cannot specify the formal objectives and plans of a new curriculum and carry them out. Establishing a new curriculum, or adapting the existing one, involves experiment, trial and error, reflection on practice, and collegial discussion. It is only after discovering what is possible in the context of one's own school that any formal plans could actually be offered. Others beyond the school, however, generally fail to appreciate the rather tentative, open-ended nature of curriculum development, and might even view teachers as being highly 'unprofessional' in being unable to document in advance a reasonably detailed plan of their work. To outsiders, curriculum plans are guarantees of what teachers can be held accountable for.

Reynolds and Saunders found that some head teachers and curriculum co-ordinators were implicitly aware of this disjunction and could readily slip in and out of the two modes of working with curriculum plans, interacting to some extent between the two, and sometimes using curriculum policy plans to their own advantage. For instance, they would consider the implications of particular 'public' aims for 'private' practice and renegotiate the aim in the light of what seemed feasible or desirable, or they might have used the LEA policy document to justify existing practices, or alternatively to coerce a reluctant member of staff to change their practice in a direction the head perceived as preferable. Some head teachers and co-ordinators, however, were less 'politically aware', took the curriculum documents at face value, and were unable to relate policy development to the processes going on within their school.

Reynolds and Saunders point out a number of difficulties that arise from this adherence to the formal planning of the curriculum. In particular, the often complex task of the curriculum co-ordinator fails to be recognized. The skills of translating ideas into feasible working plans for the classroom—the kinds of creative skills already noted in several preceding chapters, together with the skills of disseminating practices within the school—are necessarily involved in any curriculum change but are often obscured from view, and underestimated. In consequence, the kinds of training and support that curriculum development requires are often not forthcoming. Like Olson and Eaton, Reynolds and Saunders suggest that we need to divert more effort to explicate exactly what curriculum development involves on the part of teachers in order to facilitate these processes further, and to enable teachers themselves to examine and develop the skills they already employ.

TOWARDS NEW UNDERSTANDINGS OF TEACHING

The chapters of this book represent a variety of perspectives on teachers' thinking. They have been inspired by different theoretical positions, ranging from psychoanalysis to symbolic interactionism, although several share a basically cognitive psychological origin. The theoretical origins of the research, however, are not absolutes. Though they may channel the way in which researchers approach an issue, they are ideally used as a heuristic rather than a directive in promoting researchers' enquiry. As teachers' thinking is more fully explored and as we come to know more of its inter-relationships, the theories can be modified, combined, or discarded altogether in favour of the improved understandings of teaching that the research itself reveals.

Inevitably the research reported in these chapters also varies in its methods and research designs. Some researchers have explored teachers' thinking through teachers' concurrent or retrospective verbalizations of their thinking, others through inferring teachers' thoughts and conceptions through observations of their actions, or through the use of specially constructed interview procedures. These different methods raise important issues about how we gain access to human thinking and the status of the data we collect. Such issues need to be aired and examined by researchers in order to identify appropriate techniques with which to pursue their explorations further and to make appropriate interpretations of the data collected (see Calderhead 1986; Morine-Dershimer 1986; Yinger 1986).

While the focus of the research throughout the book is the thinking of classroom teachers, or student teachers in training, this is studied in a variety of contexts, at different levels, and over different periods of time. Teachers' thinking is studied in planning both lessons and whole curriculum areas, their ways of conceptualizing teaching are monitored during professional training and early teaching experiences, and teachers' cognitive processes are examined in several specific areas of their classroom practice, including how they translate subject matter knowledge into classroom activities or assess the difficulties and understandings of their children. Despite these variations, the chapters provide a number of 'linking themes' or similarities in their findings and in their insights into teaching.

First of all, teaching is described as an active process in which teachers' knowledge provides the source of identifying and interpreting professional situations and responding to them. How this knowledge is conceptualized varies considerably amongst the researchers, from a network of 'implicit theories' to a series of knowledge bases covering different educational phenomena, or a repertoire of schema each focused upon a particular type of practical situation. The knowledge on which teachers' thought and action depends appears to be based to some extent upon the 'personal' or 'commonsense' knowledge that the student teacher brings to professional training. Student teachers often have quite fixed conceptions of what teaching is like, and these conceptions influence what students extract from their professional experiences. Looking across the research, however, teachers appear to have developed quite an extensive body of professionally relevant knowledge. Research that has focused on teachers' planning itemizes a series of different types of knowledge that teachers bring to the planning process. This includes knowledge of children, educational aims, subject matter, curriculum materials, teaching strategies, and classroom processes. During the tasks of planning and evaluating past practice, new professional knowledge is created, including 'pedagogical content knowledge' oriented to the teaching of particular subject matter. Research on teachers' involvement in planning at 'higher' levels also indicates the significance of some other areas of knowledge, including knowledge of 'self', 'the role of teachers', and 'the expectations of others', which are particularly influential during periods of curriculum change. Through a process of reflection on practice, knowledge has come to provide teachers with ways of perceiving classroom situations and a repertoire of associated routine responses. Teachers' perceptions and reactions, however, may also be accompanied by affect, learned from previous (possibly even childhood) experiences, which interferes with the process of teaching. This might be evident, for example, in the ways in which teachers cope with difficult or emotionally disturbed children. With most teachers, such children quickly arouse affective responses that hamper the interactions between them. Teachers who are able to work effectively and sympathetically with these children often seem to be very knowledgeable about themselves, which might enable them to control their affective responses and avoid being drawn into conflict.

A second feature of teaching regularly emphasized in the research is the fluid, interactive nature of teachers' thinking. Teachers frequently juggle competing interests, draw upon various different areas of knowledge, and mentally rehearse alternative ways of conceptualizing and responding to the situations they face. In several of the chapters, teachers' planning is depicted as a reflective, experimental process involving the elaboration of ideas in interaction with various knowledge bases. Although in the classroom much activity may be routine and apparently 'unthinking', it is suggested that one of the characteristics of expert teaching is the way in which teachers can employ and adapt routines sensitively to the situation at hand. For instance, teachers may have a set of routines for managing a class discussion, but for the discussion to be productive and satisfying the teacher may have to engage in several improvisational procedures, drawing upon their knowledge of the pupils and their interests, their knowledge of the subject matter under discussion, and their knowledge of how children react in discussion situations to guide, probe and explain at appropriate moments, maintaining the children's attention and enthusiasm, and stimulating them to think.

In the wider context of curriculum development and implementation, teachers' ability to analyse and reflect upon both the nature of the innovation and the nature of their own classroom practice, gradually relating the two through experiment and evaluation, seems to play a crucial role in the process of translating an innovation into a workable system for the teacher's own classroom. When the innovation is spurred from outside the school, there are also additional interests to cope with to satisfy demands for accountability.

Thirdly, the chapters also point to the complex, contextualized nature of teaching, and begin to unravel some of this complexity. Beginning teachers' practices are sometimes constrained by the way the teachers' task is defined within the school, and beginning teachers must learn how to negotiate and compromise in order to establish their own preferred approach to teaching. Experienced teachers' practices are also influenced by the context in which they work and the tasks they have to accomplish. The demands of whole class teaching, for instance, appear to result in teachers' assessments of pupils' difficulties and understandings becoming bound up with the structure of the lesson and teachers' comprehension of it. Difficulties and understandings are only usually noted if they have strategic significance in the lesson being taught. Similarly, the demands that teachers face in managing and controlling classroom behaviour often distort their attempts to instruct the children, resulting in a less than intellectually challenging curriculum. The context in which teachers work and how the teaching task is defined are of particular importance in attempts to change or modify teachers' practice. Curriculum innovation and teachers' professional development have to take account of the context that has shaped existing practice, for this is a likely source of inertia in the process of change.

Though research on teachers' thinking does not provide us with a comprehensive theoretical framework for thinking about teaching, it does provide us with a number of insights that have implications for how we approach various educational tasks. For instance, in the case of curriculum development, research points out how unrealistic it is to conceive of innovation as a set of pre-formulated ideas or principles to be implemented by teachers. Innovative ideas are interpreted and reinterpreted by teachers over a period of time and translated into practice in a process that involves teachers drawing upon several different knowledge bases and interpreting and manipulating various interests. By indicating the kinds of knowledge teachers draw upon and how they use it, research points out the nature of the support that curriculum innovation and implementation might require. In introducing problem-solving, for instance, which is often a crucial element of current maths, science, and computing curricula, teachers need help in understanding the concept of 'problem-solving' itself and what it entails in terms of teachers' actions and the activities that are planned for pupils. They may also need support to reconcile the demands of introducing problem-solving into the curriculum with existing classroom managerial demands: problem-solving activities might involve more group work, and more talking and movement in the classroom. Teachers may need support and new skills to analyse those aspects of their own practice that need changing, and are capable of change in the given context. In addition, teachers may require assistance in carrying out a thorough and honest evaluation, throughout the implementation period, that helps them confront their own practice and go beyond the images they wish to present to others or the theories they hold that defend unproductive routines. They may also need help to identify the benefits and the costs of the innovation to assist in guiding future actions. Research suggests that efforts directed in these areas would be likely to enable teachers to understand, monitor, and adapt their classroom practice.

Research on teachers' knowledge bases and how they are used also helps us conceptualize the processes of professional development and how these processes might be enhanced through pre-service and in-service education. Student teachers approach professional training with an existing body of knowledge that shapes what they extract from the training experience and how they use this knowledge in developing their own practice. Professional education normally takes little account of teachers' or student teachers' preconceptions about teaching or the knowledge bases they have, for example, about themselves, pupils, or classroom contexts. Furthermore, unless courses are designed to challenge teachers' thinking about practice and encourage them to analyse and appraise their professional thinking, existing poor practices may be perpetuated and students left relatively unaffected by training itself. Teachers' professional training might also be structured around some of the teaching processes or skills that research has identified, such as the processes by which subject matter is transformed into plans for classroom activity, or the processes of identifying or framing problems and drawing upon different knowledge bases in planning, and those of adapting the teachers' repertoire of classroom routines to suit the individual characteristics of the situation at hand. In this context, the value of videotapes, stimulated recall commentaries, field reports, critical incident training, and structured professional discussions amongst teachers and students has yet to be fully explored in teacher education.

Learning to teach is an active process involving considerable interaction between thought and action. Recent policy in teacher education has begun to recognize the crucial role of thought and reflection in professional development, as is evident in calls for 'reflective teacher education' or for training 'thinking teachers'. However, notions as to the nature of this type of education vary widely. Much of so-called 'training in reflective teaching' takes little account of the knowledge and predispositions of students entering teacher education. Korthagen (1985), for instance, found that in a teacher education course aimed to develop skills of critical reflection on practice, the only students to be influenced by this type of course appeared to be those who were already disposed towards critically analysing their practice anyway. However, research on teachers' thinking is beginning to provide a sounder theoretical foundation, which might help to inform the design of such courses, indicating the kinds of knowledge bases that student teachers need to examine and develop and the skills that may be needed to use them.

Research on teachers' thinking is also beginning to address the issue of pupils' learning. One of the major purposes of teaching is that pupils acquire knowledge and skills in consequence. The processes by which these knowledge and skills are transmitted are not well understood, but we know that teachers have to take account of the different preconceptions and interests with which children come to school. Teachers acquire knowledge about children's errors and difficulties and design class work to overcome them. Pupils' responses to classroom activities, however, are somewhat unpredictable. One of the frustrations (or challenges) of classroom teaching is that, even when pupils appear to have demonstrated their knowledge of a concept or mastery of a skill, they can still appear shortly afterwards to have forgotten it again! Learning in classrooms rarely occurs in the predictable, sequential manner that some learning theories would lead us to believe. Children piece together new understandings on the basis of their prior knowledge and experience and sometimes misconceptualize what the teacher is attempting to communicate. It has also been found that children can apparently master the curriculum yet be unable to relate it to previous commonsense misunderstandings, which persist and interfere with future learning. For instance, it is not too unusual to find children who have studied basic physics still believing that heavy objects sink in water whereas lighter objects float, or to find young children who can successfully complete exercises on time in maths lessons, yet still encounter difficulties in telling the time from a clock in the home. Much of teachers' instructional work in the classroom is directed towards the identification of these difficulties and misunderstandings as they relate to the task in hand, followed by teachers' thinking about how these difficulties can be overcome and how new understanding can be achieved. Teachers need to acquire expertise in identifying and reasoning about these difficulties, working on them to enable children's understandings and skills to be nurtured. Unfortunately, such expertise sometimes has little opportunity to develop. Teachers can be swamped with managerial concerns that take precedence, eventually dictating the nature of the classroom activities and pupil learning, stultifying creativity and experimentation.

Research on teachers' thinking has begun to uncover some of the complexities of teachers' work and to identify a structure of teaching that helps us better understand educational processes and consider how to respond to problems within them. There is still clearly much for research to explore. Our understanding of how professional knowledge bases develop and are influenced, how they interact in professional planning, and how teachers' knowledge becomes embedded in action and informs classroom routines is limited. However, it is through such explorations into teachers' thinking that new conceptualizations of teaching are emerging, which in turn can guide our efforts to support and improve the quality of teachers' professional practice.

REFERENCES

Calderhead, J. (1986) *Developing a Framework for the Elicitation and Analysis of Teachers' Verbal Reports*. Paper presented at the American Educational Research Association conference, San Francisco, 1986.

Doyle, W. (1986) 'Classroom Organization and Management'. In Wittrock, M. C. (ed.) *Handbook of Research on Teaching*, 3rd edition. New York: Macmillan.

Hargreaves, D. H. (1980) 'The Occupational Culture of Teachers'. In Woods, P. (ed.) *Teacher Strategies*. London: Croom Helm.

Jackson, P. W. (1968) *Life in Classrooms*. New York: Holt, Rinehart and Winston.

Korthagen, F. A. J. (1985) *Reflective Teaching as a Basis for Teacher Education*. Paper presented at the American Educational Research Association conference, Chicago, 1985.

Lortie, D. C. (1975) *Schoolteacher*. Chicago, IL: University of Chicago Press.

Morine-Dershimer, G. (1986) *What Can We Learn from Thinking?* Paper presented at the American Educational Research Association conference, San Francisco, 1986.

NIE (1975) *Teaching as Clinical Information Processing*. Report of Panel 6, National Conference on Studies in Teaching. Washington, DC: National Institute of Education.

Schon, D. A. (1983) *The Reflective Practitioner*. London: Temple Smith.

Yinger, R. J. (1986) *Examining Thought in Action: A Theoretical and Methodological Critique of Research on Interactive Teaching*. Paper presented at the American Educational Research Association conference, San Francisco, 1986.

1

INDIVIDUAL, INSTITUTIONAL, AND CULTURAL INFLUENCES ON THE DEVELOPMENT OF TEACHERS' CRAFT KNOWLEDGE[1]

Kenneth M. Zeichner, B. Robert Tabachnick and Kathleen Densmore

This chapter examines the empirical literature related to the variety of individual, institutional and cultural influences on the development of teachers' craft knowledge before, during, and after their participation in formal preservice teacher education. Teachers' craft knowledge is used throughout the chapter as a rubric for describing a number of different approaches to studying the psychological context of teaching, from the more conventional studies of teachers' attitudes and beliefs to the more recent attempts to describe the 'implicit theories' of teachers, from the teachers' point of view and in the teachers' own language. According to Clark and Peterson (1986), this psychological context is composed of a mixture of theories, beliefs, and values about the teachers' role and about the dynamics of teaching and learning.

Following an analysis of the literature on teachers' craft knowledge, which considers both its nature and its development, the work in this area will be illustrated by describing the conceptual orientation, methodological approach, and findings from our recently completed two-year longitudinal study of prospective and beginning teachers in the US (Tabachnick and Zeichner 1985). Given the wide variety of conceptual and methodological approaches that are evident in this literature, this one study, which employed the symbolic interactionist construct of perspectives, cannot be considered as representative of the full range of approaches that have been employed in the study of the psychological context of the teachers' work. This study is, however, consistent with most of the studies in the newly emerging area of inquiry on teachers' implicit theories in that it operated from the assumption that 'a teacher's cognitive and other behaviors are guided by and make sense in relation to a personally held system of beliefs, values, and principles' (Clark and Peterson 1986, p. 287). The purpose of this study, in common with all studies of teachers' implicit theories, was to make explicit and visible the complex, practically oriented and socially derived frames of reference and perspectives through which teachers actually shape and direct the work of teaching (Elbaz 1983). This study also attempted to draw linkages between the psychological and social contexts of the teachers' work by examining a variety of individual and social influences on the development of teachers' craft knowledge.

THE NATURE OF TEACHERS' CRAFT KNOWLEDGE

In addition to the historically dominant approach, which has sought to understand teachers' attitudes and beliefs through the use of surveys and questionnaires containing a variety of categories predefined by the researcher, more recent studies have sought to understand teachers on their own terms and in their own language by attempting to elicit the often implicit and only partially articulated elements of teacher knowledge that guide teachers' actions in specific contexts. Sharp and Green (1975) have criticized studies of teacher attitudes and beliefs, which attend to teacher knowledge at a very high level of abstraction, for their failure to address the action-oriented frameworks and perspectives by which teachers make sense of and interpret their experience and act in specific situations. As Keddie (1971) has shown, we cannot assume a direct correspondence between teacher attitudes and beliefs, which exist apart from consideration of specific situations, and the perspectives that serve as the basis for a teacher's daily practice. By focusing almost exclusively on teacher attitudes and beliefs, these studies have given us a very limited view of the nature of teachers' craft knowledge and of the processes by which it is developed and maintained over time.[2]

Following the lead of Becker et al's (1961) study of medical socialization in *Boys in White*, several researchers have recently employed the interactionist construct of 'perspectives' to understand the nature and development of teachers' craft knowledge (e.g. Janesick 1977; Tabachnick and Zeichner 1985). Examples of alternative approaches to the study of teachers' craft knowledge include Duffy and Anderson's (1982) study of teachers' 'conceptions of reading', Elbaz's (1983) study of the structure and content of teachers' 'practical knowledge', Bussis, Chittenden and Amarel's (1976) study of teachers' 'construct systems' (related to curriculum, learners, and their working environment), and Marland's (1977) and Conners' (1978) studies of the 'principles' that guide teachers' classroom practice.[3]

Methodologically, this work on teachers' 'implicit theories' is also very diverse and has departed from the exclusive reliance on questionnaire data. These studies have relied, as Feiman-Nemser and Floden (1986) point out, primarily on research strategies that get teachers to talk about their work in clinical interviews (e.g. Elbaz 1983; Bussis, Chittenden and Amarel 1976) and in teacher seminars (e.g. Lampert 1985), and on the use of such methods as stimulated recall (e.g. Marland 1977), the repertory grid technique (e.g. Ingvarson and Greenway 1984), and semantic taxonomy interviews (e.g. Young 1981). These efforts to get teachers to talk about their work are frequently used in conjunction with extended observations of teachers' work (e.g. Janesick 1977;

Tabachnick and Zeichner 1985). Whatever approaches are used, the researchers attempt on the basis of these verbal and/or observational data to draw inferences about the content, organization, and development of teachers' craft knowledge.

There is much disagreement within the literature as a whole about the nature of teachers' craft knowledge at both an individual and occupational level. One of these differences is concerned with the degree of internal consistency in the craft knowledge of individual teachers and with the degree of homogeneity in craft knowledge in the occupation as a whole. Studies on teacher attitudes and beliefs have, for the most part, stressed the internally consistent nature of an individual teacher's knowledge and the uniformity of teacher knowledge in the occupational group. On the other hand, studies of teachers' implicit theories have emphasized the contradictions embedded in the craft knowledge of individual teachers and the heterogeneous 'teacher cultures' existing in various segments of the occupational group.

Although the classification of teachers' craft knowledge into dichotomous categories such as 'progressive/traditional', 'formal/informal', 'custodial/humanistic', etc. has been criticized for many years as overly reductionist (see Travers 1971), this practice still dominates the literature on teacher socialization. According to this view, the various dimensions of an individual teacher's knowledge are internally consistent and the categories themselves (e.g. 'progressive/traditional') are mutually exclusive. Additionally, it has been commonly assumed that most teachers share a uniform teaching culture and that the degree of diversity in the occupation is very small.

Several criticisms have been raised in the literature with regard to the validity of both of these views. First, Hammersley (1977a) urges researchers to be cautious in assuming that there is necessarily a logical consistency between the various components of a teacher's craft knowledge and that there are no similarities among teachers who hold different perspectives on some dimensions. There is evidence from several empirical studies (e.g. Bussis, Chittenden and Amarel 1976) that bipolar unidimensional characterizations of teachers' craft knowledge have greatly oversimplified differences within and among teachers. With regard to the mutual exclusivity of categories and the assumption of homogeneity within categories, Berlak and Berlak (1981) and Tabachnick and Zeichner (1985) have documented significant overlap between and significant variance within the conventional categories of 'progressive and traditional'. The typical assumption of internal logical consistency among the various dimensions of an individual teacher's craft knowledge has also been challenged by empirical research. For example, Duffy and Anderson (1982) found that the conceptions teachers hold about the teaching of reading did not fit neatly into their research-based typology and that these conceptions were more complex and eclectic than anticipated. Berlak and Berlak (1981) argue that it is not surprising to find these contradictions and inconsistencies in the craft knowledge of individual teachers since contradictions are embedded in the society and institutions in which teachers work.

It has also been conventional to assume a high degree of homogeneity in the craft knowledge of the occupation as a whole. According to this view, teachers are socialized into a uniform 'teacher culture'. Feiman-Nemser and Floden (1986, p. 507) conclude that this assumption of cultural uniformity in the occupation is untenable:

> Teachers differ in age, experience, social and cultural backgrounds, gender, marital status, subject matter, wisdom and ability. The schools in which they work also differ in many ways

as do the groups of students they teach. All of these differences may lead to differences in teaching culture.

This conclusion is supported by several empirical studies where diverse teaching cultures were discovered within single schools (e.g. Gracey 1972; Metz 1978), within the same subject areas (e.g. Munby 1983) and among teachers who shared a commitment to a particular approach to teaching (e.g. Bussis et al 1976). This existence of diverse teaching cultures has important implications for the study of the development of teachers' craft knowledge. Once one accepts this view, it logically follows that teachers are faced with conflicting pressures to think and to act in different ways, and the internalization of a particular set of norms becomes problematic. Whatever conclusions are reached with regard to the literature on the development of teachers' craft knowledge to be reviewed below, the nature of this knowledge needs to be viewed as more complex and subtle than has typically been the case.

THE DEVELOPMENT OF TEACHERS' CRAFT KNOWLEDGE

Lortie (1973, p. 488) concludes in his examination of the riddle of teacher socialization that 'there are several credible explanations of the socialization process available and that the socialization of teachers is undoubtedly a complex process not readily captured by a simple, one-factor frame of reference.' When one approaches the problem of the development of teachers' craft knowledge through the lens of the teacher socialization literature, Lortie's conclusion is strongly confirmed. There is clearly a lack of consensus in the literature with regard to the potency and influence of various socializing agents and mechanisms. A number of different explanations must necessarily be considered in attempting to understand the process of teacher socialization. This section briefly summarizes several alternative explanations regarding the development of teachers' craft knowledge. This analysis addresses the socialization of teachers: (1) prior to formal training: (2) during pre-service teacher education; and (3) during the early years of a teaching career. Throughout this analysis, an attempt will be made to identify the strength of the empirical evidence supporting particular points of view and to suggest areas where there is a particular need for further work to be initiated. The scope of this review covers studies conducted in the US, England, and Australia.

Pre-training influences

There are many who argue that experiences predating formal training are more influential in the making of a teacher than the efficacy of either pre-service training or socialization in the workplace during a career. The apparent persistence of particular forms of pedagogy over time (e.g. see Sirotnik 1983) is frequently explained by the failure of school reform initiatives and the curriculum of teacher education to overcome the effects of this anticipatory socialization.

Feiman-Nemser (1983) summarizes the arguments related to the three most prevalent explanations of the influence of pre-training experiences on teacher development. First, Stephens (1967) proposes an 'evolutionary' theory to account for the socialization of teachers and emphasizes the role of 'spontaneous pedagogical tendencies' in explaining why teachers think and act as they do. According to this view:

> Human beings have survived because of their deeply ingrained habits of correcting one another, telling each other what they know, pointing out the moral, and supplying the answer. These tendencies have been acquired over the centuries and are lived out in families and classrooms. Thus, children not only learn what they are told by parents and teachers, they also learn to be teachers. (Feiman-Nemser 1983, p. 152)

A second position outlined by Feiman-Nemser (1983) is the 'psychoanalytic' explanation found in the work of Wright (1959) and Wright and Tuska (1967, 1968). These studies suggest that teacher socialization is affected to a considerable extent by the quality of relationships teachers have as children with important adults (e.g., mother, father, teachers) and that becoming a teacher is to some extent a process (sometimes unconscious and sometimes deliberate) of trying to become like the significant others in one's childhood. According to this view, early relationships with significant others are the prototypes of subsequent relationships throughout life and the kinds of teachers that education students become are governed by the effects this childhood heritage has on their personalities (Wright and Tuska 1967). These studies offer empirical data in support of this 'Childhood Romance Theory of Teacher Development', including statements written by teachers that illustrate the significance of a conscious identification with a teacher during childhood (Wright 1959). According to this view, the 'reality shock' that is apparently experienced by many beginning teachers (Whiteside et al 1969) is explained by the failure of formal teacher education to overcome these early fantasies about teaching and teachers.

A third viewpoint on the role of pre-training experience on the socialization of teachers emphasizes the influence of the thousands of hours spent by teachers as pupils in what Lortie (1975) refers to as an 'apprenticeship of observation'. According to this view, teacher socialization occurs largely through the internalization of teaching models during the time spent as a pupil in close contact with teachers. According to Lortie (1975), the activation of this latent culture during formal training and later school experience is a major influence in shaping teachers' conceptions of the teaching role and role performance. Formal teaching education is viewed as having little impact in altering the cumulative effects of this socialization.

Lortie's argument is based, in part, on several studies where teachers attested to the tangential role of their formal training and where they frequently referred to the continuing influence of their earlier mentors (see Lortie 1975). Generally, however, there is little empirical evidence that directly supports either Lortie's specific position or the other two theoretical explanations. Most of the empirical evidence in support of the potent influence of pre-training experiences is indirect in nature and demonstrates a continuity in teacher perspectives during formal training without supporting a particular theoretical explanation. Studies conducted by Petty and Hogben (1980) and Hogben and Lawson (1983) in Australia, by Maddox (1968) and Mardle and Walker (1980) in England, and by Zeichner and Grant (1981) and Tabachnick and Zeichner (1984) in the US clearly indicate that biography exerts a powerful influence on teacher development, but much work remains to be done to clarify the particular source of this influence.

The impact of pre-service teacher education

Sarason et al's (1962) characterization of pre-service preparation as 'an unstudied problem' remains as true today as it was twenty years ago despite the literally hundreds of studies that have been conducted on the impact of education courses and field experiences. Generally these studies have not provided much information about the substance of pre-service preparation beyond descriptions of course titles and credit distributions (see Zeichner 1985), and they have provided even less information about how the knowledge and skills communicated to prospective teachers during training are received and are incorporated into the perspectives of teachers (see Zeichner in press, and Feiman-Nemser and Floden 1986).

There are two major elements in the professional education component of a pre-service teacher preparation program: (1) the educational methods and foundation courses; and (2) the field experiences that are typically carried out in elementary and secondary school classrooms. With regard to the influence of the formal knowledge distributed in education courses on teacher development, there is much evidence that the pedagogical methods and content knowledge introduced to students in campus courses has little influence on the subsequent actions of students even during initial training (e.g. Hodges 1982; Grant 1981; Katz and Raths 1982). There is also evidence that, when attempts are made to train prospective teachers in the performance of specific teaching skills through micro-teaching and other systematic procedures, the continued use of the skills by prospective teachers outside the laboratory is highly dependent on whether the ecological conditions in classrooms are conducive to the use of the skills. Copeland's (1980) work suggests that the impact of education courses cannot be assessed apart from these ecological conditions.

These and similar studies are all concerned with the impact of the overt curriculum of initial preparation on teacher development. Dale (1977a, b) and Bartholomew (1976) argue, on the other hand, that the chief impact of initial training comes not through the formal knowledge and skills imparted to teachers, but through the *hidden curriculum* of teacher preparation programs. For example, Dale conducted a content analysis of typical British courses on the psychological, sociological and philosophical foundations of education and concluded that initial teacher training fosters a cognitive style of 'liberal individualism', which predisposes prospective teachers to see the world in particular ways, to become conscious of it having particular properties and possibilities, and to reject or never recognize other properties or possibilities. Dale (1977a) specifically argues that this cognitive style directs teachers to seek the source of their problems in individuals (e.g. pupils) and not in the institutions in which they work.

Bartholomew (1976) analyzes other aspects of the hidden curriculum of pre-service preparation (the pedagogical practices and social relations in programs, and the social organization of programs) and concludes that despite the fact that teacher education encourages students to use liberal phrases and to affirm liberal slogans in places other than the university, the facts of socialization *within* the university (e.g. the separation of theory and practice) encourage the development of 'objectivist' conceptions of knowledge, fragmented views of curriculum, and views of learners as passive recipients of officially approved knowledge. According to Bartholomew (1976) and others such as Giroux (1980), Ginsburg (1984, 1985), and Popkewitz (1985), the real impact of pre-service preparation lies in these images of teacher, learner, knowledge, curriculum, and professional, which are subtly communicated to prospective teachers through the covert processes of the hidden curriculum of teacher education programs. Thus, despite the overwhelming evidence related to the low impact of the formal curriculum of teacher education, one must be cautious in generalizing those findings to the impact of pre-service preparation as a whole.

Generally, however, arguments related to the impact of the hidden curriculum in pre-service preparation have been offered on logical and theoretical grounds with very little supporting empirical evidence. With the exception of Ginsburg's studies of the development of teacher perspectives toward professionalism (Ginsburg 1984, 1985) and the evidence provided by Connell (1985) of the 'psychologisation' of social relations by teachers, we do not have very strong empirical evidence that confirms that teachers actually incorporate elements into their perspectives in ways consistent with the theoretical arguments.

The second aspect of pre-service preparation that has received much attention in the literature in relation to teacher development is the field experience component. Here those who have analyzed the empirical literature have consistently characterized the knowledge base related to the socializing impact of those experiences as weak and ambiguous (e.g. Zeichner 1980; McIntyre 1983; Griffin et al 1983). Today, despite the existence of numerous individual studies that have suggested specific effects of field experiences on the development of teachers, there continues to be a great deal of debate about the actual role these experiences play.

Generally, studies related to the socializing role of field experiences have not attended to the quality or substance of these experiences and have not identified the particular kinds of field programs and components within programs (e.g. characteristics of placement sites) that are related to different socialization outcomes for individual students (Zeichner 1986). Studies for the most part have relied exclusively upon the pre- and post-administration of questionnaires and surveys for their data and have not examined what actually takes place during the experience itself—how professional life is interpreted and acted upon as students participate in its ongoing affairs. We have learned from studies that have attended to the ongoing and socially constructed reality of field experiences that these experiences seem to have different effects on prospective teachers depending upon the nature of the program, the institutional contexts in which it exists, and the characteristics, dispositions, and abilities of individual students (Zeichner 1986), but we currently know very little about these context-specific effects beyond the conflicting scenarios that have been constructed from analysis of central tendencies in the literature (Zeichner and Tabachnick 1981). What we have learned is that field experiences entail complex sets of interactions among program features, settings, and people (the ecology of field experiences), and that research that seeks to understand field experiences as occasions for learning to teach must reflect in its conceptualizations and methodologies the dynamic and multidimensional nature of the events being studied. The question of the impact of field experiences on the processes of learning to teach must be recast in the future to one where attempts are made to link specific dimensions of programs and specific types of programs, together with various contextual dimensions of programs, to socialization outcomes for individual students. The current practice of attempting to explain the socializing role of field experiences *in general* has not been very productive to date, nor is it likely to become more so in the future.

In summary, the question of the socializing impact of pre-service teacher education has several dimensions. Studies of the influence of the formal curriculum of programs suggest that pre-service programs are not very powerful interventions. On the other hand, studies of the influence of the hidden curriculum of programs suggest, without much empirical evidence, that the impact of pre-service training may be far greater than has been thought. Finally, studies of field experiences indicate that these experiences have differential effects on teacher development, but do not illuminate the particular characteristics of programs or individuals that are related to specific effects. This whole area is clearly one where a great deal of empirical work remains to be done.

The impact of school experience

Pollard (1982) has developed a conceptual model describing three levels of social contextualization, which is helpful in understanding the socializing influence of the workplace of the school subsequent to pre-service preparation. According to Pollard, teachers develop coping strategies that represent active and creative responses by teachers to the constraints, opportunities, and dilemmas posed by the immediate contexts of the classroom and the school, and it is through these immediate determinants that the wider structure of society and the state have their impact.

At the *interactive* level within the classroom, Pollard (1982) describes several different kinds of influences on teacher development. Two of these influences—the socializing role of pupils, and the influence of the ecology of the classroom—will be considered here. First, the position emphasizing the significant role of pupils in the socialization of teachers is supported both on logical grounds and by empirical evidence. Haller (1967) and Doyle (1979) argue, for example, that the important role of pupils in teacher socialization is understandable given the typical isolation of teachers from their colleagues and supervisors and given the transitory and invisible nature of the learning process. These and other 'logical' explanations of the importance of pupils in the occupational socialization of teachers are consistent with the widely accepted bidirectional models of childhood socialization (e.g. Dreitzel 1973; Baumrind 1980) and are supported by a substantial number of empirical studies on the nature of classroom influence (e.g. Brophy and Evertson 1981). According to Doyle (1979), the influence of students ranges from effects on the general teaching approach and patterns of language that teachers use in classrooms to the type and frequency of specific teaching methods utilized by teachers. Furthermore, the individual characteristics of both teachers and students seem to affect the ways in which pupils influence teacher development.

As a result of these classroom studies as well as studies on teacher socialization, there is little question that classroom influence is reciprocal in nature and that teachers' perceptions of pupils' characteristics, expectations, and behaviors influence the nature of teacher development. Despite this general knowledge, however, we currently have very little understanding of how the specific characteristics of teachers and pupils mediate the process of teacher development.

Doyle (1979) argues that pupil effects are just one facet of the larger question of the effects of classrooms on teachers. Doyle (1977, 1979), Copeland (1980), and others have emphasized the role of the ecology of the classroom in teacher socialization. Doyle and Ponder (1975, p. 183) define the ecological system of the classroom as 'that network of interconnected processes and events which impinge upon behavior in the teaching environment'. Doyle (1979) has identified five distinctive features of classrooms that he feels are crucial in shaping the course of teacher development: multidimensionality, simultaneity, immediacy, unpredictability, and history. Others such as Dreeben (1973), Westbury (1973), Sharp and Green (1975), Dale (1977a, b), Denscombe (1980, 1982) and Connell (1985) all discuss various factors related to the material conditions and social organization of the classroom and how they affect teachers' work. Among these are teacher–pupil ratios, limited resources, and time.

According to this view of classrooms as ecological environments, learning to teach involves 'learning the texture of the classroom and the sets of behaviors congruent with the environmental demands of that setting' (Doyle 1977, p. 31). It is felt that the environmental demands posed by current classroom arrangements establish limits on the range of teacher behaviors that can be successful in particular settings, and that 'successful' teachers must learn a set of coping strategies appropriate to particular settings. These ecological classroom conditions, however, not only act as constraints on the actions of teachers, but they also exert positive pressures to act in certain ways (see Hammersley 1977b). Although there seems to be little doubt at present that the characteristics of the classroom need to be closely examined in any attempt to understand teacher development, the analysis cannot remain at the level of the classroom alone because these ecological conditions are themselves products of policy decisions and political actions at levels beyond the classroom.

At the *institutional* level of analysis, socializing influences related to the characteristics of schools as workplaces come into focus. Fenstermacher (1980) has argued that teachers' experiences with the institutional characteristics of schools are the most potent determinants of their perspectives toward teaching. In a similar vein Dreeben (1970, 1973) has written extensively about how certain organizational properties of schools (e.g. internal spatial arrangement, authority relationships) have implications for the character of teachers' work. There are many others of various theoretical persuasions (e.g. Larkin 1973; Gitlin 1983) who have described how particular institutional characteristics of schools affect the course of teacher development. Two aspects of school-level socializing influences on teachers will be considered here: (1) the influence of teaching colleagues; and (2) the influence of evaluators.

Although there is substantial evidence that beginning teachers view their more experienced colleagues as highly influential in the process of learning to teach (e.g. Eddy 1969; Grant and Zeichner 1981), and some evidence that indicates that norms within the teacher peer group exert a powerful influence on teacher development (e.g. Hoy 1968), there is also evidence that suggests that the influence of 'teacher cultures' is mediated by certain characteristics of beginning teachers (McArthur 1978) and that formal attempts by teachers to influence the work of their colleagues occur only under certain limited conditions (e.g. McPherson 1972). The literature suggests that most of the influence of colleagues on the socialization of beginning teachers, with the possible exception of those relatively few schools where norms of collegiality predominate (Little 1982), probably occurs informally and as part of the normal course of working in a school (e.g. Newberry 1977).

There is little question that the influence of colleagues needs to be taken into account in attempts to understand teacher socialization, despite the existence of an ethos of privacy and individualism within many schools (Denscombe 1980). Given that teachers work under generally similar conditions, collegial influence is probably closely tied to the common circumstances that teachers face in the structural characteristics of schools and in the ecological conditions of classrooms. It is also clear, however, as studies by Carew and Lightfoot (1979) and Metz (1978) have shown, that several diverse 'teacher cultures' often exist even in a single school and that teachers may face conflicting pressures by colleagues to influence them.

Edgar and Warren (1969) challenge this view of the strong socializing role of colleagues and argue that colleagues *per se* and the contextual effects of the workplace are less important in explaining teacher socialization than are the attitudes of significant evaluators—those having power over teachers in terms of their potential to apply organizational sanctions. However, despite the existence of this one study, which addressed the socialization of teachers with regard to their perspectives toward autonomy in the teachers' role, the empirical literature does not generally confirm the view that teachers' superordinates contribute substantially to teacher socialization. On the contrary, there is overwhelming evidence that teachers generally receive very little direct assistance and advice from their superiors and that teachers can insulate themselves from the directives and sanctions of significant evaluators when they choose to do so (Zeichner and Tabachnick 1985). This is not to say that the classroom is an impregnable sanctuary where teachers are free from administrative influence. The literature does suggest, however, that it is more through the structural imperatives of the job than through the influence of individual administrators that teaching perspectives are developed and maintained over time. Studies conducted by Zeichner and Tabachnick (1985) and by Connell (1985) indicate that there is a great deal of variation both among and within schools in the degree to which significant evaluators influence teachers' work.

At the *cultural* level of analysis, attempts have been made to link the perspectives of individual teachers and the micro level of the classroom and school to ideologies, practices, and material conditions at the macro level of society (e.g. inequalities in wealth and power). Here there have been two main types of analysis. First, those such as Wise (1979), Apple (1983) and Gitlin (1983) have explored how practices and policy initiatives outside the school affect the material resources available to teachers and the character of teachers' work. According to this view, teacher perspectives represent active and creative responses by teachers to constraints, dilemmas, and opportunities that are determined externally at a societal level and mediated through institutional structures and processes. Here studies have amply documented how such factors in a culture as a whole such as the bureaucratization of work, the deskilling of labor, cultural stereotypes of women, and the social division of labor (see Feiman-Nemser and Floden 1986; Ball and Goodson 1985) have affected the circumstances of teachers' work, although the frequently alleged linkages to the perspectives of individual teachers have not been well documented empirically.

A second type of analysis of the relationship between cultural forms and teacher socialization has attempted to link the perspectives of individual teachers to forms of meaning and rationality that are dominant in a society. Dale's (1977a, b) arguments related to the development of a cognitive style of 'liberal individualism', Giroux's (1980) analysis of the development of a 'technocratic rationality', and Popkewitz's (1985) thesis regarding the socializing influence of the professionalization of knowledge and the ideology of professionalism are examples of recent attempts to demonstrate the effect of 'cultural codes' on the development and nurturance of individual teachers' perspectives. As was argued above, however, there is currently very little, if any, empirical evidence available that substantiates these claims and that documents that individual teachers actually incorporate forms of meaning and modes of rationality into their perspectives in ways consistent with the macro-level theories.

Generally, the cultural level of analysis has received the least attention of the three levels in relation to teacher socialization (Atkinson and Delamont 1985). Although many of the analyses at a macro level are very persuasive on analytical grounds and although some definite influences have been amply documented regarding the link between the cultural and institutional contexts, there is much work that remains to be done regarding empirical substantiation of theories of the influence of 'cultural codes' and the material conditions of a society on the socialization of teachers.

In summary, this analysis of workplace influences on teacher socialization at three different levels has revealed that there is some evidence in the literature supporting the view that pupils, the ecology of the classroom, colleagues, and institutional characteristics of schools all play significant roles in the socialization of teachers. The specific nature of these influences has been described (e.g. the informal and contradictory nature of colleague influence) together with areas where more research is particularly needed. It has also been concluded that research has not generally confirmed Edgar and Warren's claim that 'significant evaluators' play a substantial role in teacher socialization. Finally, although some evidence has been accumulated related to the socializing influence of various factors in the culture as a whole on the conditions of teachers' work, the links between these cultural factors and the socialization of individual teachers has not been firmly established.

Amid this debate over the relative contribution of specific people and contextual factors to the socialization of teachers, there has also been much disagreement over the degree to which the development of occupational perspectives by teachers is influenced by individual or institutional factors. On the one hand, some have argued that individual teacher characteristics, dispositions, and capabilities are more influential in determining the course of teacher socialization than are the various institutional characteristics associated with teacher education and schooling. Other studies have emphasized the potency of institutional influence and have ignored the role of individual and biographical factors. A third position, exemplified by the work of Lacey (1977) and Pollard (1982) in England, by Zeichner and Tabachnick (1985) in the US and by Ingvarson and Greenway (1984) and Connell (1985) in Australia, has emphasized the interactions of individual and institutional factors in the socialization of teachers. The study that will now be described addressed both the nature of teachers' craft knowledge viewed through the lens of 'teacher perspectives' and the individual and social influences on its development.

STUDYING THE DEVELOPMENT OF PROFESSIONAL PERSPECTIVES TOWARD TEACHING

During the past five years we have been studying the way teachers acquire perspectives toward teaching. This has been part of a more general effort to understand the process by which neophytes become professional teachers, the effects of their personal histories and characteristics, the effects of their university teacher education program (especially the final student teaching semester), and the effects of their experiences with school characteristics during student teaching and the first year of teaching.

We conducted a two-phase study over a two-year period. The first phase examined the final (student teaching) semester of a university teacher education program. The second phase followed four of the student teachers into their first year of teaching.

The construct 'perspectives toward teaching' plays an important part in both studies. Becker et al (1961) defined *perspectives* as 'a coordinated set of ideas and actions a person uses in dealing with some problematic situation'. According to this view perspectives differ from attitudes since they include actions and not merely dispositions to act. Unlike values, perspectives are understood by Becker and his colleagues to be specific to situations rather than to represent generalized beliefs.

An important assumption, underlying the use of teaching perspectives as a key construct for our study, is the idea that teacher behavior and teacher thinking are inseparable and part of the same event. Perspectives toward teaching are expressed in the behavior of teachers as well as in the language teachers use to talk about their work. Both language and behavior are needed for a complete expression of perspectives.

This view of the meanings of social interaction leads us to gather naturalistic data through observers' reports, which aim to describe ongoing events and social interaction in classrooms, and also through interviews with participants, to learn their interpretations of the observed events. We treat the situational specificity of teacher perspectives as problematic, that is, we do not assume that behavior and interpretations of behavior are merely specific to situations and we do not generalize to other situations. We also do not assume that the observed behavior and participants' interpretations of that behavior explain all there is to understand about the social meanings of classroom interaction. To the extent that our data permit, we try to link those meanings to structural characteristics of schools and universities, the communities in which these exist, and the communities that exist within them.

Phase 1: Teacher perspectives during student teaching

One purpose of this first phase of our study was to discover the ways in which the student teaching experience influenced the development of perspectives. Did students change their perspectives in response to pressures coming from their schools or from the university? Did students become more alike in their perspectives toward teaching? A second purpose of this phase was to begin to explore what it was that seemed to influence perspectives—the student's background and personality, characteristics of university or schools?

Methodology

The subjects for this study were 13 student teachers (all women) who were enrolled in an elementary student teaching program at a large university in the midwestern part of the United States during the spring semester of 1981. Student teaching and a weekly campus seminar take up a full university semester (15 weeks), which is the final semester in a four-semester professional sequence leading to certification in grades kindergarten through eight.

During December 1980, a 47-item *Teacher Belief Inventory* (TBI) was developed by the staff of the research project on the basis of our own previous work on teacher perspectives (Tabachnick et al 1979–80) and on the basis of the literature on teachers (Bussis et al 1976). This instrument attempts to assess student teacher beliefs related to six specific categories: (1) the teacher's role; (2) teacher–pupil relationships; (3) knowledge and curriculum; (4) student diversity; (5) the role of the community in school affairs; and (6) the role of the school in society.[4]

In January 1981, the TBI was administered to all 40 student teachers enrolled in the elementary student teaching program. Following this administration, 13 students (a 28 per cent sample) were selected for more intensive study. These students were chosen to give us a group who appeared to have markedly different beliefs within each category measured by the TBI and whose overall profiles differed markedly from one another. We also sought a representative sample in terms of: (1) the characteristics of the settings in which the student teachers worked (urban, suburban), and (2) the grade levels at which the student teachers taught (primary, intermediate). Finally, we attempted to include a variety of school organizational patterns in our sample (e.g. teaching teams or units, self-contained classrooms) and to select a group of schools that offered the maximum possible diversity in community and pupil characteristics.

Between January and May 1981, each of the 13 student teachers was interviewed at least five times and observed while teaching at least three times. The student teachers were provided with transcriptions of all of their own interviews and were invited to clarify, elaborate, or suggest changes to their original responses. Three of the five interviews also included a line of questioning based on the specific lessons observed, which sought to clarify the observers' perceptions of the lessons, the student teachers' intentions for the lessons, and how student teachers interpreted their actions. The classroom observations lasted for a minimum of one half-day. Each observer constructed narrative descriptions of events in a student's classroom with a particular focus on one or more of the six orienting categories during each observation.

In addition to identifying the substance and dimensions of the perspectives of the 13 student teachers, we sought to examine through interviews with student teachers, co-operating teachers, and university supervisors the sources of influence related to the development of perspectives and how (if at all) perspectives changed during the course of the semester. The co-operating teacher(s) and university supervisor for each student were interviewed once at the end of the semester regarding their views about the teaching perspectives of their student teachers, their perceptions of changes that occurred in these perspectives over the course of the semester, and about how they attempted to influence, and felt they did in fact influence, their students.

Nearly 1,500 typed pages of protocol materials were generated from the interviews and from the records of classroom observations. The first step in the data analysis was the development of 13 individual profiles that attempted to describe the most salient aspects of each student's perspective toward teaching. While the original six orienting categories provided the basis for this analysis, the dimensions within each category were recast to reflect the data that were collected about each student.

Perspectives toward teaching

Students readily expressed their ideas and were observed in teaching behaviors related to the components of teacher perspective that we had labeled teacher role, teacher–pupil relations, knowledge and curriculum, and pupil diversity. Students had obviously thought much less about, had less to say about, and were observed rarely in situations in which they acted on the components of teacher perspectives that dealt with community–school relations and school-in-society.[5]

Our initial analysis led to the grouping of students into three sets of perspectives that might roughly be characterized as conservatively traditional, progressive, and a group whose members had a mixture of some of the characteristics of conservatively traditional and of progressive perspectives. The most disturbing consequence of forming groups in this way was that differences within each group that might be important, or at least intriguing, were obscured. In order to enable us to recognize and identify important differences within each perspective and important similarities between students in different groups, we made two decisions. First, we decided to examine each individual student's perspective separately and not to group students into the three categories. Second, we turned to the concept of dilemma as developed by Berlak and Berlak (1981) as a way of describing student perspectives toward teaching. We identified 18 dilemmas related to the four remaining orienting categories of perspectives that all 13 student teachers recognized, discussed, and acted upon in their classrooms. These appeared to be genuine dilemmas for most students, as they were pulled in contradictory directions by conflicting appeals within each dilemma.

These 18 dilemmas were used to construct a set of profiles, each of which described the teaching perspectives of a student teacher. Each student's characteristic way of resolving each of the 18 dilemmas was ascertained through analysis of the interview and observational data, and teaching perspectives were defined according to students' dominant modes of resolving the 18 dilemmas of teaching. Table 1.1 illustrates the nature of these profiles by presenting the profiles of four student teachers.

The four students in Table 1.1 demonstrate the extent to which interesting similarities and differences are suppressed when students are grouped. Emily and Marilyn would be grouped together as 'conservatively traditional', while Donna and Constance would be grouped together as having a 'progressive' perspective toward teaching.

Emily and Marilyn are alike in their resolutions of dilemmas related to knowledge and curriculum. They act toward knowledge as though it can exist independently of the people who have it. Their curriculum was designed to get correct pupil responses that confirmed whether pupils had learned what their teachers wanted them to know. Curriculum was arranged into teachable bits, where possible, for efficiency of transmission. In other ways they differ. Emily's relations with pupils are coolly correct, detached, controlling, while Marilyn's relations with pupils are more personal, warmer. Marilyn is somewhat less bureaucratic than Emily, acting to interpret rules rather than simply obeying them as best she can.

Donna and Constance are also much alike in their ways of acting on knowledge and curriculum. They view knowledge as more problematic, strongly influenced by the personal meanings of learners. They aim to help pupils capture whole configurations of knowledge and encourage individual and inventive pupil responses emphasizing processes of learning and discovery as well as learning products. Their relations with

Table 1.1 *Four student teacher profiles based on dominant modes of resolving eighteen dilemmas of teaching[a]*

Dilemmas	Emily	Marilyn	Donna	Constance
Knowledge and curriculum				
1. Public knowledge—personal knowledge	Public	Public	Public–personal[b]	Public–personal[b]
2. Knowledge is product—knowledge is process	Product	Product	Product–process[b]	Product–process[b]
3. Knowledge is certain—knowledge is problematic	Certain	Certain	Problematic–certain[b]	Problematic–certain[b]
4. Learning is fragmented—learning is holistic	Fragmented	Fragmented	Holistic	Holistic
5. Learning is unrelated—learning is integrated	Unrelated	Unrelated	Integrated	Integrated
6. Learning is individual—learning is collective	Individual	Individual	Individual	Individual–collective[b]
7. Teacher control over pupil learning: high—low	High	High	Low	Low
Teacher–pupil relationships				
8. Distant—personal	Distant	Personal	Personal	Personal
9. Teacher control over pupil behavior: high—low	High	Low	Low	Low
The teacher's role				
10. In determining *what* to teach: bureaucratic—functional—independent	Bureaucratic	Bureaucratic	Functional	Functional
11. In determining *how* to teach: bureaucratic—functional—independent	Functional	Functional	Functional	Functional
12. In relation to *school rules and regulations*: bureaucratic—functional—independent	Bureaucratic	Functional	Functional	Functional
Student diversity				
13. Children as members of a category—children as unique	Category	Unique	Unique	Unique
14. School curriculum: universalism—particularism	Universalism	Universalism	Universalism	Particularism
15. Pupil behavior: universalism—particularism	Universalism	Particularism	Particularism	Particularism
16. Allocation of school resources: equal—differential	Equal	Equal	Differential	Differential
17. School curriculum: emphasis on common culture—emphasis on subgroup consciousness	Common culture	Subgroup consciousness	Common culture	Subgroup consciousness
18. Career orientation: restricted—little restriction	Restricted	Restricted	Restricted	Little restriction

[a]The operational definitions for the 18 dilemmas are presented in Tabachnick, Zeichner et al (1982).
[b]The designation of a student teacher's perspective in a particular area represents her dominant mode of resolving a dilemma. The notations for dilemmas as public–personal, product–process, problematic–certain, individual–collective indicate a resolution that includes *both* poles of these dilemmas.

pupils are close and their control of pupils is firm but unobtrusive. Both see teachers as making important contributions to how and what to teach and both expect to interpret organizational rules in light of the needs of their pupils. It is in their reactions to student diversity that Donna and Constance reveal interesting differences from each other. Indeed, each of the four student teachers has a reaction to student diversity different from the others, picking and choosing to act in accordance with personal interests and their particular situations.

The role of student teaching in teacher development

To what degree did the teaching perspectives of student teachers change during the course of the 15-week semester? To what degree did any initial differences in student teachers' perspectives disappear by the end of the semester? What was the relative influence of individual intent and institutional constraint in the development of teacher perspectives during student teaching?

First, our data clearly indicate that student teaching did not result in a homogenization of teacher perspectives. Students came into the experience with different teaching perspectives, and significant differences among students remained at the end of the semester. Our analyses of interviews and observations with students, and of interviews with co-operating teachers and university supervisors, overwhelmingly indicate that student teaching did not significantly alter the substance of the teaching perspectives that the 13 students brought to the experience. On the contrary, with the exception of three students, teaching perspectives *solidified* but did not *change* fundamentally over the course of the 15-week semester. For the most part, students became more articulate in expressing, and more skillful in implementing, the perspectives that they possessed in less developed forms at the beginning of the experience. The following description by one university supervisor of the development of one of her students is typical of the perceptions of both university supervisors and co-operating teachers regarding changes in perspectives:

> I felt that she pretty much had her mind made up as to what she was going to do, how she was going to do things, and what she believed in. She was open to suggestions, but I felt she already had a pretty well established teacher identity. Her experience more or less solidified for her what she had already found out. [Interview with Ellen's supervisor]

Despite the lack of significant shifts in the substance of student teacher perspectives, there were several kinds of changes that did occur for most students. Generally, students came into the experience with fairly well-defined 'proto-perspectives' but lacked confidence and often lacked the skill to implement their preferred pedagogies effectively. Furthermore, although students came into student teaching with a background of two pre-student teaching practicums, the shift to full-time status in a school as a student teacher resulted in a more realistic perception of the work of teaching and of the teacher's role. In addition to gaining a more realistic perception of the job of teaching, most student teachers grew increasingly comfortable with their initial positions, more confident in their abilities to handle a classroom in their preferred styles.

This growing confidence and the development of teaching perspectives in a direction consistent with the latent culture brought to the experience describes 10 of the 13 students. Three students whose perspectives did not develop along the lines that would be predicted from the latent perspectives that they brought to the experience employed what Lacey (1977) has referred to as a strategy of 'strategic compliance'. Each of the students reacted strongly against the constraints posed by their placements, but because of the severe nature of the constraints and their status as student teachers they generally acted in ways demanded by their situations while maintaining strong private reservations about doing so. In these three cases, the behavioral conformity to situations that was in conflict with the students' entering perspectives was contradicted by the lack of an underlying value commitment to the apparently compliant behavior. Teaching perspectives did not develop or change for these three students, and at the end of the semester their perspectives remained at essentially the same point that they were at the beginning.[6]

Next there is the important question of the relative influence of individual intent and institutional constraint on the perspectives of student teachers. There are some who suggest that student teachers respond in a willing fashion to whatever the situation demands and who would deny that individual intentions make a substantial contribution to the perspectives of student teachers. It is our belief that individual intention and institutional constraint both played significant roles in affecting the development of student perspectives in the present study.

Most student teachers purposefully selected themselves into situations where they would be able to act in certain ways and reacted somewhat uniquely to their situations even when placed in the same school and faced with common institutional constraints.[7] There is little evidence in our data that would support the kind of passive response to institutional forces that is frequently suggested in the literature (e.g. Hoy and Rees 1977), or an unthinking acquiescence to institutional demands.

Findings related to the socialization of student teachers cannot be interpreted apart from consideration of the nature of the student teaching program that provides the context for the investigation. As Gaskill (1975) points out, one cannot assume that all student teaching programs pose the same constraints and encouragements for students and that the socialization of student teachers takes the same form and has the same meaning in different institutions. The substance of particular student teaching programs (e.g. forms of supervision, expectations, and requirements for students), the characteristics of specific elementary and middle school placement sites (Becher and Ade 1982), and the place of student teaching in the overall pre-service preparation program all necessarily affect the form and outcomes of student teacher socialization.

Each of the schools made demands on the students to learn and conform to acceptable patterns of school teacher behavior. These patterns differed from school to school, as did the constraints imposed by the availability of materials and the presence of more detailed or more open curriculum plans. More detailed plans forced students to implement teaching goals established by others, while more open plans constrained students to invent goals and activities and, possibly, to search out appropriate materials of instruction. For 10 of the 13 students, these varying constraints were cheerfully accepted, since they had chosen their student-teaching placements as models for the kind of teaching–learning settings they wanted to experience.

In the university teacher education program studied here, students had opportunities to give direction to their experience both before and after the placement process was completed. For example, field requirements for student teachers and the specific expectations for their performance were largely determined individually for each student through a formal process of negotiation ('Letter of Expectations') at the beginning of the semester involving the student teacher, co-operating teacher, and university supervisor (see Grant 1975). The university prescribed very few requirements that all student teachers were expected to fulfill and encouraged students to take active roles in determining the specific form and substance of their student teaching. The university's stance toward program content as 'reflexive' rather than as 'received' (Zeichner 1983a) was consistent with the student's active role in the placement process and probably contributed to some extent to the resilience of student teachers' perspectives during the 15-week semester.

The nature of supervision in this program also encouraged students to clarify their perspectives toward teaching and, probably, to develop in a direction consistent with their entering perspectives. The weekly student teaching seminars with supervisors, the 'inquiry-oriented' field assignments that students were required to complete, and the student-teacher journals that formed an essential part of the supervisory process generally encouraged greater clarity about the substance of teaching perspectives, a reflective or analytic stance toward teaching practice, and they pushed students to employ personal discretion and independent judgement in their work (see Zeichner and Teitelbaum 1982). All of this suggests that under certain conditions it may be possible to help student teachers control their situations rather than being passively controlled by them.

Phase 2: Professional perspectives and craft knowledge during the first year of teaching

Whatever the pressures to conform to norms for teacher behavior, they might be presumed to be greater for beginning teachers than for student teachers. Although there are considerable differences in behavioral expectations and norms from one school to another, and although the demands of universities and schools are often consistent and mutually supportive of each other (Zeichner and Tabachnick 1981), beginning teachers could be expected to hear one socializing voice only, that of their schools. Students would be scattered as beginning teachers, often the only inexperienced teacher in a school, and therefore cut off from the student peers who were available earlier for emotional and professional support. A few professionals think of teaching as a continual process of development, with the early years, especially, being an extension of university teacher education. The conventional view, probably the view of the majority of teachers and administrators, is that any fully licensed teacher should be expected to be a 'completed' teacher, fully capable of meeting all the obligations and demands of a classroom. The frequent observations and analytic discussions of the student's teaching would be gone. The fledgling teacher must usually sharpen his or her skills through self-monitoring, while working near experienced, apparently self-confident, often opinionated colleague teachers and administrators, and while faced with the expectations of pupils and parents, expectations acquired through experiences with other teachers.

The second phase of our study followed four of the 13 students into their first year of teaching. We tried to answer two major questions:

(1) *How were the teaching perspectives that were recognizable at the end of student teaching strengthened or modified during the first year?* We wished to explore the network of related knowledge and beliefs about teaching together with the craft behaviors that were expressions in action of those ideas. Would we find a smooth development, no development, or abrupt shifts and changes, possibly in response to heavy pressures to conform to different norms than those present during student teaching?

(2) *Who and what influence the development of teacher perspectives during the first year?* We wished to identify the personal characteristics of the beginning teachers and the characteristics of the schools in which they worked that appeared to encourage resistance to or compliance with particular institutional pressures regarding teaching. We explored how and from whom these teachers learned about institutional norms and the extent to which these teachers adapted to the existing institutional regularities in their schools. We also explored whether and how schools attempted to monitor and elicit compliance with particular institutional norms.

During this second phase of our work, we continued to use the four orienting categories of teacher perspectives to describe teacher actions and ideas. Each of the four orienting categories was further defined in terms of several specific 'dilemmas' of teaching that had emerged from analyses of the data in the first phase of the study. (Table 1.1 identifies the 18 dilemmas of teaching that were associated with the four orienting categories. These 18 dilemmas gave direction to our data collection efforts during the second phase of the study.)

Between August 1981 and May 1982 we spent three one-week periods in the schools of each of the four teachers. A specific research plan was followed during the three weeks of data collection for each teacher. The three weeks were distributed throughout the school year. During four days of each week, an observer constructed narrative descriptions of events in each classroom using the four orienting categories and related 'dilemmas' as an orienting framework. All of the teachers were interviewed several times each day regarding their plans for instruction (e.g. purposes and rationales for particular activities) and their reactions to what had occurred. One day each week, an observer constructed a narrative description of classroom events with a particular focus on six pupils in each classroom who had been selected to represent the range of student diversity existing in each classroom. In addition to the daily interviews with each teacher focused on particular events that had been observed, a minimum of two in-depth interviews were conducted with each teacher during each of the three data-collection periods. These interviews sought in part to explore teachers' views regarding their own professional development in relation to the four orienting categories of perspectives, and also addressed additional dimensions of perspectives, unique to each teacher, that had emerged during the second phase of the study.

Additionally, we sought to investigate the influence of several institutional elements of school life on the development of teacher perspectives (e.g. school ethos and tradition, teacher culture, administrative expectations about the teacher's role). During each of the in-depth interviews we asked the teachers about their perceptions of the constraints and encouragements that existed in their schools and about how they learned what was and what was not appropriate behavior for teachers in their schools.

We also interviewed each principal at least once and interviewed two other teachers in each school concerning their views of the degree to which each beginning teacher was free to employ independent judgement in her work. Finally, we also collected many kinds of formal documents in each school, such as curriculum guides and teacher handbooks.

Through the classroom observations and teacher and administrator interviews we sought to monitor the continuing development of teacher perspectives and to construct in-depth portraits of life in each of the classrooms. Tape-recorded interviews and classroom observations were transcribed to facilitate a content analysis of the data. Several analyses of these data led to the construction of case studies that describe the development of each teacher and the individual and social influences on their development from the beginning of student teaching to the end of their first year of teaching.

Although there was individual variation, the four teachers were relatively alike in their apparent perspectives toward teaching when they began their first teaching positions. The four teachers worked in a variety of settings—one in an urban, one in a rural, and two in suburban schools—and in schools that served very different kinds of communities (e.g. one school served children of upper-middle-class professionals and managers, a second school served children of industrial workers, etc.). Three teachers worked in self-contained classroom settings with minimal departmentalization, while the fourth teacher worked in an architecturally open-plan school with total departmentalization within teaching teams. Three were the only first-year teachers in their respective buildings, while one teacher had ready access to other beginners. Two were the only teachers at their respective grade levels, while two teachers worked with other teachers who taught the same grade or, in one case, the same pupils. Three of the four teachers taught at the seventh- or eighth-grade level (approximately 12–14-year-old pupils) and one teacher taught at the fourth-grade level (9–10 year olds). Three of the teachers worked in settings very different from those they experienced as student teachers. Table 1.2 summarizes selected characteristics of the settings that the four individuals worked in as student teachers and as first-year teachers.

Case studies from the first year of teaching

In presenting data about the four first-year teachers, we have chosen, in responding to limitations of space, to give very brief summary presentations for two of the teachers and then longer more detailed case studies for the other two. The interpretive and analytic comments that follow these data will refer to all four teachers. The two cases presented at length represent teachers who developed in different ways, employing different social strategies in response both to institutional mechanisms for social control and to pressures from formal and informal school cultures.

Sarah: internalized adjustment in a conventional school environment
Sarah was a student teacher in a middle-class community suburban to a moderate-size city (pop. 200,000). Together with her co-operating teacher she taught about a dozen 6-year-old children who had been judged unready to move from kindergarten to a regular first-grade classroom. The curriculum was invented by both teacher and student teacher during the semester, responding to their judgements about their pupils' abilities and levels of understanding. Much of the work was designed for individual pupils or groups of two or three, with a heavy emphasis on improving reading,

Table 1.2 *The four teachers: student teaching and the first year*

	Student teaching	The first year

Hannah	4th–5th grade
	Total departmentalization
	  within teams
	Suburban
		8th grade
		Self-contained/minimal
		  departmentalization
		Rural
		Only teacher at her grade level
		Only first-year teacher in her school

Rachel	4th–5th grade Self-contained class Urban	7th grade Self-contained/minimal departmentalization Urban Only teacher at her grade level Only first-year teacher in her school

Beth	5th grade
	Self-contained class
	
	Urban
		8th grade
		Heavy departmentalization within
		  teams
		Suburban
		One of nine teachers at her grade
		  level
		Only first-year teacher in her school

Sarah	Junior primary
	(pre-first grade)
	
	Suburban
		4th grade
		Self-contained/minimal
		  departmentalization
		Suburban
		One of three teachers at her grade level
		One of three first-year teachers in
		  her school

language, and arithmetic skills and on learning social behavior needed to succeed in a regular classroom.

During her first year, Sarah taught fourth graders (9–10 year olds) in an upper-middle-class community suburban to a city of about 500,000. The school was organized into self-contained classrooms of about 20–25 pupils. Sarah taught all subjects but music, art, and physical education. During reading instruction pupils were re-grouped among the three fourth-grade teachers, resulting in Sarah having a very large group (for that school—about 30 pupils) of apparently average fourth-grade reading ability.

Sarah's school was similar to the one in which she student taught, especially in the happiness of the pupils to be in school and their interest in being taught. Her pupils were different in being not only older but also in being highly verbal and high achievers. They were eager to pick up ideas and follow her leads and suggestions. They were fairly easy to keep on the task at hand.

The style of teacher–pupil interactions was warm and personal. Sarah was crisp and direct but also easily available to listen, to help; she obviously cared about pupils. The pace was quick but pupils seemed to follow right along. In most respects the curriculum was determined by textbooks or committees of teachers working in previous years. There were some initiatives taken by Sarah too, however. A very subtle initiative was her tendency to probe the obvious in a lesson, to question in such a way that pupils could more easily connect 'school knowledge' to their own lives. She stressed the process of knowing, understanding why an answer is right or wrong. The product, a correct answer or a justified answer, was also important to Sarah though. She was inventive, aiming to infuse ordinary activities with interest while staying close to the curriculum as laid out in guides or implied by the textbook.

Sarah consciously searched for the rules and limits for her behavior as teacher, intending for the most part to do what was required of her. She was frustrated to discover that these were not so easy to learn as she had expected. Explicit rules for behavior and responsibilities were provided, but many more were implied, as when the principal gives teachers articles about how much school time is wasted (in other schools) through such routines as taking attendance. Teachers suggested that discipline is best done by the teacher, that the principal would be displeased if pupils were sent to him to be disciplined. Lesson plans for the next week must be provided at the end of each week. However, one of Sarah's colleague fourth-grade teachers told the observer (Sarah was not present) that she simply ignored this 'rule' as it seemed to her not to serve any useful purpose. From another of her colleague teachers, Sarah learned that she could occasionally avoid the supposedly inflexible 'rule' about teachers staying until 4:00 p.m. every day.

Sarah felt harassed by pressure to cover many topics in what seemed to her to be too little time. She was intimidated by the reputation of parents in that school for making forceful demands of the school's professional personnel whenever parents were unhappy with the school program. (They wanted solid 'basics', with a dash of imagination and intellectual challenge.) She was frustrated by her lack of ability to get as much out of her pupils as she thought she should. She resented some of the constraints and lack of help coming from her principal and she felt she had lost some of her earlier idealism. Yet, in general she continued to internalize the same, basically eclectic perspective toward teaching as she did as a student teacher. This is consistent with the prevailing formal and informal beliefs in her school, including both its routine, product orientation as well as values placed on a controlled creativity, on attention to the process of pupil learning, on directive but humane and warm teacher relations with pupils, and on a pragmatic interpretation of formal rules and procedures.

Rachel: an attempt to redefine teaching in a private religious school
Rachel was a student teacher in a fourth–fifth-grade classroom (9–10 year olds) in a school serving a middle-class neighborhood in a city of about 200,000. Many of the parents worked in the nearby university. The school had a reputation for encouraging lively and inventive teaching. Its pupils, articulate and intellectually capable, regularly scored well on the annual citywide standardized achievement tests.

The program developed by Rachel's co-operating teacher was diversified, with many different activities going on at once—a group of pupils reading while another group wrote a story together, while individuals worked on science projects or finished math assignments. Rachel managed her part of this program competently, including the week when she was required to take on overall management of the classroom. A few words, to pupils who were too noisy or otherwise drifting off task, were enough to keep pupils focused and productive. The children reacted well to Rachel's evident personal interest in the subject being taught, especially social studies and composition, and to her initiatives that aimed to make their work intellectually challenging and interesting. Pupils seemed to accept Rachel's manner, which was friendly though not close.

Rachel's first teaching position was in a private religious school, one of those managed by the Catholic Archdiocese. The school enrolled about 200 children from kindergarten to eighth grade. Each class was self-contained and enclosed in a conventional room. The principal was a Sister but all the regular teachers were lay teachers. The school drew its pupils from working-class parents, many of whom were skilled workers in a large factory about a 15-minute walk from the school. Unemployment was very high (over 15 per cent) during the period of observation in the small industrial city (about 50,000) where the school was located.

The prevailing pattern of teaching was one in which teachers exercised tight control over what pupils did, emphasizing a uniform 'product' with a narrow range of correct responses. Pupils sat at desks in rows, listened to their teacher explain, answered when called, wrote what they were directed to write, read what they were directed to read.

Rachel was the only teacher in the school who challenged this pattern. There was some constraint imposed by the principal, who personally monitored the noise and movement levels in the classroom (the standard was to have little of either). There were textbooks supplied by the Archdiocese, which were approved for use. Yet there were few restraints on curriculum and few formal constraints altogether as long as pupils were quiet and seemed busy at work to anyone walking through the building.

Unfortunately, Rachel was unable to keep her pupils quiet or focused for very long at a time. She found her efforts to encourage pupil initiative rejected or abused by students who had been socialized to expect teacher demands and close control in a social context in which adults and children were natural enemies. This was part of the ethos of the informal teacher culture as well. From her colleagues Rachel had the scant consolation that previous teachers too had found her class difficult to manage. Rachel did not have the skill to overcome the pupils' long period of induction into patterns of response different from the self-motivated learning she hoped to encourage. Her doubts about asserting her authority and her inclination to avoid too close relationships with her pupils made it difficult for her to get their attention. Her interest in mobilizing parent support and co-operation was thwarted by lack of knowledge of the cultural content of her pupils' homes and her inability to talk to people who did not feel confident speaking English. Her fear of her principal's disapproval led her to early attempts to act the authoritarian teacher that she believed her principal wanted her to be. However, her inability to get her pupils to behave when she tried to be strict helped her to reaffirm her earlier perspective. Rachel's constant demands for quiet, for attention, interjected into almost every sentence, fragmented the ideas she presented, undermining her efforts to focus attention on the meanings of the material being presented to her pupils.

Rachel's colleagues were very friendly and Rachel found it enjoyable to be with them socially, at break times and out of school. They were aware that Rachel was having trouble but they had little professional help to give that could move her closer to her own goals for teaching. (The eighth-grade teacher was stern and forbidding; her rigidly controlled class disintegrated as soon as Rachel entered to teach them social studies. Surprisingly sympathetic, she advised Rachel to be patient. Another colleague told her that teaching was only a job, not her whole life; Rachel learned to repeat this to herself as a sustaining incantation.)

Despite her lack of professional support from colleagues, the rejecting and continuously disruptive responses of her pupils, and her own feelings of despair, Rachel was sustained by a few successes and continued to act as she thought a teacher should, trying again and again to justify her faith that if she could make the work interesting enough, involve students in active learning, they would be intrinsically motivated to learn and even become better behaved.

Beth: adjusting to teaching in a closely controlled school environment
Beth was a student teacher in a moderate-sized city (about 200,000) in a self-contained fifth-grade classroom, in an elementary school with grades kindergarten to fifth grade. In that community this meant that her co-operating teacher was responsible for instruction in all subjects except art, music, and physical education. The prevailing style of teaching in her classroom was characterized by warm personal relationships, and some judicious sharing of curriculum decisions with pupils. Though most of the teaching was fairly routine (reading to answer questions about the text, drill in arithmetic), there was a genuine effort to encourage pupils' creative thinking and problem solving. Beth was encouraged to invent activities that would further these more diffuse goals as well as to further routine classroom learning activities with more precisely targeted goals. Students were from a mixed socioeconomic background, mostly middle class, but some from economically poorer homes. The principal supported an 'active' curriculum that encouraged and displayed the results of pupils' creative efforts. The teachers and principal believed that they had firm community and parent support for such an approach.

As a first-year teacher Beth taught eighth graders in a middle school enrolling pupils in grades six through eight (approximately ages 12–14). The school served a middle-class community suburban to a large city (500,000). Homes could be characterized as middle or upper middle class. The school's organization was quite different from Beth's school during her previous (student teaching) year. Groups of 75–100 children were taught all the subjects by teams of three or four teachers. Art, music, and physical education were taught by specialists, and other specialists were available for advice on teaching reading and language and for help in working with poorly achieving or psychologically disturbed children.

Beth and her two co-teachers together taught approximately 80 pupils. Their teaching was directed by lists of 'performance' in each subject. The curriculum was referred to by the teachers and the principal as Performance Based Education (PBE) with pupil achievement being judged on the basis of Criterion Referenced Tests (CRTs). The lists of performances and the CRTs had been developed some years before by committees of teachers. Teachers were discouraged from changing or adding topics. A CRT identified student inabilities, mainly in reading, language, and mathematics skills, and in social studies and science information. Beth and her colleagues decided which of the teachers would be responsible for different groups of students in each subject, the timing of instruction, and the scheduling of tests. Deviation from these time plans was discouraged. For example, taking longer to explore a topic or 'going off on a tangent' (adding topics not specified in the PBE lists) might force one's colleagues to wait and waste time, since all pupils had to be tested at the same time. The school was built to an architecturally open plan so teachers could easily keep track of what was happening in other segments of the area housing their class. The principal frequently walked around the school and did not hestitate to discipline students or to point out to teachers deviations from established school procedures, either on the spot or in a later conference.

At the beginning of her first year as a regular teacher, Beth referred appreciatively to her student teaching when, from time to time, she decided on a topic to be taught, researched its content, and invented teaching strategies. Beth said she believed an 'open and easy' approach to teaching was valuable because it stimulated pupils to think. In some interview statements she referred to the routine, or at least 'follow-the-present-pattern' nature of her teaching. In other statements she said she selected some of the topics for study, aimed at stimulating pupils to 'sit down and think about things', tried to think of ways to present the content that would capture the interest of pupils. However, she was observed to teach in a very controlled style. Her planning at the beginning of the year was almost entirely limited to deciding which textbook pages to use in working with groups of 10–25 pupils, which and how many math solutions to demonstrate, whether to repeat teaching on a topic or go on to the next item on the PBE list. (Beth was under considerable strain at first, finding her way into the system. This was noticed by the principal who tried to get her to relax, boosting her self-confidence.)

One instance was recorded, in five consecutive days of observation, of the 'open and easy' style of teaching: the most capable math group was encouraged to find alternative solutions to problems. The pupils responded eagerly and Beth smiled and said to the observer, 'I love this!' But the bulk of her teaching behavior followed from (1) earlier decisions about how many questions to ask or problems to explain; (2) on-the-spot reactions to time remaining, to student actions (redirecting misbehavior, answering questions, correcting errors with on-the-spot explanations); and (3) the existence of available materials (booklets, film strips) with previously developed worksheets or test questions. Post-teaching behavior was mainly correcting tests and selecting the next day's questions, worksheets, drill practice.

At mid-year, five days of observation revealed no equivalent to the exciting math lesson. All the observed teaching was guided by getting through the PBE lists of objectives. Beth said the main influences on what happened in her classroom were:

> the school curriculum in that they say what should be taught … us teachers in deciding who teaches what … and then me, myself as a teacher, as in how I'm going to teach it.

Selecting or identifying goals was *not* an important effort. She said her goals:

> [are] real sketchy … I really don't have any big ones set out … I'd like them to understand what I'm talking about, sure … and to retain some of the things that I've taught, definitely. But that would be it for goals.

Beth said she was satisfied with the amount of freedom she had to control what happened in her class, 'It sets out things you should be doing, which is nice', she says, 'because you know what's expected.' She commented that she could generally teach the kind of curriculum that she thought was important, 'as long as it includes what has been set out for me to teach'.

At the same time, Beth said she thought her talents were under-utilized. She said,

> School isn't just the place for basic learning, you know; the teacher talks and you learn or absorb it. [It should be] more of an interesting kind of place … but it's just not coming through anymore. I guess I just don't take the time to sit down and think about it like I used to. Or I don't have the time to design some of the things that I designed that were really neat.

Asked about preparation time, Beth said she had enough.

At the end of the school year, Beth's teaching was observed to have changed little from the mid-year description, except that she was more self-confident and practiced in implementing the PBE curriculum. With the end-of-year tests to face, all of her class-room behavior was focused on getting her pupils to perform well. Observations described days filled with assigning drill and practice, giving information, and testing recall.

Beth's statements about her thinking during planning, during teaching, following teaching, had changed in that they no longer contained references to selecting topics, or aiming to stimulate pupil creative thinking and pupil reflection, as had appeared in earlier statements of that type. She began with the PBE lists of objectives, used materials for which there were information and recall exercises (reading, social studies, science), or decided which and how many math solutions to present, choosing items from the textbook to illustrate. Decisions were often made on the spot regarding what to say about a math problem or what questions to ask, for example, about a story or a section of a science booklet. Consideration for team decisions about time schedules were the strongest determinant for whether to extend or abbreviate teaching, give more time to slower learners or not.

What had also changed were Beth's statements about her perspectives toward teaching and about what she thought she *should* be doing. Her statements of belief now indicated that she had learned that she could be successful as a teacher without doing much detailed planning and without the need to do much (or any) research on the topics she intended to teach. Presumably, she found enough in the Teachers' Guides and the pupil materials to support the explanations and presentations she gave. Beth's thinking about teacher classroom behavior had also changed in that she no longer saw much value in open discussions and 'hands-on' pupil activities. She intended to move more quickly the following year, to spend less time explaining the work, leaving out discussions of topics that were not 'on the test', and 'covering more areas', especially areas that are tested.

Hannah: redefining teaching in a loosely managed school
Hannah was a student teacher in a small village located near a middle-sized city (about 200,000) and worked as part of the one of two fifth/sixth-grade teams in a grade 4–6 middle school enrolling about 500 children. There were four teaching teams in this school, each one of which was responsible for the instruction of approximately 120 children in all subject areas except art, music, and physical education. Hannah worked on a team with four certified teachers and had her own classes of around 30 pupils for each subject. During a typical week she taught almost all of the 120 pupils on her team, since the instructional program was totally departmentalized. The school community included few minorities and had a mix of parents ranging from a few who were very poor to some who were highly paid professionals. The majority of the parents were moderately well off financially. Although the pupils were younger, the school and its curriculum were similar in organization to Beth's school during her first year of teaching.

Throughout the semester Hannah questioned the departmentalized school structure, the rationalized curricular form, and the distant and formal relations between teachers and pupils, which were a part of the taken-for-granted reality of her school, and felt she was being asked to fit into a teacher role that she did not like. Despite isolated efforts, which continued throughout the semester, to implement what she felt was a more varied and lively curriculum and to relate to her pupils in a more personal way than was common in her school, Hannah for the most part complied outwardly with the accepted practices in her school and did not act in a manner consistent with her expressed beliefs. At the end of the semester, despite the lack of confirmation from her experience as a student teacher, Hannah was more convinced than ever ('having learned a lot of things of what not to do') that warm and close relations between pupils and teachers, getting pupils excited about learning and feeling good about themselves as people (e.g. by integrating their personal knowledge into the curriculum), were the keys to good teaching.

Hannah's first year in a regular position was spent as the only eighth-grade teacher in a nine-classroom K–8 public school enrolling about 190 pupils. The school was located in a rural farm community a few miles outside of a small city with a population of 9,000. Hannah taught all subjects except civics to her eighth-grade class and also taught science to the seventh-grade class. The parents of the children in her class were very diverse socioeconomically, ranging from farm owners and professionals to farm workers. All of the teachers lived in the immediate area with the exception of Hannah and one other teacher who commuted from a city 45 minutes away. Hannah was the youngest and the only first-year teacher in the school and the only one who had not completed a teacher education program at one of the relatively small state teachers colleges, which were now part of the state university system.

The culture, tradition, and organization of this school were quite different from the school in which Hannah completed her student teaching. There was a very strong tradition of individualism in the school, which sanctioned each teacher's right to do things in his or her own way, and there was very little co-operation or co-ordination among the staff. All of the classrooms, with the exception of Hannah's and the seventh-grade class, were totally self-contained, and each teacher was responsible for all of the instruction for a group of around 25 students. The principal of the school was also a full-time teacher and did not observe or confer with teachers except during weekly staff meetings.

Consistent with the individualistic tradition of the school, very few overt controls were exerted on teachers with respect to the planning and teaching of the curriculum. Teachers were given curriculum guides and textbooks for each subject area and were permitted to cover the content specified in the guides in whatever order, at whatever pace, and with whatever methods they thought were most appropriate. Teachers were also free to supplement the texts with any other materials and to go beyond what was listed in the curriculum guides as long as the curriculum was covered by the end of the year.

The only explicit controls placed on teachers' handling of the curriculum were in the areas of grading and testing. All of the teachers were expected to give each child 30 'marks' for each subject during each of three report periods and to grade pupils' work according to a standard grading scale. A great deal of emphasis was also placed upon pupil performance on a national standardized test given each spring.

Alongside the tradition of individualism in the school, there was also a very strong and mostly unspoken agreement among all but Hannah and one colleague in the seventh-grade class about the ways in which teachers should relate to their pupils. This approach was characterized by one teacher as 'the old school method ... you can't have someone here who is too soft with the kids'. Hannah became aware of this consensus on teacher–pupil relations ('In this school it's the teacher's role to be the disciplinarian') through observation of other teachers, through her pupils' comments, and indirectly through the school 'grapevine'. Other teachers would rarely confront Hannah directly with criticisms of her more informal style of relating to pupils. On several occasions, however, teachers complained to the principal, who in turn passed the word to Hannah that she had violated the preferred formality between teachers and pupils. All of the classrooms, with the exception of the seventh and eighth grades, were very tightly controlled by teachers, and this strong, informal agreement among the staff initially made Hannah feel isolated and alone.

> You begin to try new things; everything is not out of the textbooks or worksheet oriented. They look down on that. But they don't constrain you and say you can't do things. They would never say you can't do things. They'll do it in a roundabout way... when it comes back to you, you feel that everyone else is against you.

The community was characterized by Hannah and several other teachers as extremely conservative, as suspicious of new ideas, and as holding expectations for teachers to maintain very tight controls over pupils. Hannah initially felt more pressure from the parents than from her colleagues to conform to the unspoken tradition regarding the teacher's role and was initially reluctant to act on her intuitions because she felt that she was perceived as an outsider. From the beginning of the year, Hannah made many efforts to win the trust and confidence of the parents and to learn more about the ways and mores of the community. She visited the homes and farms of several students and joined a bowling team made up of local parents. During one memorable weekend she invited several farm girls in her class to spend the night at her apartment in town.

At the beginning of the year, despite the lack of close supervision and formal controls, Hannah relied heavily on the textbooks in planning her curriculum; however, she also made efforts from the very beginning to establish warm and close relationships with her pupils in violation of the school's tradition. Hannah continued to describe her basic orientation to teaching as 'humanistic' and emphasized the affective and inter-personal dimensions of her work. She felt strongly that a positive self-concept is the key to learning and wanted to find ways to make school enjoyable for herself and her pupils. Hannah tried very hard to present herself to her pupils as a 'human being' by openly admitting her mistakes and her ignorance with regard to content, and by freely sharing aspects of her personal life with her pupils. She also made many efforts to understand the personal lives of each child in her class and to gain her pupils' trust and confidence.

Initially, Hannah's pupils were very suspicious of her efforts to break down the conventional barriers between teachers and students, and there was a lack of support from her colleagues. Hannah became confused and uncertain during the first three months of the school year about the direction she should take, and established several classroom practices and rules that violated her own vision of 'humanistic' teaching. Despite these isolated instances where Hannah flirted with more conventional methods of controlling her pupils, for the most part she exerted relatively little direct control over pupil behaviors, and the pupils gradually began to respond to her efforts.

Despite her efforts to establish warm and personal relations with her pupils, which were gradually becoming more and more successful, Hannah was frustrated with her heavy reliance on textbooks and with her inability to establish a more varied and lively instructional program. While she was very sure of herself in dealing with children in interpersonal matters, she felt that she did not have a clear idea of how to implement her expressed preference for a more integrated curriculum that incorporated children's personal experiences, that gave pupils concrete experiences in relation to ideas, and that elicited their enthusiasm and excitement about solving problems in relation to the world around them. 'I just feel like I'm spoon feeding them and opening their heads and pushing the knowledge in.'

Knowing that her pupils had been taught 'right out of the textbook' in the past and that they would probably be taught so in the future, and not confident that she was able to explain to others how particular methods were meeting specific academic goals, Hannah worried a lot about handicapping her students and about not giving them what they were 'supposed to learn'. By December, Hannah was so frustrated that she considered quitting teaching and accepting another job outside education.

As the year progressed, Hannah became more and more satisfied with her classroom program, and her actions began more and more to reflect her expressed beliefs about teaching. She continued to rely mainly on the texts in planning her lessons, but she gradually made more independent decisions, which resulted in a greater emphasis on providing concrete experiences for children and on incorporating their personal lives into the curriculum.

By April, Hannah felt confident enough to drop the basal readers, having her pupils read novels instead, and to let two pupils teach a unit on engines to the class that drew upon their experiences in repairing farm vehicles. Throughout the year Hannah continued to expose all of her pupils to the same curricular content and stayed fairly close to the texts in some subjects (e.g. math), but her work in language, reading, and science reflected the active pupil involvement and problematic approach to knowledge that she had hoped to create since the beginning of her student teaching. By the end of the year Hannah felt that she had come closer to her ideal, where pupils are thinking critically and constantly and where they are always asking questions and trying to apply their in-class learnings to everyday life. In May, Hannah's pupils got the highest scores of all the eighth-grade classes in the school district on the nationally standardized achievement test they were given.

Hannah maintained her beliefs regarding the importance of 'humanistic' teaching throughout her student teaching and her first year of teaching with little or no formal support from her schools, and gradually, as her pupils and their parents began to respond positively to her approach, Hannah was able to find ways, by acting on her intuitions and through trial and error, of modifying her behavior to bring it into closer agreement with her beliefs about teaching.

Interpreting data from the first year of teaching

In the second phase of the study we find further support for an interactive view of teacher socialization. During this phase, we found it necessary to elaborate Lacey's (1977) conceptual framework in order to account for the two different institutional contexts that each teacher had experienced. Although we retained Lacey's categories of internalized adjustment, strategic compliance, and strategic redefinition, we added a contextual factor to the definition of each social strategy; this considered the overall similarity or dissimilarity between the institutional contexts experienced during student teaching and the first year. For example, the two cases of internalized adjustment in our sample were different from one another because one teacher had adjusted to a school situation very much like her school during student teaching, while the other teacher adjusted to a very different situation. The implications of this additional dimension are important for understanding the development of teacher perspectives over time.

A second elaboration of Lacey's conceptual framework broadens the meaning of strategic redefinition, or at least describes a dimension of its meaning that is not explicit in Lacey's discussion. While Lacey seems to reserve this term for only those attempts at redefinition that are successful, we broadened the definition to include both those attempts that were successful and those that were not. In this way the framework can account for all instances of overt deviance. Obviously, one cannot determine which of the two types of strategic redefinition has occurred until the process has been completed. Furthermore, each of the two varieties of strategic redefinition may lead to different actions. For example, if an individual fails in a change attempt, he/she may choose to leave the organization or to engage in one of the two strategies of situational adjustment. On the other hand, if the attempt is successful, the behavior might now fall within the range of acceptable responses within the school.

Table 1.3 summarizes the eight possible social strategies within this elaborated version of Lacey's (1977) model when the differences between successful and unsuccessful strategic redefinition are also taken into account.

Table 1.3 *Eight possible social strategies*

	Similar school context	Dissimilar school context
Internalized adjustment	X	X
Strategic compliance	X	X
Successful strategic redefinition	X	X
Unsuccessful strategic redefinition	X	X

Despite the variety of social strategies employed by each teacher, there was also a dominant strategy that characterized the experience of each teacher. Specifically, two of the four teachers (Hannah and Rachel), who were both in 'dissimilar situations' (different from the context of their student teaching), attempted to redefine significantly the range of acceptable behaviors in their schools in various ways (e.g. in relation to teacher–pupil relationships, the curriculum), while the other two teachers (Beth and Sarah) experienced adjustment to the dominant norms in their schools in terms of both values and behaviors. Sarah, who was in a situation very similar to her school during student teaching, was able to continue to develop her teaching perspectives in a manner consistent with her development during student teaching. Beth, on the other hand, who taught in a school very different from the one that she had worked in as a student teacher, appeared to shift away from her entering perspectives toward perspectives that were consistent with those encouraged by the dominant formal and informal cultures in her new school. Beth was the only one of the four teachers who appeared to 'give up' perspectives that seemed clearly developed (they were certainly clearly articulated) by the end of student teaching, and both her actions and statements indicated that this shift was one of internalized adjustment.

Hannah, one of the two students whose dominant strategy was one of strategic redefinition, was successful in her efforts even under strong pressures to conform, while the other teacher, Rachel, failed for various reasons in her efforts to establish her 'dominant' teaching style. There were many reasons why attempts at strategic redefinition either failed or succeeded. Among these were the degree to which teaching perspectives were developed at the beginning of the year and the strength with which they were held, the 'coping skills' and political sensitivity of the teachers, the degree of contradiction between formal and informal school cultures, and the reactions of the pupils to the teachers. We were particularly impressed with the tenacity with which both Rachel and Hannah clung to their entering perspectives under strong pressures to change and with the key role played by pupil responses in strengthening or modifying these perspectives.

Table 1.4 *The dominant social strategies employed by the four teachers during student teaching and the first year*

	Student teachers	The first year
Hannah	Strategic compliance	Successful strategic redefinition (dissimilar context)
Rachel	Internalized adjustment	Unsuccessful strategic redefinition (dissimilar context)
Beth	Internalized adjustment	Internalized adjustment (dissimilar context)
Sarah	Internalized adjustment	Internalized adjustment (similar context)

Table 1.4 summarizes the dominant social strategies employed by all four of the teachers during student teaching and the first year. Without going into detail here about the combinations of specific factors in each case that led to the adoption of a particular social strategy or to its success or failure, we feel that this study clearly demonstrates that the adaptation of beginning teachers to institutional regularities cannot be taken for granted and that first-year teachers, under some conditions at least, can have a creative impact on their workplaces and survive.

These findings also call into question the definition of teaching perspectives as situationally specific. Despite the fact that three of the four teachers worked in very different situations as first-year teachers than as student teachers (different in terms of the kinds of constraints and possibilities they presented teachers, different in terms of school traditions and cultures), two of these three teachers attempted to implement a style of pedagogy similar to that evidenced during student teaching. Only one teacher (Beth) significantly changed her perspectives in response to differing institutional demands. Although Sarah talked about having to follow the textbook more and about feeling less in control of her classroom as a first-year teacher, she found herself in a situation very similar to that experienced as a student teacher and continued to develop her perspectives in a manner consistent with her initial predispositions.

In summary, despite differing organizational contexts during student teaching and the first year, beginning teachers under some conditions at least were able to maintain a perspective that was in conflict with the dominant institutional cultures in their schools. One possible explanation for the resilience of beginning teachers in the face of institutional pressure is that the pressure of the organization is often contradictory in nature. Despite arguments by Hoy (1968) and others that there is a homogeneous school culture into which neophytes are socialized, we found, consistent with the studies of Carew and Lightfoot (1979), Metz (1978), and Hammersley (1977b), that school cultures were often diverse, that various 'subcultures' were easily identifiable in all but one school, and that these subcultures at times attempted to influence the beginning teachers in contradictory ways. In the one case where a teacher was able to redefine various aspects of her school situation successfully, these contradictions within the school culture (particularly contradictions between the formal and informal school cultures) played a significant role in enabling Hannah to implement successfully a style of teaching that was very different from that which went on around her. However, in the one case of unsuccessful strategic redefinition, a very strong and homogeneous school culture in opposition to the teacher's preferred style played a significant role in blocking Rachel's efforts to succeed in a manner consistent with her initial predispositions. School cultures are apparently not always diverse and contradictory within any one setting, but when they are the contradictions seem to provide room for beginning teachers to implement a 'deviant' pedagogy, or at least to establish individual expressions of teaching. In any case, whatever the explanation, it seems clear the beginning teachers give some direction to the strength and quality of their socialization into teaching. There is very little evidence in our data that would support the kind of ready acquiescence to institutional demands that has been described frequently in the literature of both student teaching (Gibson 1976) and teaching (Schwille et al 1979).

INSTITUTIONAL CONTROL AND THE SOCIALIZATION OF BEGINNING TEACHERS

The second interest in Phase 2 of our study was to discover how the particular characteristics, dispositions, and abilities of the beginning teachers and the various people and institutional characteristics in their schools influenced the development of teaching perspectives during the first year. We focused especially on how institutional control mechanisms within the four schools affected the work of the beginning teachers.

All organizations, and schools are no exception, employ mechanisms of control to exact greater productivity from workers and to try to ensure that organizational members follow accepted procedures within the organization. Etzioni (1965, p. 650) defines an organizational control structure as the 'distribution of means used by an organization to elicit the performance it needs and to check whether the quantities and qualities of such performances are in accord with organizational specifications'. Richard Edwards (1979) identifies three different forms of organizational control (personal, bureaucratic, and technical) in his analysis of the struggles of management and labor to exert control within the workplace. These three forms of control are defined in relation to three specific aspects of the work process: (1) the *direction* of work (e.g. the specification of what needs to be done, in what order, with what degree of precision, and in what period of time); (2) the *evaluation* of workers' performance (e.g. how work is supervised and how the performance of each worker is assessed); and (3) *discipline* (e.g. how workers are sanctioned and rewarded in attempts to elicit co-operation and enforce compliance with 'management's' direction of the work process).

First, with *personal or direct control*, superordinates (which in the case of the school would be the principal) personally supervise the activities of workers and through close monitoring of workers' actions ensure that workers comply with organizational norms. Secondly, with *bureaucratic control*, control is embedded into the social structure of the workplace and is enforced through impersonal bureaucratic rules and hierarchical social relations. Sanctions and rewards under bureaucratic control are dictated by officially approved policies to which workers, in particular role groups, are held responsible. Finally, with *technical control*, an organization's control over its members (direction of work tasks, evaluation of work done, and rewarding and disciplining of workers) is embedded into the physical structure of the labor process, and jobs are designed in such a way as to minimize the need to rely on workers' compliance with impersonal bureaucratic rules.

This framework for examining various forms of organizational control was very helpful to us in understanding how the first-year teachers learned what was expected of them, how desired behaviors were reinforced, and how organizational sanctions were applied. Generally, we found that there was very little direct and close supervision of the first-year teachers by their principals. Although all of the principals articulated expectations of what the teachers were supposed to teach and of how they should manage their classroom, there was very little effort (with the exception of Beth's principal) to attempt to ensure teacher compliance by directly monitoring behaviors in the classroom. Furthermore, none of the four teachers looked to their principals for guidance and assistance on a regular basis.

On the other hand, as one would expect, there were numerous bureaucratic rules and regulations in each school that attempted to dictate to teachers how and what to teach, procedures for managing pupil behavior in and out of the classroom, and such general activities as when teachers could leave the school buildings at the end of the day. We found that these rules and regulations (e.g. articulated in curriculum guides and teacher handbooks) gave the beginning teachers varying degrees of information about what was expected of them and of the limits beyond which organizational sanctions would be applied. We also found, consistent with Weick's (1976) notion of schools as 'loosely coupled systems' and with Bidwell's (1965) construct of 'structural looseness', that the first-year teachers were frequently able to ignore or even to openly violate bureaucratic rules when they wanted to do so. The self-contained classrooms in three of the four schools together with the minimal amount of personal supervision by principals in these three schools weakened the controlling effects of a bureaucratic organization. For example, despite a policy in her school that required teachers to grade pupils according to a standardized grading scheme based entirely on the percentage of correct responses, Hannah frequently raised the marks of her pupils when she thought that they had put their best effort into the work. There was minimal interaction among teachers in this school about classroom-related matters and the principal, who was also a full-time classroom teacher, did not have the time personally to supervise Hannah's activities in the classroom.

While the teachers complied with formal school rules and regulations on a regular basis, only Beth adopted a 'bureaucratic perspective' toward her role as a teacher. In Beth's school there was considerable pressure on all teachers to conform to a perspective preferred by the administration and the majority of teachers. This pressure took the form of the principal's more frequent supervision, though it was often casual and indirect, the bureaucratic organization into teaching teams, each team of teachers planning for and teaching 80–100 or more pupils, and pupil and teacher success judged by success on pre-set tests. There was some 'slippage' even here, and some teachers resisted these constraints to some extent, though Beth did not.

The most pervasive and powerful factor in determining the level of institutional constraints in all of the schools was *technical control* exerted through the timing of instruction, the curriculum and curricular materials, and the architecture of the school. Technical control reached through the walls into every teacher's classroom. It was most powerful for Beth, where the pace and form of instruction, the open architectural plan, the precise time schedules, and the performance-based curriculum all made deviation from the preferred patterns of teaching very difficult. While present as a factor in all the other schools, technical control was less complete, was not as strongly reinforced by other forms of control (direct supervision or strong bureaucratic structures), and was more easily manipulated or ignored by the teachers.

Apple (1983), Gitlin (1983), and Wise (1979) have recently argued, and have provided some empirical support for the view, that technical control is a significant aspect of the way in which teachers are socialized into their work and of how institutional norms are maintained over time. Our research supports their arguments, particularly with reference to Beth, and underscores the importance of examining how different forms of institutional control contribute to communicating institutional expectations to teachers and to the monitoring and evaluation of teacher's work activities. However, as with any other form of attempted institutional control, technical control does not constitute an irresistible pressure for teacher conformity. Even beginning teachers can manage to avoid or redirect elements of technical control if they have personal goals and the political skills to realize these. Technical control is an issue that has not received much attention in the literature to date and should be taken into account in future studies of beginning teacher socialization.

Finally, it should be pointed out that Edwards' (1979) conceptual framework did not provide a complete picture of how the four institutions sought to elicit compliance with particular norms regarding teaching. Specifically, while this framework illuminated important aspects of the *formal* institutional control structures, it did not enable us to address the ethos and tradition in a school that were communicated to each beginning teacher through the *informal* teacher, pupil, and school cultures present in each setting. Informal school cultures were often tacit rather than explicit. Even when explicit, the informal culture was less visible than the formal culture, being expressed in private conversations between teachers, casual remarks not intended for wide distribution, interpretations of the publicly acknowledged formal culture expressed not in words but in teacher, principal, and pupil actions. There was usually one formal school culture, but there were several different and often conflicting versions of the informal school culture within a single school; one or more of these informal school cultures were often in conflict with the officially sanctioned one. It was the interaction of these formal and informal cultures rather than the presence or absence of any particular control mechanism by itself that determined the institutional constraints and opportunities presented to each teacher.

For example, in the one case where strategic redefinition was largely successful (Hannah), an informal school tradition to let each teacher function on his or her own without interference from other teachers weakened the influence of formal attempts to co-ordinate curricular activities within the school, and provided opportunities for Hannah to attempt to implement her preferred and 'deviant' style of teaching.

Colleague teachers were the major source of information about the informal culture. They also provided a 'shaded' view of the formal school culture that brought the practical reality of formal school pronouncements into sharper relief. Not so explicit, but quite forceful in their influence on the behavior of three of the teachers in our study, were the actions and reactions of pupils—the acquiescence of some, the rebellion of others. In the case where strategic redefinition was unsuccessful (Rachel), the agreement and mutual reinforcement between the formal and informal school cultures made it very difficult for Rachel to find any support for her attempts to implement her 'deviant' teaching style. In particular, the powerful expression (in their actions) of pupil traditions of resisting teacher initiatives prevented Rachel from realizing a style of teaching that was based on mutual teacher–pupil co-operation and on pupils accepting responsibility for much of their own learning.

Many factors influenced the strength of the informal traditions within each school (e.g. the number of years a staff had worked together) and their impact on the four teachers (e.g. the degree to which pupils had internalized informal school traditions). Many factors in each instance also contributed to the success or failure of particular actions of the beginning teachers. Although a discussion of all of these influences is beyond the scope of our data, it should be emphasized that an understanding of institutional control in the four schools cannot be derived from an analysis of formal control mechanisms alone.

NOTES

1. The research reported in this chapter was funded by the Wisconsin Center for Education Research, which is supported in part by a grant from the National Institute of Education (Grant No. NIE-G-81-0009). The opinions expressed in this paper do not necessarily reflect the position, policy, or endorsement of the National Institute of Education.
2. See Zeichner and Tabachnick (1985) and Olesen and Whittaker (1970) for discussions of the limitations of teacher attitude studies.
3. See Clark and Peterson (1986) and Feiman-Nemser and Floden (1986) for reviews of these studies on the nature, content and structure of teachers' craft knowledge.
4. This instrument and the profiles of 13 student responses to the TBI are included in the complete report of the study (Tabachnick and Zeichner 1985).
5. Because of this we decided to drop the categories 'the role of the school in society' and 'the role of the community in school affairs' from our analysis and based our descriptions of student teacher perspectives on the data related to the four remaining categories of perspectives.
6. While space does not permit documentation of the existence of this 'strategic compliance' or the internalized adjustment and development which characterized the majority of students, further documentation of these socialization 'outcomes' can be found in Tabachnick, Zeichner, et al (1982).

7. Egan's (1982) case study analysis of three of the 13 students demonstrates that diverse perspectives existed even in a single school. See Zeichner (1983b) for a detailed analysis of the specific agents and institutional mechanisms which influenced the socialization of the 13 students.

REFERENCES

Apple, M. (1983) 'Curricular Form and the Logic of Technical Control: The Building of the Possessive Individual'. In Apple, M. and Weis, L. (eds) *Ideology and Practice in Education*. Philadelphia, PA: Temple University Press.

Atkinson, P. and Delamont, S. (1985) 'Socialisation into Teaching: The Research Which Lost Its Way'. *British Journal of Sociology of Education*, **6**(3), 307–22.

Ball, S. and Goodson, I. (1985) 'Understanding Teachers: Concepts and Contexts'. In Ball, S. and Goodson, I. (eds) *Teachers Lives and Careers*. London: Falmer Press.

Bartholomew, J. (1976) 'Schooling Teachers: The Myth of the Liberal College'. In Whitty, G. and Young, J. M. (eds) *Explorations in the Politics of School Knowledge*. Driffield, Yorks: Nafferton Books.

Baumrind, D. (1980) 'New Directions in Socialization Research'. *American Psychologist*, **35**, 639–62.

Becher, R. and Ade, W. (1982) 'The Relationship of Field Placement Characteristics and Students' Potential Field Performance Abilities to Clinical Experience Performance Ratings. *Journal of Teacher Education*, **33**, 24–30.

Becker, H., Geer, B., Hughes, E. and Strauss, A. (1961) *Boys in White*. Chicago, IL: University of Chicago Press.

Berlak, A. and Berlak, H. (1981) *Dilemmas of Schooling: Teaching and Social Change*. London: Methuen.

Bidwell, C. (1965) 'The school as a formal organization'. In March, J. (ed.) *Handbook of Organizations*. Chicago, IL: Rand McNally.

Brophy, J. and Evertson, C. (1981) *Student Characteristics and Teaching*. New York: Longman.

Bussis, A., Chittenden, E. and Amarel, M. (1976) *Beyond Surface Curriculum*. Boulder, CO: Westview Press.

Carew, J. and Lightfoot, S. L. (1979) *Beyond Bias: Perspectives on Classrooms*. Cambridge, MA: Harvard University Press.

Clark, C. and Peterson, P. (1986) 'Teachers' Thought Processes.' In Wittrock, M. C. (ed.) *Handbook of Research on Teaching*, 3rd edition. New York: Macmillan.

Connell, R. W. (1985) *Teachers' Work*. Sydney, Australia: Allen & Unwin.

Conners, R. D. (1978) *An Analysis of Teacher Thought Processes, Beliefs, and Principles during Instruction*. Ph.D. thesis, University of Alberta, Canada.

Copeland, W. (1980) 'Student Teachers and Cooperating Teachers: An Ecological Relationship'. *Theory into Practice*, **18**, 194–9.

Dale, R. (1977a) 'Implications of the Rediscovery of the Hidden Curriculum for the Sociology of Teaching.' In Gleason, D. (ed.) *Identity and Structure: Issues in the Sociology of Education*. Driffield, Yorks: Nafferton Books.

Dale, R. (1977b) *The Structural Context of Teaching*. Milton Keynes, Bucks: The Open University Press.

Denscombe, M. (1980) 'The Work Context of Teaching: An Analytic Framework for the Study of Teachers in Classrooms'. *British Journal of Sociology of Education*, **1**, 279–92.

Denscombe, M. (1982) 'The Hidden Pedagogy and Its Implications for Teacher Training'. *British Journal of Sociology of Education*, **3**, 249–65.

Doyle, W. (1977) 'Learning the Classroom Environment: An Ecological Analysis'. *Journal of Teacher Education*, **28**, 51–5.

Doyle, W. (1979) 'Classroom Effects'. *Theory into Practice*, **18**, 138–44.

Doyle, W. and Ponder, G. (1975) 'Classroom Ecology: Some Concerns about a Neglected Dimension of Research on Teaching.' *Contemporary Education*, **46**, 183–8.

Dreeben, R. (1970) *The Nature of Teaching:*

Schools and the Work of Teachers. Glenview, IL: Scott, Foresman.

Dreeben, R. (1973) 'The School as a Workplace'. In Travers, R. (ed.) *Second Handbook of Research on Teaching*. Chicago: Rand McNally.

Dreitzel, H. P. (1973) *Childhood and Socialization*. New York: Macmillan.

Duffy, G. and Anderson, L. (1982) *Conceptions of Reading Project: Final Report*. East Lansing, MI: Institute for Research on Teaching, Research Series No. III.

Eddy, E. (1969) *Becoming a Teacher*. New York: Teachers College Press.

Edgar, D. and Warren, R. (1969) 'Power and Autonomy in Teacher Socialization'. *Sociology of Education*, **42**, 386–99.

Edwards, R. (1979) *Contested Terrain: The Transformation of the American Workplace in the 20th Century*. New York: Basic Books.

Egan, K. B. (1982) *The Power of Personal Context in Making Students Teachers: Three Cases*. A paper presented at the annual meeting of the American Educational Research Association, New York City, March.

Elbaz, F. (1983) *Teacher Thinking: A Study of Practical Knowledge*. London: Croom Helm.

Etzioni, A. (1965) 'Organizational Control Structure'. In March, J. (ed.) *Handbook of Organizations*. Chicago, IL: Rand McNally.

Feiman-Nemser, S. (1983) 'Learning to Teach'. In Shulman, L. and Sykes, G. (eds) *Handbook of Teaching and Policy*. New York: Longman.

Feiman-Nemser, S. and Floden, R. (1986) 'The Cultures of Teaching'. In Wittrock, M. (ed.) *The Third Handbook of Research on Teaching*. Chicago, IL: Rand McNally.

Fenstermacher, G. (1980) 'What Needs to Be Known about What Teachers Need to Know?' In Hall, G., Hord, S. and Brown, G. (eds) *Exploring Issues in Teacher Education: Questions for Future Research*. Austin, TX: University of Texas Research and Development Center for Teacher Education.

Gaskill, P. (1975) *Patterns and Changes in the Perspectives of Student Teachers*. Unpublished doctoral dissertation, Harvard University.

Gibson, R. (1976) 'The Effects of School Practice: The Development of Student Perspectives'. *British Journal of Teacher Education*, **2**, 241–50.

Ginsburg, M. (1984) *Reproduction and Contradictions in Preservice Teachers' Encounters with Professionalism*. A paper presented at the annual meeting of the American Educational Research Association, New Orleans, LA.

Ginsburg, M. (1985) *Reproduction, Contradiction, and Conceptions of Professionalism: The Case of Preservice Teachers*. A paper presented at the annual meeting of the American Educational Research Association, Chicago, IL.

Giroux, H. (1980) 'Teacher Education and the Ideology of Social Control'. *Journal of Education*, **162**, 5–27.

Gitlin, A. (1983) 'School Structure and Teachers' Work'. In Apple, M. and Weis, L. (eds) *Ideology and Practice in Education*. Philadelphia, PA: Temple University Press.

Gracey, H. (1972) *Curriculum or Craftsmanship*. Chicago IL: University of Chicago Press.

Grant, C. (1975) *The Role of the Letter of Expectations in Facilitating Communication in the Student Teaching Triad*. A paper presented at the annual meeting of the Wisconsin Educational Research Association, Madison, WI, December.

Grant, C. (1981) 'Education That Is Multicultural and Teacher Preparation: An Examination from the Perspectives of Preservice Students'. *Journal of Educational Research*, **75**, 95–101.

Grant, C. and Zeichner, K. (1981) 'Inservice Support for First-Year Teachers: The State of the Scene'. *Journal of Research and Development in Education*, **14**, 99–111.

Griffin G. et al (1983) *Clinical Preservice Teacher Education: Final Report of a Descriptive Study*. Austin, TX: University of Texas Research and Development Center for Teacher Education.

Haller, E. (1967) 'Pupils' Influences in Teacher Socialization: A Socio-linguistic study'. *Sociology of Education*, **40**, 316–33.

Hammersley, M. (1977a) *Teacher Perspectives*. Milton Keynes, Bucks: The Open University Press.

Hammersley, M. (1977b) *The Social Location of Teacher Perspectives*. Milton Keynes, Bucks: The Open University Press.

Hodges, C. (1982) 'Implementing Methods: If You Can't Blame the Cooperating Teacher, Whom Can You Blame?' *Journal of Teacher Education*, **33**, 25–9.

Hogben, D. and Lawson, M. (1983) 'Attitudes of Secondary School Teacher Trainees and Their Practice Teaching Supervisors'. *Journal of Education for Teaching*, **9**, 249–63.

Hoy, W. (1968) 'The Influence of Experience on the Beginning Teacher'. *Journal of Educational Research*, **66**, 89–93.

Hoy, W. and Rees, W. (1977) 'The Bureaucratic Socialization of Student Teachers'. *Journal of Teacher Education*, **28**, 23–6.

Ingvarson, L. and Greenway, P. (1984) 'Portrayals of Teacher Development'. *The Australian Journal of Education*, **28**, 45–65.

Janesick, V. (1977) *An Ethnographic Study of a Teacher's Classroom Perspective*. Ph.D. thesis, Michigan State University.

Katz, L. and Raths, J. (1982) 'The Best of Intentions for the Education of Teachers'. *Action in Teacher Education*, **4**, 8–16.

Keddie, N. (1971) 'Classroom Knowledge'. In Young, M. (ed.) *Knowledge and Control*. London: Collier-Macmillan.

Lacey, C. (1977) *The Socialization of Teachers*. London: Methuen.

Lampert, M. (1985) *Teachers' Strategies for Understanding and Managing Classroom Dilemmas*. A paper presented at the annual meeting of the International Study Association on Teacher Thinking, Tilburg University, The Netherlands, May.

Larkin, R. (1973) 'Contextual Influences on Teacher Leadership Styles'. *Sociology of Education*, **46**, 471–9.

Little, J. W. (1982). 'Norms of Collegiality and Experimentation: Workplace Conditions of School Success'. *American Educational Research Journal*, **19**, 325–40.

Lortie, D. (1973) 'Observations of Teaching as Work'. In Travers, R. (ed.) *Second Handbook of Research on Teaching*. Chicago, IL: Rand McNally.

Lortie, D. (1975) *Schoolteacher: A Sociological Study*. Chicago, IL: University of Chicago Press.

McArthur, J. (1978) 'What Does Teaching Do to Teachers?' *Educational Administration Quarterly*, **14**, 89–103.

McIntyre, D. J. (1983) *Field Experiences in Teacher Education*. Washington, DC: Foundation for Excellence in Teacher Education and the ERIC Clearinghouse in Teacher Education.

McPherson, G. (1972) *Small Town Teacher*. Cambridge, MA: Harvard University Press.

Maddox, H. (1968) 'A Descriptive Study of Teaching Practice'. *Educational Review*, **20**, 177–90.

Mardle, G. and Walker, M. (1980) 'Strategies and Structure: Critical Notes on Teacher Socialization'. In Woods, P. (ed.) *Teacher Strategies*. London: Croom Helm.

Marland, P. W. (1977) *A Study of Teachers' Interactive Thoughts*. Ph.D. thesis, University of Alberta, Canada.

Metz, M. (1978) *Classrooms and Corridors*. Berkeley, CA: University of California Press.

Munby, H. (1983) *A Qualitative Study of Teachers' Beliefs and Principles*. A paper presented at the annual meeting of the American Educational Research Association, Montreal, Canada, April.

Newberry, J. (1977) *The First Year of Experience: Influences on Beginning Teachers*. A paper presented at the annual meeting of American Educational Research Association, New York City, April. (ERIC Document Reproduction Service No. ED 137 299)

Olesen, V. and Whittaker, E. (1970) 'Critical Notes on Socialization Studies of Professional Socialization'. In Jackson, J. A. (ed.) *Studies of Professional Socialization*. London: Cambridge University Press.

Petty, M. and Hogben, D. (1980) 'Explorations of Semantic Space with Beginning Teachers: A Study of Socialization into Teaching'. *British Journal of Teacher Education*, **6**, 51–61.

Pollard, A. (1982) 'A Model of Classroom Coping Strategies'. *British Journal of Sociology of Education*, **3**, 19–37.

Popkewitz, T. (1985) 'Ideology and Social Formation in Teacher Education'. *Teaching and Teacher Education*, **1**(2), 91–107.

Sarason, S., Davidson, K., and Blatt, B. (1962) *The Preparation of Teachers: An Unstudied Problem*. New York: Wiley.

Schwille, J. et al (1979) *Factors Influencing Teachers' Decisions about What to Teach* (Research Series No. 62). East Lansing, MI: Institute for Research on Teaching.

Sharp, R. and Green, A. (1975) *Education*

and Social Control. London: Routledge & Kegan Paul.

Sirotnik, K. (1983) 'What You See Is What You Get: Consistency, Persistency and Mediocrity in Classrooms'. *Harvard Educational Review,* **53**, 16–31.

Stephens, J. (1967) *The Processes of Schooling.* New York: Holt, Rinehart & Winston.

Tabachnick, B. R., Popkewitz, T., and Zeichner, K. (1979–80) 'Teacher Education and the Professional Perspectives of Student Teachers'. *Interchange,* **10**, 12–29.

Tabachnick, B. R., Zeichner, K., Densmore, K., Adler, S., Egan, K. B. (1982) *The Impact of the Student Teaching Experience on the Development of Teacher Perspectives.* Madison, WI: Wisconsin Center for Education Research.

Tabachnick, B. R. and Zeichner, K. (1984) 'The Impact of the Student Teaching Experience on the Development of Teacher Perspectives.' *Journal of Teacher Education,* **35**(6), 28–36.

Tabachnick, B. R. and Zeichner, K. (1985) *The Development of Teacher Perspectives: Final Report.* Madison, WI: Wisconsin Center for Education Research.

Travers, R. (1971) 'Some Further Reflections on the Nature of a Theory of Instruction'. In Westbury, I. and Bellack, A. (eds) *Research into Classroom Processes.* New York: Teachers College Press.

Weick, K. (1976) 'Educational Organizations as Loosely coupled systems'. *Administrative Science Quarterly,* **21**, 1–19.

Westbury, I. (1973) 'Conventional Classrooms, "Open" Classrooms, and the Technology of Teaching'. *Journal of Curriculum Studies,* **5**.

Whiteside, M. T., Bernbaum, G., and Noble, G. (1969) 'Aspirations, Reality Shock and Entry into Teaching'. *Sociological Review,* **17**(3), 399–414.

Wise, A. (1979) *Legislated Learning: The Bureaucratization of the American Classroom.* Berkeley, CA: University of California Press.

Wright, B. (1959) 'Identification and Becoming a Teacher'. *Elementary School Journal,* 361–73.

Wright, B. and Tuska, S. (1967) 'The Childhood Romance Theory of Teacher Development'. *School Review,* **25**, 123–54.

Wright, B. and Tuska, S. (1968) 'From Dream to Life in the Psychology of Becoming a Teacher'. *School Review,* **26**,

183–93.

Young, R. E. (1981) 'The Epistemic Discourse of Teachers: An Ethnographic Study'. *Anthropology and Education Quarterly.* **12**(2), 122–44.

Zeichner, K. (1980) 'Myths and Realities: Field Experiences in Preservice Teacher Education'. *Journal of Teacher Education,* **31**, 45–55.

Zeichner, K. (1983a) 'Alternative Paradigms of Teacher Education'. *Journal of Teacher Education,* **34**, 3–9.

Zeichner, K. (1983b) 'Individual and Institutional Factors Related to the Socialization of Beginning Teachers'. In Griffin, G. and Hukill, H. (eds) *First Years of Teaching: What Are the Pertinent Issues?* Austin, TX: University of Texas Research and Development Center for Teacher Education.

Zeichner, K. (1985) 'Preparation for Elementary School Teaching'. In Burke, P. and Heideman, R. (eds) *Teacher Competence: Issues in Career-long Teacher Education.* Springfield, IL: Charles Thomas.

Zeichner, K. (1986) 'Content and Contexts: Neglected Elements in Studies of Student Teaching as an Occasion for Learning to Teach'. *Journal of Education for Teaching,* **12**, 5–24.

Zeichner, K. (in press) 'The Ecology of Field Experience: Toward an Understanding of the Role of Field Experiences in Teacher Development'. In Haberman, M. and Backus, J. (eds) *Advances in Teacher Education, Volume 3.* Norwood, NJ: Ablex.

Zeichner, K. and Grant, C. (1981) 'Biography and Social Structure in the Socialization of Student Teachers'. *Journal of Education for Teaching,* **1**, 198–314.

Zeichner, K. and Tabachnick, B. R. (1981) 'Are the Effects of University Teacher Education Washed out by School Experience?' *Journal of Teacher Education,* **32**, 7–11.

Zeichner, K. and Tabachnick, B. R. (1985) 'The Development of Teacher Perspectives: Social Strategies and Institutional Control in the Socialization of Beginning Teachers'. *Journal of Education for Teaching,* **11**, 1–25.

Zeichner, K. and Teitelbaum, K. (1982) 'Personalized and Inquiry-oriented Teacher Education'. *Journal of Education for Teaching,* **8**, 95–117.

2

WAYS OF THINKING ABOUT STUDENTS AND CLASSROOMS BY MORE AND LESS EXPERIENCED TEACHERS

David C. Berliner

A number of writers in this volume explore the way craft knowledge or practical knowledge about teaching is obtained by classroom teachers. In general, the old aphorism that experience is the best teacher is borne out, though this could be much more accurately stated: experience that is reflected upon is a very good teacher.

This restatement allows for the recognition of two facts. First, it recognizes that some individuals apparently never learn much from their experience. Although we find few individuals who are designated experts in a field who do not have extensive experience, and definitions of expertise almost always mention the term experience (both words emanating from the same roots), none the less experience should not be a synonym for expertise. In our view experience is a necessary but certainly *not* a sufficient condition for expertise. Education, as it happens, is a field where there is a widespread belief that experience and expertise are quite different. Teachers, as opposed to pilots, welders, surgeons, and many others, are not believed to gain in proficiency as they serve more clients or accrue more hours on the job. In education there is a very ill-defined system for passing from apprentice to journeyman to master of the teaching field. First-year teachers are often given equal or more difficult assignments than 10-year veteran teachers, and they are expected to perform as if they were very experienced. Although there are fields in which experience and expertise are highly correlated, we would hypothesize that in all fields mere personal experience probably teaches very little. We have no doubt, however, that personal experience that is reflected on and examined, in order to derive ways to improve one's own performance, is a very valuable teacher.

Learning from experience probably requires the application of what we now call metacognitive skills. These skills include the ability to ask questions of oneself as one is performing some activity; monitoring one's own and other's behavior in a setting: seeking alternative solution strategies to problems; systematically encoding cues in the environment that provide information about the pace of the activity, sequence of activity, the adjustments to be made in the activity; and so forth. Whether learning to fly planes, cut hair, play chess, or teach children, experience will probably only instruct those who have the motivation to excel in what they do and the metacognitive skills to learn from their experience. We believe that individuals with that kind of motivation to learn and in possession of a set of strategies for learning from experience are literally transformed by their experience. They become something else. They become experts in their field. We will discuss, below, the unique ways of thinking that are demonstrated by a group of teachers who were transformed into expert classroom teachers by virtue of their motivation to succeed and their experience as classroom teachers.

The second reason for restating how experience teaches is to reflect more accurately another fact, namely, that other kinds of events besides personal experience can be very instructive. Individuals possessing rich, relatively complete schemas about certain phenomena need very little personal experience to learn easily, quickly, and retain well information pertaining to those phenomena. A well-developed schemata allows very efficient learning from verbal and written discourse on a topic about which much is known. Experience, in such cases, does not seem nearly as crucial an element in learning as it is for those with incomplete schemata. Another way to say this is that reflected-on experience is, perhaps, the best teacher only for those with very little experience.

This desire to rewrite the aphorism about how experience teaches is not due to any lack of reverence for folk wisdom. Rather, it is based on what has been learned from personal experience. My colleagues[1] and I study scientists and mathematicians with different degrees of experience as classroom teachers. By using standardized tasks in laboratory settings we can compare how these different groups of individuals think about classroom phenomena. We believe we are uncovering the ways experience in teaching changes apprentices into journeymen and journeymen into master teachers. Our work is guided by the quite reasonable belief that experienced teachers, whom we have judged also to be expert teachers, should have different, more sophisticated, and more utilitarian ways of thinking about classrooms than do individuals with little or no classroom teaching experience. Our data generally, but not always, support that notion. What is also clear to us is that the issue is more complex than we thought it would be. To explore these ideas further we will briefly discuss our program of research and elaborate on some of our findings. Next, a number of research issues concerned with how experience influences teachers' thinking about classroom teaching will be discussed. The policy and teacher training issues addressed by this kind of research will also be considered.

THE RESEARCH PROGRAM

Until recently, most of the extant research on how experienced/expert members of some field differ from minimally experienced/novice members of that field has been conducted outside of education (see Glaser in press a, b; Chi et al in press). This is partly because educational phenomena have been considered too ill defined to study adequately the changes brought about by experience, and educational criteria have been too narrowly conceived to identify with any certainty a sample of teachers who might possess expert knowledge. We have nothing in education like the championship matches in chess, or the olympics in sports, to identify our finest teachers. But things are changing. Researchers are finding ways to study these issues despite problems that are unique to the field of education (see Leinhardt and Greeno 1986; Housner and Griffey 1985). Investigators have learned that expertise in dozens of disparate fields appear to have some similar characteristics. Thus, it was heartening to find in a review of existing studies of experienced/expert teachers (Berliner 1986) that expert teachers acted very similarly to experts in many other fields. It appears that in the process of reflecting on one's thousands of hours in classrooms, or on one's thousands of hours in chess matches, cognitive changes occur in the ways information is processed. The research reported on below illustrates this point. This program of research is characterized by a unique sample of subjects and a unique set of tasks, by means of which our subjects inform us of their thoughts about pedagogical issues. This research also ties into the existing cognitive science research on expertise in different fields and sheds some light on contemporary policy issues for education.

A general strategy in our work, though not always held to, is to compare the performance of three groups of subjects on a standardized task. One group of subjects we have designated as experienced/expert classroom teachers. They are mathematics and science secondary school teachers who were nominated as excellent by their principals and whose classroom teaching was judged by two or three independent and knowledgeable observers to be excellent. In this group the minimum amount of time spent as a classroom teacher is five years. A second group of subjects are highly rated student teachers and first-year teachers of mathematics and science. This group, who are minimally experienced in classroom teaching, we call novices. A final group of even less experienced individuals is comprised of mathematicians and scientists from local industrial and research organizations who would like to obtain certification for teaching, but who do not want to take any education courses. Those individuals generally have had some experience in the instruction of young people by coaching, scouting, or teaching for a church. But these people have no formal classroom teaching experience. We call this group postulants. They believe they have sufficient knowledge and skill to enter teaching without taking most of the courses that novices take.

In our research, different tasks have been used to assess the performance of the experienced/expert teachers, the minimally experienced/novice teachers, and the inexperienced/postulant teachers. One task requires looking very briefly at slides of mathematics and science classes, and describing what was seen (Cushing et al 1986). Another task requires looking at multiple-choice items from a nationally standardized test to estimate the percentage of 13- and 17-year-old students who would get such items correct and to explain why certain distractors would be frequently or infrequently chosen (Stein et al 1986). Another task requires the viewing of three television screens, simultaneously, each one showing different parts of a classroom during a lesson. Subjects had to comment on what they were seeing and hearing and were asked questions about their viewing when the lesson was over (Sabers et al in progress). Still another task was a simulated planning activity (Sabers et al 1986). This task was very informative and can be used to describe in greater detail the kinds of data we obtain and the kinds of conclusions that can be reached from investigations of this kind.

A design to look at the role of experience and expertise in thinking about planning

An experimental task resembling the kind often encountered by teachers was developed. For this task, each of nine experts, six novices, and six postulants was presented with the following scenario. Five weeks into the school year he/she had been assigned an additional class to teach. The previous teacher had left abruptly, and her classes were being distributed among existing staff members. Experts and novices who were science teachers were given the assignment of teaching a biology class; those who were math teachers were assigned an algebra class. Postulants were assigned at random to be science or mathematics teachers. Subjects were given a short note left by the previous teacher, a grade book with grades and attendance recorded, student information cards containing demographic information on one side and teacher comments about the student on the other, corrected tests and homework assignments, and the textbook. The subjects were given 40 minutes to prepare for a debriefing session and to write a lesson plan for the first two days of instruction. They were instructed that they should do no more or no less than they would actually do to prepare for the class. In addition, subjects were encouraged to take notes that might enable them to recall general and specific information about the class and individual students. All subjects were observed through a one-way mirror as they planned. They had been informed during the initial instructions for the task that they would be observed.

Subjects from each of the different subject pools were asked to recall general and specific information about the students and to make generalizations about instruction, management, and classroom organization based on the information provided. Subjects were also requested to explain their lesson plans and to select or develop a seating chart for the class. The protocols obtained from these questions provided the basic data in the study.

Thinking about the students to be taught

From studying the protocols we found that the most notable contrast in ways of thinking about students was between *experts* and *postulants*. Experts were notably less interested in remembering specific information about students than were postulants. Moreover, experts did not seem to believe specific student information would be particularly salient for their task of taking over a new class (though some indicated that they might want more information about students after they got 'going'). When they *did* react to student information cards, it was at a comparatively more general level. Experts seemed to merge information about students into a 'group picture' that they defined as more or less 'typical', 'normal', or 'usual'. Some illustrative excerpts from expert protocols follow:

> *Expert*: I don't sit there and spend my first week wondering who is who and who does what, and who doesn't do this. I'm not into that aspect of it. I just figure I can win them over. I'm going to give them the best shot first, and then we will see who can't do it.

Expert: I just don't think names are important as far as this point in time. I haven't met the kids; there is no reason for me to make any value judgments about them at this time. And so she [the previous teacher] had a whole little packet of confidential material that I looked at, and it had trivial little things about where the parents worked and this kid was cute or nice or something like that, and that to me is not relevant.

Expert: Especially when I start fresh, I start from a clean slate. I usually always try to ... I like getting a little background on the students in that there are going to be severe problems or someone may need special attention on certain things, you know, learning areas, but, in general, it's a conglomeration of the students. I like to learn from them and develop my own opinions.

Expert: Some of the students were shy, and you had your usual variety.

Expert: They seemed to be typical of what I would expect, I guess.

Expert: I really didn't [try to remember information about students] because if I were going into that room, in 40 minutes, I might try to pick out students that had potential severe problems, hearing problems, or something along those lines that stood out.

Expert: I didn't read the cards. I never do unless there's a comment about a physical impairment such as hearing or sight or something I get from the nurse. I never want to place a judgement on the students before they start. I find I have a higher success rate if I don't.

Our expert teachers apparently did not want to know much about the children they would soon teach. They intended to negotiate their own relationships with each child. Furthermore, in a sense, they seemed already to know all about them. They did not have to delve very long into the assorted class records that we had diligently prepared for them in order for some of them to decide that these students were 'like other kids'. This finding replicates one by Calderhead (1983). In Calderhead's study he noted that experienced teachers seemed to have a different schemata for students than did novice teachers. Calderhead used interviews and the repertory grid technique to study experienced, student, and novice teachers. He reported that the experienced teachers seemed to know the kinds of home backgrounds of students, they knew what to expect in the way of knowledge and skills in their classrooms, they had an image of the likely number of students who would need help, they had an image of the types of behaviors and discipline problems that could be expected. They knew what the students might possess in the way of previous experience, skills, and knowledge. And the teachers had a sense of what kinds of activities the children engaged in outside school. As Calderhead put it, the experienced teachers had amassed a large quantity of knowledge such that they did, in a sense, know their new class even before they got to meet them. This knowledge is not derived from pre-service experiences or from merely observing in classrooms. This kind of pedagogical knowledge is learned from thousands of hours of instruction, and tens of thousands of interactions with students. It is knowledge that influences the running of the classroom. It influences the pace, the intellectual level, affect, work orientation, and so forth. It is knowledge that influences classroom organization and management and is the basis for interpreting the curriculum. Such knowledge is complex, often tacit, only derivable from extensive experience, and in most other fields of endeavor would be called expert knowledge.

But what of the novices and postulants? The protocols of the postulants, our most inexperienced group of subjects, were very different than those of the experts.

Postulants' protocols indicate much more serious attention is given to information about individual students. They appeared to use individual student information to 'slot' students into two or three categories. Examples from protocols of the postulants' comments illustrate this point.

> *Postulant*: I sorted the bad kids from the good kids from some of the ones that were just good natured, if they like to work, that type of thing. And I would do that if I started writing my own comments. If I had the class for a while, I would tend to still categorize them. I always wanted to have my eye out for the cause of the trouble, and I think that's natural.

> *Postulant*: I went through her student cards and also went through the test scores and tried to divide the students into three groups, one group which I thought might be disruptive, one group which I thought would not be disruptive and that wouldn't need intense watching. The third group I really didn't know because the back of the card was blank. So it was classified later. I realized not all the disruptive students were getting bad grades. I decided to sort of rank cards from what I thought would be the best student from top to the obviously poorer students going down the stack just to get some sort of an idea of ranking.

> *Postulant*: Thirty some people I'm not going to remember right off the bat, but I'm going to try to identify who these people are. You know, your top side and your bottom side.

> *Postulant*: I went over their test scores and looked up the ones that had low scores.

> *Postulant*: The only analysis I made on these students was what the distribution of boys and girls were and whether or not they came from a white collar background or a blue collar background.

While postulants expressed this clear preference to use student information for categorizing students, their rationales for doing so were often sparse or non-existent. As one postulant indicated,

> It seemed like the thing to do [he laughs]. I get lost ... yeah, it just somehow seems like the thing that should be done. I'm not really sure why.

Novices (all were in their first year of teaching) resembled experts in their unwillingness to focus on student information as they planned to take over a new class. However, their rationales seemed to us to be less rich than were those of the experts. Basically, novices were hesitant to make judgements about students before they met them because they 'didn't want to be biased' or felt negative statements from the previous teacher might be explained by 'personality conflicts' with students. Experts worried about these points as well, but their rationales included statements about features that were more important than student information (e.g. getting students involved in the work, getting organized, setting the tone for the class, thinking about the whole class, making decisions about what content should be covered, giving the class some rules to follow to get started, letting the students know the new teacher's philosophy, and the like). In other words, experts' 'detachment' from the information about individual students seemed to be embedded in a set of understandings about what considerations were more important for getting on with the task of running the class.

Thinking about the validity of information used to describe students

All of the most experienced teachers, our expert teachers, indicated that they would likely disregard most of the information left by the previous teacher. Expert protocols suggest that, more than any other group, they like to get their own, very personal feeling for the students and the classroom. In describing this preference, experts suggested:

> *Expert*: I wouldn't want to take someone else's word for these things.

> *Expert*: I would sooner leave her value system and try and introduce the kids to what I value in science. My expectations going in aren't the same as everybody [else].

> *Expert*: So if I bias that by any knowledge other than the fact that I presume they can succeed, then I feel that I might not give them a fair chance going into the class.

These kinds of statements seemed to be attached to experts' notions of what 'I' want to know, what 'I' would do, what 'I' think about, how 'I' start, or what 'I' try. A positive sense of their self-worth as teachers permeated their responses, and led, inevitably, to a downgrading of the unknown teacher's opinions.

Postulants more readily accepted the validity of the information provided them. They, in fact, suggested that they were 'guided' by the observations of the previous teachers. Their descriptions of students are particularly revealing: they had developed clear images and expectations about performance from descriptions about students whom they had never met. For example:

> Kim Wong looks like an excellent student. He made an 89 on that test. And then the background sort of goes with that. His father is a scientist of some sort, and his mother does some kind of computer software. On the other hand, the other extreme is that Sue Gallegos. I think, supposedly that's her name. I think she made a 22 on the test; she was the low end of the score. She's going to be a real problem ...

Postulants indicated that they tried to tie together the various pieces of information left by the previous teacher. Postulants saw their job as connecting what they did with the previous teacher's ideas and actions, an obvious sign of attributing high validity to the unknown teacher's opinions.

Novices' beliefs about the validity of student information were not as easy to categorize. As might be expected, they seemed less sure of themselves than the experts did. Nevertheless, they seemed not as ready to accept the opinions of an unknown teacher as easily as the postulants did.

Thinking about the meaning of 'labels' for students

When questioned about the students, subjects in all groups talked about those who were 'discipline problems', 'good students', 'shy students', etc. Yet the protocols suggested subtle differences across groups about the *meaning* these student labels carried for participants. For experts, these categories appeared to be embedded in rich episodic memories about particular students of the particular type under discussion. The labels serve as broad sense-making categories for thinking about groups of students *and* planned actions in classrooms. The labeling (categorizing) and an action connected to that categorization were noted more often in the responses of experts than in the other two groups. Student categories seemed to be connected to teachers' broader understandings of classroom events, causes, and consequences. Representative examples from the protocols follow:

Expert: Paul Long is having problems, He's in the back, and I guess potentially he would be a discipline problem because he doesn't understand, and he's in the eleventh grade [most student are ninth graders] and maybe never understands.

Expert: [There's] the unmotivated student who will always be the problem ... they'll sleep like the one student [in this class] because he works; he's tired. I've had students like that, and I talk to them and say, 'What are we going to do?' You have to ... Luckily, the high school kids, you can talk to them as adults, but junior high is a totally different approach to how you treat them and the level that you're at with teacher–student relationships.

Expert (on failing students): A lot of them had been let go too long without homework; there was no system to catch up on your homework. It would be impossible for them to pass because they hadn't participated in any of their classwork. So they couldn't pass the test.

Expert: There's probably five to ten per cent that are off-task no matter what you're doing. They're going to drift on you, and you just have to constantly be working at corralling them in.

Memory for information about students

We believe our most experienced group of subjects had learned to be more discriminating in the types of information they remembered about students than were novices or postulants. The experts found different kinds of information more salient and useful than did postulants or novices. For example, when asked to recall who was the best student in the class, novices and postulants recalled the name of the student with the highest scores on the two tests. Experts, on the other hand, weren't willing to accept that this student would necessarily be the best student. The following excerpt serves as an illustration.

Expert: Let's see, as far as just pure score, Wong. What I mean is he was able to read the textbook and answer the questions. But can he relate it? Does he know what he's doing? Can he apply these elements?

Experts also recalled fewer details about individual students and the class as a whole than did subjects from the other two groups. Whether general or specific questions were asked, the experts were more likely to remember the information if it were related to planning and to preparing for teaching the class. When asked a series of nine specific questions about the class, experts, as a group, attempted to respond to only one question. This question (which the majority of the experts answered correctly) asked how many students were in the class. The number of students in the class is a very important bit of information to have. The experts viewed it as having significant implications for instruction (e.g. whether small group, whole group, or individual instruction might be more appropriate). Questions eliciting information about the number of students who were in specific grades, the number of males and females in the class, and the ethnicity of the students were apparently not as salient to the experts. As one expert teacher remarked: 'Those things I never take into consideration.'

The overriding concern of experts appeared related to assuming the responsibility for teaching the *group* of students, and therefore specific information about individual students was relatively less important than was information that could affect group instruction. That was why the size of the class was such a salient bit of information for them. There was an exception, however, that proved the rule. When asked a series of seven specific questions about special students in the class, the experts appeared to be concerned with answering only the one question regarding a visually impaired student. Even the experts who did not remember the handicapped student's name commented that such information was important to remember. Given the expert's interest in instruction-related data, it is not surprising, then, that experts would view information concerning a handicapped student important to remember, even while other kinds of specific information about individual students was considered unimportant.

Novices were more inclined to believe they should have remembered all of the information presented to them in the student files. Their protocols suggested that they were more anxious about not having committed all the information to memory even though they answered considerably more questions than the experts. Novices complained at the end of the task that they really needed more time to learn about the students. None of the experts was concerned about that. Protocols from the postulant sample indicated that their thinking and perceptions resembled those of the novices. Novices and postulants alike rarely judged the relevancy of one piece of information against another or generated instructional plans based on the information they had.

Interestingly, our group of novices may have remembered more information than our experts, but the novices appeared not to assign differential value to the various pieces of information. We found no evidence that they tried to remember information that had particular significance for instruction. An expert apparently knows what is important, and what is not. A characteristic of a novice is this lack of ability to separate important from unimportant events. That is probably why novices in many fields talk about being overwhelmed, while experts are not and are judged to be cool, calm, and collected. The experts simply do not pay attention to everything. The experts, therefore, probably remember less student information because they never paid attention to it in the first place. They only perceive and remember information that is judged by them to be meaningful or important. They simplify their world. It is a world of essentials, uncluttered by non-essentials.

We obtained another bit of evidence about the role of pedagogical experience in learning what is and what is not important from another study in our project. We showed experts, novices, and postulants some slides of classrooms for a very brief period of time. The subjects were then asked to tell us what they saw. The postulant or novice responses were clearly descriptive, and usually quite accurate.

> *Postulant*: A blond haired boy at the table, looking at papers. Girl to his left reaching in front of him for something.

> *Novice*: [It's] a classroom. Student with back to camera working at a table.

> *Novice*: A room full of students sitting at tables.

In contrast to the literal descriptions that were given regularly by the novices and postulants, our most experienced/expert teachers often responded with inferences about what they saw.

> *Expert*: It's a hands-on activity of some type. Group work with a male and female of maybe late junior high school age.

Expert: It's a group of students maybe doing small group discussion on a project as the seats are not in rows.

For experts, the blondness of a student's hair or similar raw description was simply unimportant as information worth obtaining from the visual field. The only information that was deemed important was information that had instructional significance. Identifying the means of instruction was very important because experts know that many other important classroom events and teaching behaviors co-vary with an activity. If it is a small group discussion, then perhaps 20 other students are unattended at that time. If it is a hands-on project, there are bound to be unique management issues concerned with preparation for work, putting things away at the end of work, classroom cleanliness, and noise level in the classroom. Experts know what co-varies, and in which way, when a particular kind of instruction is used. Thus, a good deal of information is known about a classroom the minute the means of instruction (or the task structure or activity structure) is correctly identified (Berliner 1983).

The experts also correctly identified the slide as coming from a classroom in the upper junior high school grades. Once again, the experts extracted an important piece of instructional information even though their glimpse of the classroom was quite brief. Upper junior high school students, in comparison to lower-grade students or high school seniors, require different forms of instruction, nurturance, directions, structure, autonomy, etc. Thus, the experts keyed in on age/grade issues as important, and again we believe it is because age/grade information has instructional significance. Our experts see classrooms differently than do novices or postulants because they no longer see classrooms literally. They appear to us to weight information differentially according to its utility for making instructional decisions. Almost without conscious thinking they make inferences about what they see and no longer merely see. This is not unlike experts in chess. Studies of grandmasters and less highly ranked chess players revealed extraordinary differences of the kind we find in comparing teachers with different levels of experiences (de Groot 1965).

> The swift insight of the chessmaster into the possibilities of a newly shown position ... are only understandable ... if we realize that, as a result of his experience he quite literally 'sees' the position in a totally different (and much more adequate) way than a weaker player. The vast differences between the two in efficiency ... need not, and must not be primarily ascribed to large differences in 'natural' power for abstraction. The difference is mainly due to differences in perception. (p. 306)

Out of his monumental study of expertise in chess, de Groot concludes that a result of 'experience' is 'seeing' differently. Our data indicate the same thing is true of experienced teachers. They see different things and therefore they remember different things than do less experienced teachers.

Thoughts about taking over a class

Important differences were revealed when we compared the ways that our experienced/expert teachers, our minimally experienced/novice teachers and our inexperienced/postulant teachers planned to take over a new teaching assignment.

(1) Our experts were more critical of the previous teacher than were subjects from the other two groups.

(2) The experts held a different conception of how to begin with the class.

(3) The experts had established routines for beginning the class.

(4) The experts held a different conception about the kinds of information students could provide them.

(5) Some experts planned for a more 'genuine' relationship with the students.

Each of these differences in ways of thinking about classrooms and students will be discussed further.

Critical comments.   Our expert group, which we had anticipated might be the most tolerant of another teacher, were comparatively more judgemental than novices or postulants about the approaches they thought had been taken by the previous teacher. Experts made a number of inferences about the previous teacher and her teaching from the various sources of information provided them for the experimental task. When talking about the homework and tests, several experts expressed concern that the students were not required to show their work when solving algebraic equations; the students wrote just the answers. The experts' concern was on the loss of information about how a student was attempting to solve the problem. They believed that the previous teacher should have required students to show all their work, a practice they planned to initiate immediately. A number of experts mentioned that the things the previous teacher did seemed 'strange' to them. They willingly volunteered a number of changes they would make. For example:

> *Expert*: [She had a] strange method of scoring. I didn't like that; I would change that immediately.

> *Expert*: I would have liked to have seen quizzes, occasional quizzes, to get more feedback before a test, and I thought that was strange if there were so few grades, just the two tests after five weeks.

> *Expert*: I think it's better just to turn over a new leaf and say, 'look, we're starting over again'.

Experts often described their proposed changes in terms of their own histories in classrooms and in terms of what sorts of action plans would likely be 'workable', such as the plan mentioned above (i.e. requiring students to show all their work when solving algebraic equations).

It appeared to us that novices also felt they might want to make these kinds of changes, but they did not volunteer this information nearly as often as experts. Their judgements about the previous teacher appeared to be somewhat 'softer'.

Postulants differed from experts and novices. They seemed less concerned about broader organizational and curricular issues (perhaps because they knew so little about them) and more concerned about the impact of their actions on individual students. They mentioned that they did not want to embarrass shy students or to be seen as making unfair demands on students. The protocols led us to believe that they simply wanted to get to know the students and to help them as much as possible.

Beginning over.   All of our experts made much out of starting the class afresh. The term *new* was heard frequently, as in *new* leaf, *new* start, *new* rules, *new* instructional systems, and *new* relationships to establish. To the directive 'Tell me about your lesson plan for the first day of instruction', experts responded with clear statements about beginning over. For example:

Expert: The first thing that came to mind was the organization matters. I have to be organized before I feel comfortable. It can't be chaotic; I can't run a class when I don't know what's going on. I've got to be with it, what's going on, and have a routine set up the kids respond to, when they know what's expected ... It's like training a two year old; they have to know what is expected. So I put a lot of emphasis at the beginning of the year training the students.

Expert: Well, day one, I just wanted to meet the kids and find out who they were. I would lay down what my rules are, what my grading system would be, and my policies. Then I would need to question them to find out what chapters they had covered in this book. And then what I wanted to do was verbally review with them and ask questions to find out the techniques they've been taught or how they solved their greatest common factor in solving equations. From there I was going to give them all review sheets that I made because I wasn't sure where it was they had left off.

Expert: On day one I would go in and introduce myself and maybe give an activity with the kids, a short one where they would get to know me a little better, I'd go over the class rules and assertive discipline with them. Then I'd go over their requirements for grades since most kids in high school are interested in grades.

In these excerpts, routines for beginning the class are apparent. More will be said of this below. At present, we are focusing on the expert teachers' plans to start over as quickly and as efficiently as possible. The experts indicated in many ways that they would make it clear to their students that 'a different teacher is in charge'.

The novices saw a need to introduce themselves, too, but did not appear to have the same sense that the creation of a new beginning was a crucial pedagogical act. The following protocol illustrates this.

Novice: I would first introduce myself and then give a brief history of myself, and I don't know it depends on the class, but I might have them introduce themselves. Then I would ask them what their prior teacher expected from them and how she ran the class and what they liked or disliked about it.

Postulants indicated they would introduce themselves to the class and would talk about the rules for the class, but their major concern appeared to be a desire to hurry back to the book and teach what needed to be taught. As a group, they appeared to be more interested in where the students were in the book than in assessing what the students might have learned during the previous weeks. For example:

Postulant: When I was scribbling out some notes to myself, trying to figure out where they were in the book, I guess my biggest problem with the lesson plan was to figure out where they are now and where they were going.

This brief narrative provides an insight into how this postulant viewed the class. First, was the reliance on 'the book'. Postulants possess little knowledge about classroom organization and management but have lots of knowledge about the content of the curriculum. So it is no wonder that 'the book' is a way to start thinking about instructing the new class.

Routines.   As noted above, the experts had routines for beginning the class. They seemed to possess routines to introduce themselves, explain new rules, get lots of student information, and to 'groove' the students. Their plans were reminiscent of Geoffrey's actions in starting the school year, as described by Smith and Geoffrey (1968) in their book on teaching in an urban classroom. Geoffrey gave students relatively innocuous tasks to carry out, so that he could gently, firmly, but quickly establish that teachers give orders while students carry orders out. That was called 'grooving' the students. Our experts had almost all learned to groove their students by demonstrating authority and by having students learn the routines they were going to use. Though none of our experienced teachers had a label for this kind of knowledge, all had some sense that they had quickly to get their students into the right groove.

One of the insights coming out of our project that is compatible with the work done by others has to do with the enormously important role played by mental scripts (Shavelson 1986) and behavioral routines (Leinhardt and Greeno 1986) in the performance of expert teachers. For example, Leinhardt and her colleagues looked at an expert and a novice teacher's plans for conducting a lesson, the activity structures used in the classroom by which the plans were carried out, and the routines that were embedded in the different classroom activities. These routines are the shared, scripted, virtually automated pieces of action that constitute so much of our daily lives. In classrooms, routines often allow students and teachers to devote their attention to other, perhaps more important matters inherent in the lesson. In Leinhardt's study of how an opening homework review is conducted, an expert teacher was found to be brief, taking about one-third less time than a novice. She was able to pick up information about attendance, and about who did or did not do the homework, and identified who was going to need help in the subsequent lesson. She was able to get all the homework corrected, and elicited mostly correct answers throughout the activity. And she did so at a brisk pace and without ever losing control of the lesson. Routines were used to record attendance, to handle choral responding during the homework checks, and for hand raising to get attention. The expert used clear signals to start and finish lesson segments. Interviews with the expert revealed how the goals for the lesson, the time constraints, and the curriculum itself were blended to direct the activity. The expert appeared to have a script in mind throughout the lesson, and she followed that script very closely.

In contrast, when the novice teacher was enacting an opening homework review she was not able to discover quickly who did and did not do the homework, she had problems with taking attendance, and she asked ambiguous questions that led to inadequate assessment of the difficulty level of the homework. At one time the novice lost control of the pace, and never did learn which students were going to have more difficulty later on in the lesson. The novice showed lack of familiarity with well-practiced routines. She seemed not to have any habitual way to act. She apparently had not yet accumulated the experience to have a script in mind to guide her behavior. One consequence of this lack of experience on the teacher's part was that students were unsure of their roles.

The routines that people use are often invisible to the people using them, they are so natural, so automatic. Although they may be unnoticeable by expert teachers, musicians, or athletes, they may actually constitute, in large part, the basis for their expertise. Benjamin Bloom (1986) has recently completed a lengthy study that documented the importance of automation of procedures among experts. All of the talented individuals he studied in sports, music, or the professions talked about the great amount of practice and training time—25–50 hours per week—that they had devoted to the field in which they had succeeded by the time of their adolescence. Once their skill was developed to a high level of automaticity it could be maintained with very little practice or thought. That is the key point: automation of routines provides great economy of effort.

The automaticity of certain processes apparently enables people who have achieved eminence to transcend their daily existence and to rise to creative heights in their chosen field. Bloom, rightly, has resurrected the wonderful work done at the turn of the century on automaticity by the psychologist William Bryan and his student, the telegrapher Noble Harter (1899). In their studies of learning telegraphy they concluded:

> The learner must come to do with one stroke of attention what now requires half a dozen, and presently in one still more inclusive stroke what now requires 36. He must systematize the work to be done and must acquire a system of habits corresponding to the system of tasks. When he has done this he is master of the situation in his [professional field] ... Automatization is not genius, but it is the hands and feet of genius. (p. 375)

Given our interviews with experts, novices, and postulants, our thinking about the ways experience changes someone, and our reading of the literature on talent and expertise, we would state our views in a similar manner. Automatization of behavioral routines along with clarity in one's mental script about how things should occur is not expertise, but those factors probably constitute a great deal of the necessary conditions for the development of expertise.

Student information for beginning instruction. As already noted, and as expected, the postulants had placed great reliance on the text as a guide for where to begin instruction. Students were not important as sources of information about where to start. Finding out where the old teacher left off, and moving on through the course, was their basic strategy.

The common strategy that novices had for gearing up to begin instruction was to ask the students where they were or to review content with them. Their reviews, however, focused more on providing the students with feedback than with eliciting information from them. For example:

> *Novice*: I'd ask them where they were in the text, and the next day I'd review important concepts that they'd already covered because it didn't seem they understood it very well.

This protocol is in contrast to many of the expert protocols where there was a clear intent on the part of the teachers to have the students provide the information of what they knew or could do. For the expert teachers, the students would be asked to answer questions and work review exercises for the purpose of assessing student knowledge of the subject matter. One expert indicated he would not use any specific plans for the first two days of instruction. He explained that he would use those days to interact with the students and to assess what the students remembered, to give him 'a fairly good idea of what had happened in the first five weeks'.

Although novices planned to review student work to get information from students, just like the experts, the review apparently was seen as something like a homework check, a chance for the novice teacher to correct student errors. The experts planned to use their review procedures to probe student knowledge in order to guide instruction. This is a subtle, but we think important, difference in the way the two groups generally conceptualized how to work with students at the start of instruction.

Genuineness. In our simulation, as we had expected, the novices and postulants usually expressed more concern about discipline and management than did our experts. The experts appeared to be so confident in that area that they were almost completely unconcerned about it when planning instruction. There was no doubt in their mind, given years of successful experience, that they could manage a class. This kind of confidence allowed at least one expert teacher to plan for a personal talk with the class about his beliefs, hopes, ambitions, and the like, in order intentionally to be 'vulnerable' in front of them.

> *Expert*: I think my primary concern is to allow the students to look at me. In other words, I would want to make myself somewhat vulnerable that [first] day to the kids. So they would know ... what is acceptable behavior and what is not acceptable behavior from my value system. ... I think because teaching involves so many humanist attributes that each teacher has to do their own thing and be accepted on their own terms.

This expert's confidence in his management skills allowed his humanness and moral commitment to be featured in his introduction. We do not think novices and postulants could dare to be so open and genuine about themselves in introductory activities with their students.

Thinking about tests and homework

Experts generally appeared to attend in greater detail and at a substantially deeper level than novices and postulants to content, instructional, and curriculular issues that 'surfaced' in the homework and test information that was left for them. Experts often used these sources of information to build models or explanations for why students would succeed or fail, why they acted motivated or unmotivated, and why they achieved or did not achieve. In contrast to novices and postulants, experts sometimes were able to 'look inside' student work to pull out salient information about what content they would need to focus on, what concepts were difficult for students, and the like. One response to the question 'Anything special you remember about the test?' illustrates this characteristic of experts:

> *Expert*: The student who had four incorrect [story problems] really understood it better than the student that had two incorrect because of the questions he missed. The way he missed his, he really got the concept. He missed partial problems so he did understand it. So I felt as though the boy that had the four incorrect answers had a better understanding of the chapter. I think he could have helped most of the other students in practically all areas because he did understand those story problems.

Novices appeared to consider the tests and homework important for other reasons. They searched for comparatively more 'surface' information. Postulants' remarks about students, tests, and homework were notably vague and largely unrelated to action plans for working with students or the curriculum. Examples from the responses of novices and postulants to the question about what was notable in the tests and homework illustrate these points.

Novice: Looking at the homework, I don't know what to tell you. I couldn't examine each one. It looked like the teacher had actually corrected it herself which is pretty good; if they can do that, then that is great ... Also, it looked like a good volume of homework which means that they were used to turning it in on time, which is good. So besides that, I noticed that some were neat, thorough; some showed all the work, and some weren't. Some, most of them, were neat.

Novice: I didn't go over the tests too much, except just getting the scores. I looked at the grades the students got on the tests. I noticed their grades corresponded to some of the comments on the back [of the cards]. The one [card] said they were having problems and had a low test score. But I didn't spend a long time looking over the tests.

Novice: I just glanced [at the tests]. The tests are the least important thing in my mind for science. I looked at [the homework], but it was not something that I was going to get a lot of information from.

Postulant: There was one student that apparently had the time to write about Black Sabbath and all those rock and roll things ... She had a kind of code on the test which is a way of learning. I mean it's done a lot. She had hers visibly on there, and that's how she checked her answers. She didn't do that bad, but she apparently had a lot of time to sit and write on the back of the test, and that impressed me.

Postulant: [I noticed] one that wasn't dated. I didn't understand the grading system; I didn't really look at it too carefully. I know they were mimeographed. The homework was mimeographed, and I was annoyed at the previous teacher for not leaving lesson plans or even ... I might have my own lesson plans. But she should have at least told me where she was and how she got there. And not to mention where she came up with all the mimeographed tests, and then I got to thinking, 'Gee, when we do a test on chapter 17, where do I get this?'

RESEARCH ISSUES AND POLICY RELEVANCE OF STUDIES OF EXPERIENCE AND EXPERTISE

The interpretations of the data given above lead us to conclude that experienced teachers differ from less experienced or inexperienced teachers in profound ways. Their experience has given them mental representations of typical students. In the terminology of cognitive psychology, they have a fully developed student schemata, by means of which they operate. They find others' opinions of students untrustworthy. The labels they use have personal meanings associated with them. When a student is labeled as shy, or emotionally handicapped, the terms call up episodes and events that are the source of the personal knowledge possessed by these experienced teachers. Novices and postulants have facts, concepts, and principles, a kind of propositional knowledge, but only sketchy personal experience. The experienced teachers use their rich base of personal knowledge to instantiate concepts (labels) such as 'shy' or 'emotionally handicapped'. In ways that agree with our observations and hypotheses, Kolodner (1983) has discussed how memory evolves as one progresses from novice to expert:

> Two things happen in that evolution. First, knowledge is built up incrementally on the basis of experience. Facts, once unrelated, get integrated through occurrence in the same

episodes. Second, reasoning processes are refined, and usefulness and rigidity of rules is learned ... Because experience is vital to the evolution from novice to expert, experience is organized in long-term memory, and guides reasoning processes ... When a person has only gone to school and acquired book knowledge, he is considered a novice. After he has had experience using the knowledge he has learned, and when he knows how it applies both to common and exceptional cases, he is called an expert ... Experience serves to turn unrelated facts into expert knowledge. (p. 498)

Like experienced/expert individuals in other fields our experienced teachers show memory for information that is different from the memory of less experienced teachers. Their perception is different, thus they remember different things. And their memory is organized differently. What they remember appears to be more functional. They focus primarily on instructional events and issues. This replicates a finding from the study by Housner and Griffey (1985) that examined the planning behavior and actual teaching of experienced and inexperienced physical education teachers.

The more experienced teachers, in contrast with the less experienced teachers, appear to use their rich schemas about students, their large store of episodic knowledge, and their unique memory to analyze student work such as tests and homework differently. These same cognitive processes are also used to develop plans for instruction that are different. In short, our specially selected experienced teachers often acted like the experts we thought they were, at least in these simulated teaching tasks. Therefore, we conclude that experience as a classroom teacher leads to changes in cognition—in perception, memory, and thought—in ways that seem more sophisticated, more efficient, and more useful. That is a finding of considerable importance. It has implications for the policy-makers who hope to develop a master teacher category for the profession of teaching. It has implications for the development of career ladders and differential pay scales. Although many experienced teachers whom we observed while choosing our sample did not seem expert, we are now confident that some of the experienced teachers we did choose to work with really do deserve that appellation. This would be a nice conclusion to our work if it stood without qualification. But our conclusions need to be qualified a great deal.

First of all, the experienced teachers did not always act in unique ways. We have worked with them on some tasks where no advantage seemed to accrue to experience. Thus, a research issue that is of interest to us, and perhaps to all who study teaching, is the development of some conceptions about teaching tasks that would help us understand when advantages in performance might occur for experienced teachers, and when they might not. We believe that there must be other tasks, as well, where postulants or novices might demonstrate advantages. Some sensible hypotheses on this issue need to be put forward. There is more than scientific interest at stake in this matter. Important policy decisions about teacher certification await such knowledge.

A finding related to this policy issue, also derived from our research, is that experienced/experts, minimally experienced/novices, and inexperienced/postulants did not all act as we have portrayed them above. A good deal of clinical interpretation of the protocols we had collected was necessary in order to reach the conclusions about group differences that we reached. Such interpretive work, of course, should always lead a reader to be skeptical about objectivity, the reliability of the data, the validity of the inferences put forth, etc. Those concerns are always present. We note that in addition to (or perhaps because of) such problems, many of our subjects in the three different groups were judged to have responded in similar ways. A few of our postulants, our least experienced teachers, demonstrated to us exceptional insights about classrooms, had sensibly organized perceptual and memory systems, showed fine insights into curriculum, were very caring about students, and honored schooling and teaching. They acted experienced. They were likely, we thought, to become expert teachers very rapidly. They seemed to us to be as good as they thought they were. These individuals may be correct when they argue that they do not need much coursework before they are equipped to be functioning classroom teachers.

The novices and experts in our samples also showed considerable variation; the group differences reported above are not based on clear performance differences by all members of the two groups. This kind of overlap in ways of thinking by some postulants, novices, and experts provided us with the reason for questioning, at the start of this chapter, the statement that experience is the best teacher. Some of our experienced/ expert teachers did not always act in ways we thought they might, or in ways some of their fellow experienced/expert colleagues did. And some of our least experienced teachers showed very sophisticated patterns of thinking. Experience does not teach everyone equally well.

Another finding of interest to policy-makers, we think, is that some of our postulants appeared to be as ignorant of classroom realities as we expected they would be. Some state legislators, superintendents of instruction, and governors (as in New Jersey, Texas, and a growing number of other states) have programs to provide teaching certification to individuals, like our postulants, who possess subject matter content knowledge. Our data inform us that such a policy could be dangerous. It denies that there is any sophisticated knowledge base needed for classroom teaching. It is interesting to note that no one who has great knowledge of flying and who may even be able to pilot a Cessna airplane believes they can walk into the cockpit and fly a Boeing 747. But the myth persists that anyone who has subject matter knowledge can teach. That belief shows both ignorance and arrogance. Our work leads us to believe that most content matter specialists in mathematics and science who have only industrial and research experience are profoundly ignorant about important characteristics of classroom functioning. Some individuals from this group will, we think, become excellent teachers rapidly. But there appears to be no substitute for experience, particularly when one has not acquired any.

There are other reasons for studying how experience with classroom teaching affects the thought and action of an individual. Such studies provide us with information about the routines, the scripts, and the schema used by the experienced/expert teachers, and thereby help us in identifying the troublesome routines or scripts, or ill-formed schemata, that are characteristics of less expert/less experienced teachers. Information of that kind can influence the design of training programs for beginning teachers. It can provide guides for what beginning teachers might want to think about when they plan for or engage in teaching. The performance of experienced/expert teachers, while not necessarily perfect, provides a place to start from when novices are instructed. The experts' performance provides us, as Glaser (in press, a) has noted elsewhere, with a temporary pedagogical theory, a temporary scaffolding from which novices may learn to be more expert.

There should be no illusions about how much help this might be. The evidence thus far provides little reason to believe that such information will result in dramatic changes in how quickly or efficiently a novice can acquire the skill of an experienced/expert teacher. For example, Huberman (1985) studied the point in their careers when experienced teachers actually mastered the problems that ordinarily perplex first-year teachers. Problems of discipline, effectiveness with both slow and rapid students, sustaining the interest of poorly motivated students, having a variety of materials that students liked to work with, and establishing a satisfactory set of requirements for the classroom were all judged as requiring five years or more to solve for the majority of the experienced teachers. Of the original 18 problems that first-year teachers had identified, only five were adequately solved by the majority of experienced teachers in under three years. Thus, the role of experience in the acquisition of problem-solving skills seems clear. An answer to the question about how much experience is needed to acquire certain skills is not as forthcoming. This is, however, a researchable issue. The development of reliable knowledge about this issue has relevance to policy on teacher certification.

Although not likely to be perfect, the thoughts and actions of experienced/expert teachers can sometimes be considered exemplary. Records of such exemplary performances can be used as case studies for novice teachers to learn from. Shulman (1986, pp. 13–14) argued that beginning teachers need a complementary form of educational experience to accompany their learning of propositional knowledge. He argued for a case literature.

> A case, properly understood, is not simply a report of an event or incident. To call something a case is to make a theoretical claim—to argue that it is a 'case of something ...'
>
> Case knowledge is knowledge of specific, well-documented, and richly described events. Whereas cases themselves are reports of events or sequences of events, the knowledge they represent is what makes them cases. The cases may be examples of specific instances of practice—detailed descriptions how an instructional event occurred—complete with particulars of contexts, thoughts, and feelings. On the other hand, they may be exemplars of principles, exemplifying in their detail a more abstract proposition or theoretical claim.
>
> An event can be described; a case must be explicated, interpreted, argued, dissected, and reassembled.
>
> [Envisioned is] the use of case methods in teacher education, whether in our classrooms or in special laboratories with simulations, videodiscs and annotated scripts, as a means of developing strategic understanding, for extending capacities toward profession-al judgment and decision-making.

In the past few years, there has been some advocacy for the creation of pedagogical laboratories (e.g. Berliner 1985). Laboratories in teacher education could be places to study exemplary cases of schools, teachers, lesson planning, lesson enactments, teachers' thinking about teaching tasks and routines, and teachers' performance of those tasks and routines. The scripts that guide teaching behavior can be developed in such laboratories. Some of the many hours necessary to achieve a functional degree of automation of the classroom routines that experienced teachers use fruitfully could occur in laboratory settings rather than in more complicated real world settings.

The determination of molecular weight in a chemical reaction, the tracing of the efferent system in a frog, the following of a logic structure to determine what happens in a 'go to' statement, and the dissection of cases of classroom teaching are conceptually equivalent phenomena. They require study in laboratories uniquely designed for different professions.

A worthwhile question to ask is: When does a profession know enough to need laboratory experiences for their novice colleagues? To answer that question it is informative to try and find out when medicine, chemistry, computing, biology, and physics were able to get laboratory space in universities for training their inexperienced professionals. A working hypothesis is that training laboratories were created when the people who held the purse strings at the universities became convinced that more book knowledge, more propositional knowledge, was ultimately going to be insufficient to produce a competent practitioner. Somehow a consensus was arrived at that some forms of hands-on and intellectual experience with the subjects or objects of the propositional knowledge was patently needed. That time has come now in teacher preparation programs. If we ever do get teacher education laboratories, extensive knowledge of experienced/expert teachers will be extremely useful in designing learning experiences for novices. The performance of experienced/expert teachers can illuminate important aspects of teaching tasks, provide cases for further study, and may also serve as a guide for developing teaching simulations and games for the teacher education laboratories of the future.

Another reason to study the nature of thought and action in experienced teachers is to foster thinking about the nature of expert systems in pedagogy. The computer's success in solving well-structured problems in domains such as geology or medicine is both spectacular and well known. An expert system in these areas is a knowledge-based artificial intelligence program whose performance depends more on the explicit presence of a large body of organized knowledge than on the possession of special computational procedures. The whole enterprise of applying artificial intelligence in well-structured domains is only about 30 years old.

Solving problems in classrooms, however, is considered to be a case of problem-solving in an ill-structured domain. There are no surely right answers. A good solution depends on some consensus by other professionals, and such consensus is not always easy to find in education. Some computer modeling of problem-solving in ill-structured domains is already occurring. Voss and his colleagues (e.g. Voss and Post, in press) have presented problems of Soviet agriculture to experts in economics, politics, and agriculture. Models of the attempts to solve these social science problems are adequate and improving. Thus, we may soon see some simple expert systems for solving problems in these ill-structured domains. But it is more likely that we will see very practical expert systems for tutoring single students long before we see practical expert systems designed for solving instructional problems in large classes. Knowledgeable writers in that area (Lesgold 1985; Ohlsson 1986) have pointed out that to design an intelligent tutoring system requires a system that has versatile output. Expert tutoring systems need a wide range of instructional options to choose from, and some decision rules about when to use these options. To learn the sheer range of choices that are applicable in a particular teaching situation, and to gain knowledge about what tactic to use when, during instruction, is not easy. Such knowledge can probably be derived only from studying teachers who themselves have a variety of instructional tactics and some decision rules for their use. Experienced/expert teachers seem to have more of these qualities than do novices.

Although practical expert systems may not ever be possible as a management tool for classroom instruction, it might still pay us to act as if we could develop such a system. This point was made in *Science* by two experts in the development of expert systems (Duda and Shortliffe 1983).

> The greatest contributions of expert systems research may well go beyond the development of high-performance programs. Equally as important is the field's impact on the

systematization and codification of knowledge previously thought unsuited for formal organization. Improved approaches to formalizing and managing knowledge are certain to be of importance to a variety of ... endeavors.

There are benefits, therefore, to studying experienced/expert teachers *as if* they could lead us to design expert problem-solving systems as has been done in medicine, chemistry, and physics. Such research can help us codify, formalize, and systematize the knowledge of experienced/expert teachers, and this would be helpful even if computer forms of expert systems never become a reality for the classroom teacher. We could, perhaps, in this way put an end to the concerns of many scholars (e.g. Jackson 1968; Lortie 1975) that teachers have no shared body of knowledge upon which to call. A technical culture based on codified experience may be possible through studies of experienced/expert teachers.

There is yet another reason to study the influence of experience on the thought and action of teachers. It is accepted by many that it is the co-operating or supervising teacher who makes the greatest impact on the career development of the novice during the student teaching experience. The supervising teachers are supposed to be the models for expertise, who lead the novice to a high level of competency in teaching. Despite these lofty hopes, in all but a few institutions the methods for choosing a supervising teacher are inadequate, and sometimes scandalous. One of the things we need, therefore, is research that helps us think about differentiating mere experience from expertise in such a way that the selection of supervising teachers is improved. It is possible that, as we come to understand better an expert teacher's thoughts and actions, we will develop selection procedures for supervising teachers that are more satisfying. Furthermore, studies of this kind could influence the relationship between the novice and supervising teachers in another, perhaps even more important way. A fundamental problem for the novice is that experienced and expert practitioners often have difficulty articulating the basis for their expertise and skill. Schon (1983, p. 49) talks about the commonly found inarticulateness of people who are themselves competent performers:

> When we go about the spontaneous, intuitive performance of the actions of everyday life, we show ourselves to be knowledgeable in a special way. Often we cannot say what it is that we know. When we try to describe it we find ourselves at a loss, or we produce descriptions that are obviously inappropriate. Our knowing is ordinarily tacit, implicit in our patterns of action and in our feel for the stuff with which we are dealing. It seems right to say that our knowing is *in* our actions.
> ... every competent practitioner can recognize phenomena ... for which we cannot give a reasonably accurate or complete description. In his day-to-day practice he makes innumerable judgments of quality for which he cannot state adequate criteria, and he displays skills for which he cannot state the rules and procedures. Even when he makes conscious use of research-based theories and techniques, he is dependent upon tacit recognitions, judgments, and skillful performances.

It is likely that the inarticulateness of many professionals about their knowledge-in-action is, in part, due to their lack of consciousness about their scripts for performance. An understanding of the complexity of their behavioral routines, which run automatically, may also be unavailable to consciousness. This certainly raises problems for any apprenticeship program, like student teaching, where experienced/expert teachers try to communicate to novices the essence of the skills they possess. Analysis of transcripts of supervising teachers' interactions with novice teachers during feedback sessions shows only the lowest level of insight into instructional skills. Perhaps learning to teach from a master teacher would be less mysterious for the novice if the master teacher had some language to describe lessons. Examples of such a language are emerging from studies of classroom tasks and from cognitive psychological investigations of expert–novice differences. These include terms like goals, means/ends relationships, cues, scripts, routines, stop signals, start signals, change signals, etc. Intensive analysis about what one does and development of a language for describing what one does would seem to be a necessary condition for a supervisory teacher to influence the learning of a novice teacher. We have only the most meager start at developing such intelligent apprenticeship systems. Research on the role of experience in learning to teach might shed some light on this matter.

Finally, there is one further reason why research programs of experienced/expert teachers should be expanded—professional pride. It would be a continuing source of pride for teachers to know that some members of their profession resemble experienced/experts in other fields where more clear-cut criteria for the determination of expertise exist. Grand masters in chess, or internationally regarded bridge players, or highly reputed physicists are recognized for their expertise by criteria not normally available in the field of teaching. If similarities were to be found in the way that those experts handle phenomena in their field and the way that experienced/expert teachers handle phenomena in their classrooms, then there exists a chance to build pride in the much-maligned profession of teaching.

Finally, an apology is in order for any confusion resulting from the extensive use, above, of the combined term experienced/expert. Use of that convention reflects the writer's own difficulty in sometimes distinguishing between the two states. Researchers and policy-makers concerned with the role of experience in the profession of teaching would clearly profit from a better understanding of how to separate these two factors.

CONCLUSION

From our overall research program, particularly from analysis of protocols obtained from experienced/expert, less experienced/novice, and inexperienced/postulants in a simulated planning task, we conclude that experience is a good teacher primarily for those without much experience. Experience can change a person. Thus, we found overall performance differences between our most and least experienced teachers. Nevertheless, it was also true that many who have accumulated years of relevant kinds of experience seem not to have profited from it, at least under the conditions described in this chapter. We found, also, that many individuals who do not yet have much experience probably need less of it than we first imagined. There do seem to exist some motivated, reflective, novice and postulant teachers who are likely to excel quickly in their profession. We suggested that other novices and postulants, in comparison with experienced/expert teachers, may have a long road ahead of them. Nevertheless, we believe that if these unseasoned novice and postulant teachers can remain motivated and reflective they are likely to be transformed by their experience into expert teachers. As research grows in the two related areas discussed in this chapter—(a) the role of experience on the thoughts and actions of teachers, and (b) the nature of the skills possessed by expert teachers—we will greatly expand our knowledge base about teachers and teaching. That research is also likely to play an important role in policy pertaining to such areas as teacher training, career development, and certification.

NOTE

1. Members of the research team include Kathy Carter, co-director, and K. Cushing, J. George, D. Sabers, P. Stein, and S. Pinnegar. Funding for our research has been provided by the Spencer Foundation of Chicago.

REFERENCES

Berliner, D. C. (1983) 'Developing Conceptions of Classroom Environments: Some Light on the T in Classroom Studies of ATI'. *Educational Psychologist,* **18**, 1–13.

Berliner, D. C. (1985) 'Laboratory Settings and the Study of Teacher Education'. *Journal of Teacher Education,* **36**, 2–8.

Berliner, D. C. (1986) 'In Pursuit of the Expert Pedagogue'. *Educational Researcher,* September.

Bloom, B. (1986) 'Automaticity'. *Educational Leadership,* February, 70–7.

Bryan, W. L. and Harter, N. (1899) 'Studies of the Telegraphic Language. The Acquisition of a Hierarchy of Habits'. *Psychological Review,* **6**, 345–75.

Calderhead, J. (1983) *Research into Teachers' and Student Teachers' Cognitions: Exploring the Nature of Classroom Practice.* Paper presented at the annual meeting of the American Educational Research Association, Montreal, April.

Chi, M. T. H., Glaser, R. and Farr, M. (in press) *The Nature of Expertise.* Hillsdale, NJ: Erlbaum.

Cushing, K., Carter, K., Sabers, D., Pinnegar, S., and Berliner, D. C. (1986) *Differences in Visual Information Processing between Expert and Novice Teachers.* Paper presented at the annual meeting of the American Psychological Association, Washington, DC, August.

de Groot, A. D. (1965) *Thought and Choice in Chess.* The Hague: Mouton.

Duda, R. O. and Shortliffe, E. H. (1983) 'Expert Systems Research'. *Science,* **220**, 261–8.

Glaser, R. (in press, a). 'On the Nature of Expertise'. In *Proceedings of the In Memorium Hermannn Ebbinghaus Symposium.* Amsterdam, The Netherlands: Elsevier–North Holland Publishers.

Glaser, R. (in press, b). 'On the Nature of Expertise'. In Schooler, C. and Schaie, W. (eds) *Cognitive Functioning and Social Structure over the Life Course.* Norwood, NJ: Ablex.

Housner, L. D. and Griffey, D. C. (1985) 'Teacher Cognition: Differences in Planning and Interactive Decision-Making between Experienced and Inexperienced Teachers'. *Research Quarterly for Exercise and Sport,* **56**, 45–53.

Huberman, M. (1985) 'What Knowledge Is of Most Worth to Teachers? A Knowledge-Use Perspective'. *Teaching and Teacher Education,* **1**, 251–62.

Jackson, P. W. (1968) *Life in Classrooms.* New York: Holt, Rinehart & Winston.

Kolodner, J. (1983) 'Towards an Understanding of the Role of Experience in the Evolution from Novice to Expert'. *International Journal of Man-machine Studies,* **19**, 497–518.

Leinhardt, G. and Greeno, J. G. (1986) 'The Cognitive Skill of Teaching'. *Journal of Educational Psychology,* **78**, 75–95.

Lesgold, A. M. (1985) 'Computer Resources for Learning'. *Peabody Journal of Education,* **62**(2) 60–74.

Lortie, D. (1975) *Schoolteacher.* Chicago, IL: University of Chicago Press.

Ohlsson, S. (1986) 'Some Principles of Intelligent Tutoring'. *Instructional Science,*

14(3–4), 293–326.

Sabers, D., Cushing, K., Carter, K., and Berliner, D. C. (in preparation) *The Processing of Simultaneous Information by Expert and Novice Teachers*. Tucson, AZ: University of Arizona.

Sabers, D., Pinnegar, S., Cushing, K., Carter, K., and Berliner, D. C. (1986) *Saliency and Utility of Information for Expert, Novice, and Postulant Teachers*. Paper presented at the annual meeting of the American Psychological Association, Washington, DC, August.

Schon, D. (1983) *The Reflective Practitioner*. New York: Basic Books.

Shavelson, R. J. (1986) *Interactive Decision-making: Some Thoughts on Teacher Cognition*. Paper presented at the First International Congress on Teacher Thinking and Decisionmaking, La Rabida, Huelva, Seville, Spain, June.

Shulman, L. S. (1986) 'Those Who Understand: Knowledge Growth in Teaching'. *Educational Researcher*, **15**(2), 4–14.

Smith, L. C. and Geoffrey, W. (1968) *The Complexities of an Urban Classroom*. New York: Holt, Rinehart & Winston.

Stein, P., Carter, K., and Berliner, D. C. (1986) *The Estimation of Students' Knowledge by Expert and Novice Teachers*. Paper presented at the annual meeting of the Rocky Mountain Educational Research Association, Albuquerque, NM, November.

Voss, J. F. and Post, T. A. (in press) 'On the Solving of Ill-Structured Problems'. In Chi, M. T. H., Glaser, R., and Farr, Y. M. (eds) *The Nature of Expertise*. Hillsdale, NJ: Erlbaum.

3

TEACHER PLANNING

Christopher M. Clark and Robert J. Yinger

Teacher planning is one of the central topics of research on teacher thinking, largely because of the pivotal role it plays in linking curriculum to instruction, but perhaps also because planning is a relatively accessible aspect of the mental lives of teachers. The studies summarized in this chapter provide interesting detail about how experienced teachers plan and what relation their plans have to their classroom behavior. The literature of research on teacher planning is not sufficiently mature to provide a solid empirical basis for deciding what the best ways to plan may be. But, even in its early descriptive stage, this research offers concepts and insights that can help us see and appreciate the complexities of the teacher's role in new ways. In particular, these descriptions of teacher planning lend support to the image of the teacher as a reflective professional engaged in a complex and fluid design process. Seen in this way, research on teacher planning can be helpful in demonstrating ways in which teaching is similar to other design professions.

RESEARCH ON TEACHER THINKING

The thinking, planning, and decision-making of teachers constitute a large part of the psychological context within which curriculum is interpreted and acted upon and within which teachers teach and students learn. Teacher behavior is substantially influenced and even determined by teachers' thought processes. These are the fundamental assumptions behind the literature that has come to be called research on teacher thinking. Researchers on teacher thinking seek first to describe fully the mental lives of teachers. Second, they hope to understand and explain how and why the behaviorally observable activities of teachers' professional lives take on the forms and functions that they do. They ask when and why teaching is difficult, and how human beings manage the complexity of classroom teaching. The ultimate goal of research on teachers' thought processes is to construct a realistic portrayal of teaching for use by educational theorists, researchers, policy-makers, curriculum designers, teacher educators, school administrators, and teachers themselves.

Jackson's (1968) book *Life in Classrooms* reports one of the earliest empirical attempts to describe and understand the mental constructs and processes that underlie teacher behavior. His descriptive study departed strikingly from contemporary research on teaching and ill fit the then-dominant teacher effectiveness research paradigm. In 1968 it was difficult to see how description of life in a few classrooms could contribute much to the quest for teaching effectiveness. Jackson's contribution to research on teaching, however, was conceptual. He portrayed the full complexity of the teacher's task, made conceptual distinctions that fit the teacher's frame of reference (such as that between the pre-active and interactive phases of teaching), and called educators' attention to the importance of describing the thinking and planning of teachers toward more fully understanding classroom processes.

In Sweden, Dahllof and Lundgren (1970) conducted a series of studies of the structure of the teaching process as an expression of organizational constraints. While this work was primarily concerned with the effects of contextual factors on teaching, it revealed some of the mental categories that teachers use to organize and make sense of their professional experiences. Dahllof and Lundgren's contribution, like Jackson's, was primarily conceptual.

Of particular significance in the Dahllof and Lundgren research was the phenomenon of the 'steering group', a small subset of a class (ranging in achievement level from the 10th to the 25th percentile) that teachers used as an informal reference group for decisions about pacing a lesson or unit. During whole class instruction, when the students in the steering group seemed to understand what was being presented, the teachers would move the class on to a new topic. But when the teachers believed that the steering group students were not understanding or performing up to standards, the teachers slowed the pace of instruction for all. The steering group is important as a concept both because of its empirical verifiability and because it shows clearly how teachers' mental categories can have significant pedagogical consequences.

In June 1974 the National Institute of Education convened a week-long National Conference on Studies in Teaching to create an agenda for future research on teaching. The participants in this planning conference were organized into ten panels, and each panel produced a plan for research in their area of expertise. The deliberations of Panel 6, Teaching as Clinical Information Processing, were of particular importance to the development of research on teacher thinking. To understand, predict, and influence what teachers do, the panelists argued, researchers must study the psychological processes by which teachers perceive and define their professional responsibilities and situations.

Panel 6's report is explicit about the view of the teacher that guided the panelists in their deliberations and recommendations for research:

> The Panel was oriented toward the teacher as clinician, not only in the sense of someone diagnosing specific forms of learning dysfunction or pathology and prescribing particular remedies, but more broadly as an individual responsible for (a) aggregating and making sense out of an incredible diversity of information sources about individual students and

the class collectively; (b) bringing to bear a growing body of empirical and theoretical work constituting the research literature of education; somehow (c) combining all that information with the teacher's own expectations, attitudes, beliefs, purposes ... and (d) having to respond, make judgments, render decisions, reflect, and regroup to begin again. (National Institute of Education, 1975, pp. 2–3)

In short, Panel 6's report presented an image of the teacher as a clinical practitioner who has more in common with physicians, lawyers, and architects than with technicians who execute skilled performances according to prescriptions or algorithms defined by others. This view of the teacher has had a profound effect on the questions asked, methods of inquiry employed, and the form of the results reported in research on teacher thinking. With this as background, we now want to focus more closely on one part of the research on teacher thinking: research on teacher planning.

RESEARCH ON TEACHER PLANNING

Planning defined

As a subject of research, planning has been defined in two ways. First, planning is a basic psychological process in which a person visualizes the future, inventories means and ends, and constructs a framework to guide his or her future action—'thinking in the future tense'. This definition leads to research on the process of planning that draws heavily from the theories and methods of cognitive psychology. At another level of abstraction, planning could be defined (somewhat circularly) as 'the things that teachers do when they say that they are planning'. This definition suggests a phenomenological or ethnographic approach to research on teacher planning, in which the teacher takes on an important role as informant or even as research collaborator.

Both definitions of teacher planning are represented in the research literature either explicitly or implicitly. These differences in thought about what planning is account for the variety of methods of inquiry in use and for the challenge that reviewers of this literature face in pulling together a coherent summary of what has been learned. Planning is challenging to study because it is both a psychological process and a practical activity.

Through examining the results of selected studies of teacher planning, we hope to answer three major questions that researchers have been pursuing:

1. What are the types and functions of teacher planning?
2. What models have been used to describe the process of planning?
3. What is the relationship between teacher planning and subsequent action in the classroom?

Types and functions of teacher planning

What are the different kinds of planning that teachers do, and what purposes do they serve? The answer to both parts of this question seems to be 'many'. That is, there are many different kinds of planning in use and many functions served by these processes. More specific answers come from several recent studies of teacher planning.

Kinds of planning

Two of these studies were designed to (among other things) determine what kinds of planning experienced teachers engage in. Yinger (1977) studied the planning decisions of a single first/second-grade teacher over a five-month period. Using interviews, thinking aloud, and extensive classroom observations, Yinger determined that this teacher engaged in five different kinds of planning: yearly, term, unit, weekly, and daily. The 'activity' was found to be the basic unit of daily and weekly planning. The teacher drew heavily on routines established early in the school year that incorporated learning outcomes for students. These routines were seen as functioning to reduce the complexity and increase the predictability of classroom activities.

In a second study by Clark and Yinger (1979), 78 teachers wrote descriptions of general characteristics of their planning and also selected and described three examples of their own plans representing the three most important types of planning that they did during the year. The teachers reported that they engaged in the following eight different types of planning (in order of frequency of mention): weekly, daily, unit, long-range, lesson, short-range, yearly, and term planning. Unit planning was most often identified as the most important type of planning, followed by weekly and daily planning. Only 7 per cent of the teachers in this study listed lesson planning among the types of planning most important to them.

The dynamic relationships among different types of planning have also been studied to a modest degree. Two studies by Greta Morine-Dershimer (Morine-Dershimer 1979; Morine-Dershimer and Vallance 1976) suggest that teachers' plans are seldom fully reflected in their written plans. Rather, the details recorded on a written plan are nested within more comprehensive planning structures, called 'lesson images' by Morine-Dershimer. These lesson images, in turn, are nested within a still larger construct called the 'activity flow' by Joyce (1978–9). For elementary teachers the activity flow encompasses the year-long progress of a class through each particular subject and the balance of activities across subjects in a school day or week.

Further support for the idea that teacher planning is a nested process comes from a study by Clark and Elmore (1979). They interviewed and observed five elementary teachers during the first five weeks of the school year and found that their planning was primarily concerned with setting up the physical environment of the classroom, assessing student abilities, and establishing the social system of the classroom. By the end of the fourth week of school, a system of schedules, routines, and groupings for instruction was established. These structural and social features of the classroom then persisted throughout the school year and served as the framework within which particular activities and units were planned. Other studies of the first weeks of school also support the conclusion that, to a significant degree, the 'problem space' (after Newell and Simon 1972) within which teacher and students operate is defined early, changes little during the course of the school year, and exerts a powerful, if subtle, influence on thought and behavior (e.g. Anderson and Evertson 1978; Buckley and Cooper 1978; Schultz and Florio 1979; Tikunoff and Ward 1978).

Functions of planning

The research that speaks to the function of teacher planning suggests that there are almost as many reasons to plan as there are types of planning. In the Clark and Yinger study (1979) mentioned earlier, the teachers' written responses to a question about why they plan fell into three clusters:

- planning to meet immediate personal needs (e.g. to reduce uncertainty and anxiety, to find a sense of direction, confidence, and security),
- planning as a means to the end of instruction (e.g. to learn the material, to collect and organize materials, to organize time and activity flow),
- direct uses of plans during instruction (e.g. to organize students, to get an activity started, to aid memory, to provide a framework for instruction and evaluation).

An ethnographic study of the planning of 12 elementary teachers by McCutcheon (1980) also confirmed that some teachers plan in order to meet the administrative requirement that they turn in their plans to the school principal on a regular basis. These teachers also indicated that special plans were necessary for use by substitute teachers in the event of absence of the regular teacher. These plans for substitute teachers were special both because they included a great deal of background information about how the system in a particular classroom and school operated and because the regular teachers tended to reserve the teaching of what they judged to be important material for themselves, planning filler or drill and practice activities for the substitute teacher.

The most obvious function of teacher planning is to transform and modify curriculum to fit the unique circumstances of each teaching situation. In one of the only studies of yearly planning to date, Clark and Elmore (1981) asked a second-grade teacher to think aloud while doing her yearly planning for mathematics, science, and writing. The primary resources she used in yearly planning were curriculum materials (especially the teacher's guides), her memory of classroom interaction during the previous year, and the calendar for the coming school year. The process of yearly planning, typically done during the summer months, consisted of the teacher reviewing the curriculum materials that she would be using during the coming year, rearranging the sequence of topics within curricula, and adding and deleting content to be taught. A broad outline of the content to be taught emerged from a process of mental review of the events of the past year, combined with adjustment of the planned sequence and pace of teaching to accommodate new curriculum materials and new ideas consistent with the teacher's implicit theory of instruction.

Through her review of the past year, reflection on her satisfaction with how things went, and modifications of the content, sequence, and planned pace of instruction, the teacher's yearly planning process served to integrate her own experience with the published materials, establishing a sense of ownership and control of content to be taught (Ben-Peretz 1975). Yearly planning sessions satisfied this teacher that she had the resources available to provide conditions for learning at least equal to those she had provided during the previous year. Yearly planning decreased the unpredictability and uncertainty that attend every teaching situation.

The Clark and Elmore (1981) study of yearly planning supports the idea that published curriculum materials have a powerful influence on the content and process of teaching. In a series of studies of teacher planning for sixth-grade science instruction, Smith and Sendelbach (1979) pursued this idea at the level of unit planning. Working with the SCIS (Science Curriculum Improvement Study) curriculum, Smith and Sendelbach compared explicit directions for a unit of instruction provided in the teacher's manual with four teachers' transformations of those directions into plans, and finally with the actual classroom behavior of one of the four teachers while teaching the unit. Observation of the four teachers during planning sessions combined with analysis of think-aloud and stimulated recall interview data revealed that the principal product of a unit-planning session was a mental picture of the unit to be taught, the sequence of activities within it, and the students' probable responses. These mental plans were supplemented and cued by sketchy notes and lists of important points that the teachers wanted to be sure to remember. Smith and Sendelbach characterized the process of activating a unit plan as one of reconstructing the plan from memory, rather than of carefully following the directions provided in the teacher's guide.

Smith and Sendelbach are critical of the loose coupling between curriculum and instruction because of potential they see for distortions or significant omissions in the content of science instruction. From their classroom observations of one experienced teacher implementing her unit plan, they concluded that the quality of instruction was degraded somewhat by both planned and unintended deviations from the SCIS materials. They attributed these deviations to the teacher's limited subject matter knowledge, to difficulty in finding information in the teacher's guide, and to the presence of inherently complex and confusing concepts. The researchers suggest that the phenomenon of heavy dependence on teacher's guides in unit planning provides an opportunity to improve the quality of instruction by revising these guides to be more clear, more comprehensive, and more prescriptive.

Few studies have attempted to describe teacher planning as it occurs naturally in all its variety. Virtually all but two or three studies of teacher planning focus on a single type of planning. Educators could benefit from more studies that describe the full range of the kinds of planning that teachers do during the school year and the interrelationships between these kinds of planning.

In addition, the modest to insignificant role of lesson planning for experienced teachers is interesting. Lesson planning is the one type that is addressed directly in all teacher preparation programs. Yet it is rarely claimed as an important part of the repertoire of experienced teachers. This anomaly suggests that perhaps some of our teacher preparation practices bow more to the task demands of the university than to those of the teaching profession.

Finally, it appears that the functions of teacher planning that are not directly and exclusively concerned with a particular instructional episode have been slighted. Researchers and teacher educators should think more broadly about what teachers are accomplishing in their planning time, and avoid narrow comparisons of what was planned with what was taught as the only criterion for evaluation.

What models describe teacher planning?

The logic of an industrial production system has given educators the most widely prescribed model for teacher planning (Tyler 1950). This linear model consists of a sequence of four steps: (1) specify objectives, (2) select learning activities, (3) organize learning activities, and (4) specify evaluation procedures. This linear model has been recommended for use at all levels of educational planning, and hundreds of thousands of educators have been trained in its use. It was not until 1970 that researchers began to examine directly the planning processes in use by teachers and to compare what was being practiced with what had been prescribed.

Taylor (1970) conducted a study of teacher planning in British secondary schools. The study was directed toward examining how teachers planned syllabuses for courses. Using group discussions with teachers, analysis of course syllabuses, and a questionnaire administered to 261 teachers of English, science, and geography, Taylor came to the following general conclusions. The most common theme found across all of the modes of data collection was the prominence of pupils—their needs, abilities, and interests. Following these, in order of importance, were the subject matter, goals, and teaching methods. In planning for courses of study, evaluation emerged as being of little importance, as did the relation between one's own courses and the curriculum as a whole. Taylor concluded that most course planning was unsystematic and only general in nature and that most teachers appear to be far from certain about what the planning process requires.

Through teacher ratings of the importance of various issues in curriculum planning and a factor analysis of their responses, Taylor identified four primary factors of interest to his sample of teachers. The results indicated that, when planning, the teachers tended to consider in order of importance: (1) factors associated with the teaching context (e.g. materials and resources), (2) pupil interests, (3) aims and purposes of teaching, and (4) evaluation considerations. Rather than beginning with purposes and objectives and moving to a description of learning experiences necessary to achieve the objectives as the linear-planning theorists propose, Taylor found that these teachers began with the context of teaching, next considered learning situations likely to interest and involve their pupils, and only after this considered the purposes that their teaching would serve. Another difference between Taylor's data and the Tyler model was that criteria and procedures for evaluating the effectiveness of their course of teaching were only a minor issue. These findings led Taylor to conclude that curriculum planning should begin with the content to be taught and with important contextual considerations (e.g. time, sequencing, resources). This should be followed by considerations of pupil interests and attitudes, aims and purposes of the course, learning situations to be created, the philosophy of the course, the criteria for judging the course, the degree of pupil interest fostered by the course, and finally, evaluation of the course.

Zahorik (1975) continued this line of inquiry by examining the use of behavioral objectives and the 'separate ends–means' model, and the use of the 'integrated ends–means' model proposed by Eisner (1967), which viewed objectives as implicit in the activities. He asked 194 teachers to list in writing the decisions that they made prior to teaching and the order in which they made them. He classified these decisions into the following categories: objectives, content, activities, materials, diagnosis, evaluation, instruction, and organization. He found that the kind of decision made by the greatest number of teachers concerned pupil activities (81 per cent). The decision most frequently made first was content (51 per cent), followed by learning objectives (28 per cent).

Zahorik concluded from this study that teacher planning decisions do not always follow linearly from a specification of objectives and that, in fact, objectives are not a particularly important planning decision in terms of quantity of use. He also argued, however, that the integrated ends–means model does not appear to be a functioning reality because of the relatively few teachers (only 3 per cent) who reported beginning their planning by making decisions about activities.

More recently, researchers have turned their attention to describing teacher planning by observing and audiotaping teachers thinking aloud during planning sessions. Peterson et al (1978) examined planning in a laboratory situation as 12 teachers prepared to teach a new instructional unit to groups of junior high school students with whom they had had no previous contact. These units were taught to three different groups of eight students on three different days. During their planning periods, teachers were instructed to think aloud, and their verbal statements were later coded into planning categories including objectives, materials, subject matter, and instructional process. The primary findings of this study were that (1) teachers spent the largest proportion of their planning time dealing with the content to be taught; (2) after subject matter, teachers concentrated their planning efforts on instructional processes (strategies and activities); and (3) the smallest proportion of their planning time was spent on objectives. All three of these findings were consistent with those by Zahorik (1975) and Goodlad and Klein (1970). The third finding was also similar to results reported by Joyce and Harootunian (1964) and by Popham and Baker (1970).

The task demands on the teachers should be taken into account in interpreting these results. The researchers provided the teachers with unfamiliar materials from which to teach, and limited preparation time to 90 minutes immediately preceding teaching on each day of the study. Since the teachers did not know their students in advance, it follows that the emphasis in their planning would be on content and instructional processes. Finally, the researchers did provide the teachers with a list of six general teaching goals, expressed in terms of content coverage, process goals, and cognitive and attitudinal outcomes for students. Under these circumstances, it is not surprising that the teachers devoted little planning time to composing more specific objectives, and devoted the largest part of their planning time to studying the content and deciding how to teach it.

The findings of a study conducted in a classroom setting by Morine-Dershimer and Vallance (1976) were consistent with those of Peterson et al (1978). Morine-Dershimer and Vallance collected written plans for two experimenter-prescribed lessons (one in mathematics and one in reading) taught by 20 teachers of second and fifth grades in their own classrooms to a small group of their students. Teacher plans were described by the researchers in terms of (1) specificity of written plans, (2) general format of plans, (3) statement of goals, (4) source of goal statement, (5) attention to pupil background and preparation, (6) identification of evaluation procedures, and (7) indication of possible alternative procedures. In this study, teachers tended to be fairly specific and used an outline form in their plans. Their written plans reflected little attention to behavioral goals, diagnosis of student needs, evaluation procedures, and alternative courses of action. However, the teachers reported that writing plans for researcher-prescribed lessons was not typical of their planning, and observations of their classroom teaching behavior revealed that much of what the teachers had planned was not reflected in their written outlines (Morine-Dershimer 1979).

In his five-month field study of one teacher, Yinger (1977) drew on his observations, interview data, and think-aloud protocols to create a theoretical model of the process of teacher planning. The following is a brief description of the model (from Clark and Yinger 1977):

> Three stages of planning were represented in the planning model. The first stage, problem finding, was portrayed as a discovery cycle where the teacher's goal conceptions, her knowledge and experience, her notion of the planning dilemma, and the materials available for planning interact to produce an initial problem conception worthy of further exploration. The second stage in the planning process was problem formulation and solution. The mechanism proposed for carrying out this process was the 'design cycle'. In this cycle, problem solving was characterized as a design process involving progressive elaboration of plans over time. Elaboration, investigation, and adaptation were proposed as phases through which plans were formulated. The third stage of the planning model involved implementation of the plan, its evaluation, and its eventual routinization. This stage emphasized the contribution of evaluation and routinization to the teacher's repertoire of knowledge and experience which in turn play a major role in future planning deliberations. (p. 285)

One of the most significant contributions of this way of conceptualizing the planning process is that the model is cyclical in two senses. Internally, the model postulates a recursive design cycle similar to the processes hypothesized to go on in the work of architects, physicians, artists, designers, and other professionals. Externally, the model acknowledges that schooling is not a series of unrelated planning–teaching episodes, but that each planning event draws from prior planning and teaching experiences and that each teaching event feeds into future planning and teaching processes. The cycle is a continuous, year-long process, in which the boundaries between planning, teaching, and reflection are not sharp and distinct.

A later study by Clark and Yinger (1979) involved asking five teachers to plan a two-week unit on writing of their own devising that had never been taught before. The teachers kept journals documenting their plans and their thinking about planning during a three-week period, and they were interviewed twice each week. The journal-keeping and interviews continued and were supplemented by observations during the two-week period when the plans were being implemented.

Analysis supported the idea that unit planning was not a linear process moving from objectives through design of activities to meet objectives. Rather, it was a cyclical process, typically beginning with a general idea and moving through phases of successive elaboration. Some teachers spent a great deal of time and energy at the problem-finding stage, generating topics or ideas for their unit. The search process typical of this stage was distinctly different from the elaboration and refinement of the idea that took place in the subsequent problem-formulation/solution stage. These data are consistent with the planning process model developed earlier (Yinger 1977).

Individuals differed in their use of the model. Two of the teachers' unit plans consisted of a short problem-finding stage, brief unit planning, and considerable reliance on trying out activities in the classroom. This approach to planning was called 'incremental planning'. Teachers who planned incrementally employed a series of short planning steps, relying heavily on day-to-day information from the classroom. The remaining three teachers' unit plans were characterized as products of 'comprehensive planning', in which the teachers developed a thoroughly specified framework for future action. Comprehensive planning involved more attention to the unit as a whole, and more time and energy invested in specifying plans as completely as possible before beginning to teach. Both approaches to unit planning seemed to work well for the teachers who used them. Incremental planning saved time and energy while staying in touch with changing student states. Comprehensive planning provided a complete and dependable guide for teacher–student interaction for the whole course of a unit, reducing uncertainty and increasing the probability of achieving pre-specified objectives.

A final note on the models of planning issue comes from McLeod (1981). She approached the question of learning objectives in planning by asking not whether they are the starting point for planning but when teachers think about them. McLeod did a stimulated recall interview with each of 17 kindergarten teachers, using a videotape of a 20–30-minute classroom activity taught earlier that same day. The purpose of the interviews was to determine when intended learning outcomes were formulated in terms of four stages: (1) pre-active 1: before planning activities or selecting materials; (2) pre-active 2: after planning but before teaching; (3) interactive: during the act of teaching; and (4) post-active: during reflection after a teaching episode (after Pylypiw 1974). The interviews also revealed how different types of intended learning outcomes (cognitive, social, and psychomotor) were distributed.

Averaging the responses across the 17 teachers, McLeod found that the largest percentage of intended learning outcomes occurred during the interactive stage (45.8 per cent). This was followed by pre-active stage 1 (26.5 per cent), pre-active stage 2 (19.5 per cent), and the post-active stage (8.2 per cent). The data also indicated that 57.7 per cent of the intended learning outcomes were categorized as cognitive, 35 per cent were classified as social or affective, and 7.2 per cent as psychomotor or perceptual. Interestingly, the social/affective intended learning outcomes were primarily identified during the interactive stage, while cognitive outcomes predominated in the pre-active and post-active stages.

The McLeod study can be criticized on the grounds that possibly excessive weight was placed on the stimulated recall interviews. These data could have been supplemented to good effect by observations and by having teachers think aloud during the pre-active stages. Nevertheless, this research does much to broaden the concept of goals, objectives, or intended learning outcomes and their roles in planning and teaching. Earlier research tended to dismiss learning objectives as a rare, and therefore unimportant, element in teacher planning, even going so far as to characterize teachers as interested only in activities rather than in outcomes. McLeod's study suggests that teachers can and do think about and act to support both specific and general learning outcomes for their students, and that it is hazardous to study the process of teacher planning in isolation from interactive teaching and post-active reflection.

Teacher planning and classroom interaction

The third and final question to be addressed has to do with the link between teacher planning and action in the classroom. Studies mentioned earlier demonstrate that the content of instruction and the sequence of topics are influenced by teacher planning (e.g. Clark and Elmore 1981; Smith and Sendelbach 1979). Several other studies examine how what teachers planned to do influences what actually happens in the classroom.

Zahorik (1970) compared the effects of the presence and absence of structured planning on teachers' classroom behavior. He provided 6 of 12 teachers with a partial lesson plan containing behavioral objectives and a detailed outline of content to be covered two weeks hence. He requested that the remaining 6 teachers reserve an hour of instructional time to carry out a task for the researchers, not telling them that they were going to be asked to teach a lesson on credit cards until just before the appointed time. Zahorik analyzed recorded protocols of the 12 lessons focusing on 'teacher behavior that is sensitive to students' (p. 144). He defined this behavior as 'verbal acts of the teacher that permit, encourage, and develop pupils' ideas, thoughts and actions' (p. 144). In comparing the protocols of the planners and non-planners, Zahorik judged that teachers who had been given plans in advance exhibited less honest or authentic use of the pupils' ideas during the lesson. He concluded from this that the typical planning model—goals, activities and their organization, and evaluation—resulted in insensitivity to pupils on the part of the teacher.

Unfortunately, Zahorik did not determine the degree to which the teachers who received the lesson plans in advance actually planned or elaborated the lesson. A competing explanation for these findings is that the teachers who had no advance warning about what they were to teach were forced by the demands of the task to concentrate on their students' ideas and experiences, while those teachers who knew the expected topic of instruction for two weeks prior to teaching were influenced to focus on the content rather than on their students.

Peterson et al (1978) conducted a laboratory study of teacher planning, teaching, and student achievement. Twelve experienced junior high school teachers were given social studies materials dealing with life in a small French community along with a list of desired cognitive and affective student learning objectives. The teachers were given a 90-minute period in which to think aloud while they planned a three-hour instructional unit. After planning, the teachers were videotaped while teaching groups of eight junior high school students. At the end of the teaching day, the teachers were interviewed using a stimulated recall process in which they viewed videotaped segments of their own teaching and responded to a series of questions about their thought processes while teaching. The students completed achievement tests and an attitude inventory immediately after class. Each teacher repeated this process on three separate days with three different groups of students.

A number of positive relationships between the focus of the teachers' planning statements and their classroom behavior emerged. For all teachers, planning on the first day of teaching was heavily weighted toward the content to be covered. However, the focus shifted on the second and third days, with planning for instructional processes becoming more prominent. The proportion of planning statements dealing with the learner was positively related to teacher behavior classified as 'group focused'. The proportion of planning statements dealing with the content was positively and significantly correlated with teacher behavior coded as 'subject matter focused'. These findings suggest that teacher planning is most related to the general focus or tone of interactive teaching rather than to the specific details of verbal behavior. They also suggest that the nature of the work done during the pre-active planning period changes with situation-specific teaching experience. As the task demands on the teacher change, so does the nature of appropriate preparation.

Carnahan (1980) studied the planning and subsequent behavior of nine fifth-grade teachers who taught the same two-week mathematics unit. The quality of the teachers' written plans was determined by rating plans that focused on large groups as low in quality and plans that focused on individuals or small groups as high in quality. (This criterion was chosen because the curriculum materials that the teachers were using incorporated a similar bias.) Classroom observers rated instruction for teacher clarity, use of motivation strategies, and student engagement. Carnahan found that no statistically significant relationship existed between his ratings of plan quality and the ratings of teaching quality. However, he did find a significant positive correlation between the total percentage of written planning statements about small groups or individuals and the teachers' observed use of small groups in the classroom. This and other findings in Carnahan's report indicated that the main relationship between written plans and subsequent classroom interaction is in the domain of organization and structuring of teaching rather than in the domain of specific verbal behavior. During interactive teaching, the responses of students are unpredictable and therefore verbal dialogue is not a profitable focus for teacher planning.

The influence of teacher planning on classroom processes in the teaching of pre-school seems to be somewhat different from that observed in higher grades. Hill et al (1981) studied the planning of six teachers who constituted the staff of a university developmental pre-school. During a ten-week period the researchers observed the teachers' Friday afternoon group planning sessions, staff meetings, conferences with student teachers, materials selection from the storeroom, and their arranging of their classroom environments. They also interviewed the teachers about their planning processes and copied planning documents and records.

Hill, Yinger, and Robbins found that much of the teachers' planning centred around selecting and arranging manipulable materials. The school storeroom was an important source of ideas for learning activities, and once the appropriate materials were identified the planning process focused on how these materials were to be arranged in the classroom for use by the children, and on how the transitions into and out of these activities were to be managed. The teachers were observed to spend three or more hours per week arranging the physical environments of their classrooms. When an activity did not go well, the first improvement strategy used by these teachers was to rearrange the physical environment. Because teaching in this setting was so heavily dependent on the materials selected and arranged by the teachers, it is clear that the nature of the children's learning opportunities was heavily influenced by teacher planning. It is also clear that the nature of the planning process was influenced by the demands of teaching in this setting.

These studies, taken together, suggest that teacher planning does influence opportunity to learn, content coverage, grouping for instruction, and the general focus of classroom processes. They also highlight the fact that the finer details of classroom teaching (e.g. specific verbal behavior) are unpredictable and therefore not planned. Planning shapes the broad outlines of what is possible or likely to occur while teaching, and is used to manage transitions from one activity to another. But once interactive teaching begins, the teacher's plan moves to the background and interactive decision-making becomes more important.

THINKING FROM THE RESEARCH

We believe strongly that research on teachers' thought processes has taught us as much about how to think about teaching as it has about teachers' thinking. As we reflect upon the findings of research on teacher planning, we have been able to develop new conceptions of teaching, which in turn have led us into new areas of inquiry and theorizing. In this section we explore some of these ideas to show how the research on teacher planning has become a bridge to more powerful and productive conceptions of teaching and teachers.

Images of teaching

Throughout history the act of teaching has been described and guided by various metaphors and images drawn chiefly from the arts, agriculture, and the social sciences. Most recently, educators have been influenced by two dominant images: the teacher as skilled manager and the teacher as decision-maker.

The image of the teacher as skilled manager has its roots in the industrialization of western society. It came to fruition in the early 1950s with the emergence of an 'educational technology' based largely on the promise of behavioral psychology as a means of controlling human behavior. These notions, when combined with theories from the emerging areas of organizational development, systems science, and administrative science, led to the development of the image of the teacher as one who effectively manages the learning of his or her charges.

Like other professions, the skill of the teacher was thought to be rooted in the mastery of technique, which in turn is grounded in 'basic sciences' (for education these being the social sciences, primarily psychology). In teaching, as in most other professional fields, this image became solidified and institutionalized in the guise of a model of 'technical rationality' (Schon 1983). This model asserts that skilled professional practice is possible only when the practitioner employs technical or 'engineering' skills based on systematic knowledge that is specialized, scientific, and standardized. The model of technical rationality was exemplified in teacher education by the rise of competency-based models of training, and behavioral systems for evaluating teacher effectiveness.

In recent years the image of the teacher as skilled manager or technician has been joined by the image of the teacher as decision-maker. The coming to prominence of cognitive psychology has refocused the emphasis on technique and skill from the behavioral domain to the domain of thinking and cognition. Skills such as diagnosis and prescription, problem-solving, and decision-making have been nominated as basic teaching skills. The inclusion of cognitive skill in the image of the teacher has not replaced the manager metaphor in the thinking of most teacher educators and teachers. Decision-making has in many cases just become another skill or technique to be mastered and applied within the framework of technical rationality.

The influence of cognitive psychology has been much more apparent in the thinking of researchers who have turned their interests to studying teacher cognition. Research on teacher thinking has uncovered an unacknowledged richness and complexity in the realm of teaching practice. At the same time, it has failed to uncover the model of technical rationality in the actual practice of teachers. In fact, drastically different norms of rationality seem to be present.

The norms of rationality being documented in teaching are very similar to those being described in recent research in other professions. All professions must deal with five general features of practical situations: complexity, uncertainty, instability, uniqueness, and value conflict. Russell Ackoff, one of the founders of operations research, paints a vivid picture of the world of the professional:

> Managers are not confronted with problems that are independent of each other, but with dynamic situations that consist of complex systems of changing problems that interact with each other. I call such situations *messes*. Problems are abstracted from messes by analysis; they are to messes as atoms are to tables and charts ... Managers do not solve problems; they manage messes. (Ackoff 1979, as cited in Schon 1983)

The skills called for by these situations are not the systematic application of predetermined models or standardized techniques. These situations require from the practitioner the artful use of skills such as problem discovery and formulation, design, invention, and flexible adaptation. The orderly prescriptions of technology and science do not seem to match what professionals do in practice.

The image we see emerging from research and theory is of the teacher as professional. We use this term to refer to practitioners who specialize in designing practical courses of action to serve the needs of a particular client group. We assume, based on previous research on teaching practice, that the images that dominate education today are insufficient to fully describe the work of teachers. We see a need to break from the model of technical rationality, which seems mismatched with the world of teaching, and to explore patterns of practice and knowledge that may be used as a basis for rethinking and reasserting teaching as a profession. Our firm belief is that teaching is in great need of a new image to revive and empower those involved. We believe that teacher as professional may be that image.

Teaching as a design profession

Our goal is to develop an understanding of the ways in which educators act as professionals.

Research on teacher thinking has become established as a major and influential body of inquiry within research on teaching (Clark and Yinger 1977; Shavelson and Stern 1981; Clark and Peterson 1986). Following are some propositions that we have distilled from the research:

1. What teachers do is strongly influenced by what and how they think, i.e. little of what teachers do is merely spontaneously reactive.
2. Teaching practice is based on thoughtful and systematic (though often implicit) notions about students, subject matter, teaching environments, and the teaching process itself.
3. Effective teaching seems heavily based on the successful translation and adaptation of curricula into instructional activities suitable for diverse groups of students.

4. Teaching involves complex social and interactional processes such as clear communication, mutual negotiation of action, and joint construction of meaning.
5. Experienced teachers draw upon and successfully orchestrate tremendously large bodies of knowledge (subject matter, social, technique) in idiosyncratic contexts.

Philosophical analyses of action have in the past few years provided an intellectual scaffolding to aid in the construction of a theory of teaching that is compatible with cognitive conceptions of teaching practice. Two notions that have influenced our thinking from this work include the analysis of practical problems (Gauthier 1963; Reid 1979) and action analyses of teaching (Kerr 1981). Some propositions generated by this work include:

1. Teachers are primarily confronted by practical problems—problems about 'what to do', radically different from 'what if' theoretical questions and problems.
2. Many of the practical problems that teachers address are of the type 'uncertain practical problems', which are not solved by the application of a rule, technique, or procedure.
3. Uncertain practical problems require unique and idiosyncratic approaches to solution because of their strong ties to specific contextual factors, the uncertainty and competition among goals and the grounds for decision, and the unpredictability of uniquely configured events.
4. Teaching may be considered as a member of the class 'mediated goal-directed action', and, as such, includes three major components: the choice of a goal (a learning to encourage), the choice of means (or a plan) to reach the goal, and acting on the plan.
5. The adequacy of teaching as an act may be assessed by examining the adequacy of the component actions involved separately and apart from *post hoc* and distal measures such as student achievement.

The image that emerges from the combination of this and the previous set of propositions is of a practitioner whose success depends on his or her ability to manage complexity and solve practical problems. The skill required is that of intelligent and artful orchestration of knowledge and technique. It also portrays the richness of practice by emphasizing the importance of goal-directed action and design. This image gains further power when compared to descriptions of professional behavior in other fields.

Research on the professions (e.g. Argyris and Schon 1974: Schon 1983) has recently begun to portray the divergent activities of such professionals as planners, architects, engineers, and psychiatrists as being based on common mental operations and processes. Simon (1981) has labeled this common activity as 'design': action aimed at bringing about desired states of affairs in practical contexts. Schon (1983) has depicted the activities of the professional as a 'reflective conversation' with the immediate problem situation and has suggested that to understand the practice of professionals we need to understand their reflection in action. Some propositions that we have derived from this research include:

1. Not only can we think about things we do, we can think about doing something while

doing it. This reflection in action is central to the art through which practitioners cope with divergent situations of practice.

2. Reflection in action draws upon implicit and situation-grounded ('action-present') cognitions instead of the more explicit and deliberative cognitions associated with reflection *on* action.

3. Professional problem-solving draws upon a repertoire of practical knowledge that generates exemplars (e.g. cases, telling examples) or generative metaphors for understanding new phenomena.

4. Professional problem-solving often proceeds by reframing the initial problem, inquiry within the imposed frame, and reflection on the 'back-talk' produced by this inquiry.

Recently there has been much discussion both within and outside the teaching community about teaching as a profession. Questions abound about what a professional is, whether teachers are true professionals, and what must be done to establish teaching as a profession. We would argue that professionals are defined by the essential nature of their action, rather than their educational experiences, certification or licensing processes, or governance of standards of practice. Therefore, we see teachers as professionals already, designing practical courses of action in complex situations. What allows them to do this is a thoughtful and purposeful consideration of practice. What is needed in education is a more thorough understanding of these processes. One aspect of this conception that needs to be further developed and researched is that of the relationship between reflection and action.

The reflective professional

To say 'thoughtless professional' is to pose a contradiction. The essence of professional life is thoughtful deliberation, problem-solving, and design. To say that teaching is a profession is to attribute the same characteristics to the life of teachers. (It is a revealing commentary on the current image of teaching that to say 'thoughtless teacher' would not seem contradictory or impossible.)

It was suggested previously that one way to depict the activities of a professional is as a reflective conversation with the immediate situation. This notion of tying reflection to the immediate context is somewhat contradictory to the ways in which many writers have defined reflection.

John Dewey's writings are often the reference of first choice when discussing the nature of reflection. In his books *How We Think* (1933) and *Democracy and Education* (1966) Dewey uses the word 'reflection' almost synonymously with the word 'thinking'. Reflection, for Dewey, involves active, persistent, and careful consideration of behavior or practice. He says reflection is the means for meeting and responding to problems (reflection is also used interchangeably with problem-solving).

One of the most useful distinctions Dewey draws is between reflection and impulse and routine. To Dewey, reflection 'converts action that is merely appetitive, blind, and impulsive into intelligent action' (1933, p. 17). Not only is reflection intelligent action, it is responsible action.

The opposites ... to thoughtful action are routine and capricious behavior. The former accepts what has been customary as a full measure of possibility and omits to take into account the connections of the particular things done. The latter makes the momentary act a measure of value, and ignores the connections of our personal action with the energies of the environment. It says, virtually, 'things are to be just as I happen to like them at this instant,' as routine says in effect 'let things continue just as I have found them in the past.' Both refuse to acknowledge responsibility for the future consequences which flow from present action. Reflection is the acceptance of such responsibility. (Dewey 1933, p. 140)

Thus for Dewey and most writers who have built on his writings, reflection has become the component of thought that is most intelligent and responsible. Reflection is often portrayed as a type of rational analysis and contrasted to intuitive thought. In effect, reflection is defined as something that one does deliberately and deliberatively. One is portrayed as reflecting *on* action; the reflective posture is one of standing apart from the chaos of action and bringing reason to bear upon it.

In contrast to this 'careful consideration' view of reflection stands a body of theory on practical reasoning. Most of this writing has been done by philosophers in the area of moral philosophy. The relationship between thought and action has been portrayed as being more general and intertwined. Maxine Greene (1984), for instance, says that 'thinking about our craft often brings conscience to bear on the actions we undertake in the course of our work' (pp. 55–6).

Donald Schon has described the intermingling of thought and action as thought in action.

> When someone reflects-in-action, he becomes a researcher in the practice context. He is not dependent on the categories of established theory and technique, but constructs a new theory of the unique case. His inquiry is not limited to a deliberation about means which depends on a prior agreement about ends. He does not keep means and ends separate, but defines them interactively as he frames a problematic situation. He does not separate thinking from doing, ratiocinating his way to a decision which he must later convert to action. Because his experimenting is a kind of action, implementation is built into his inquiry. (Schon 1983, p. 68)

In describing the nature of the deliberation that occurs in practical reasoning, Wiggins (1978) supports the description offered by Schon. Wiggins describes practical deliberation as a process of searching for an 'adequate specification' of the situation, a constant re-making and re-evaluation of concerns, an evolving conception of the point of acting, and a reciprocal relation between the agent and the world. One of the keys to practical deliberation, according to Wiggins, is 'situational appreciation', what he says Aristotle called 'perception' (*aisthesis*). 'The man of highest practical wisdom is the man who brings to bear upon a situation the greatest number of genuinely pertinent concerns and genuinely relevant considerations commensurate with the importance of the deliberative context' (pp. 146–7).

Both these conceptions of reflection contain some useful notions. It is apparent that reflection can take place subsequent to action as one's thoughts return to the situation. It is also apparent that we somehow think about practice in the midst of it and that this is an important process. In reality, we know very little about how these processes take place. Reflection has long been an admirable goal of practitioners, but there have been few empirical studies of this kind of thought in action. What kinds of products can we expect to result from research in this area? Wiggins suggests that the best we can hope for from this analysis is not explanation or prediction of practical reasoning but 'a conceptual framework which we can apply to particular cases, which articulates the reciprocal relations of an agent's concerns and his perceptions of how things objectively are in the world; and a schema of description *which relates the complex ideal the agent tries in the process of living to make real in the form which the world impresses, both by way of opportunity and by way of limitation, upon that ideal'* (1978), pp. 149–50; emphasis in original).

We see the goal of research on teaching as the development of an image of teaching that provides the kind of schema Wiggins refers to. The nature of practice is such that improvement can only be fostered by the professional's own understanding of self and of the nature of the practical. Reflection obviously plays a major role here. The results of these efforts may not meet everyone's desires for a theory of practice. We side with Wiggins when he says,

> I entertain the unfriendly suspicion that those who feel they *must* seek more than all this provides want a scientific theory of rationality not so much from a passion for science, even where there can be no science, but because they hope and desire, by some conceptual alchemy, to turn such a theory into a regulative or normative discipline, or into a system of rules by which to spare themselves some of the agony of thinking and all the torment of feeling and understanding that is actually involved in reasoned deliberation.' (1978, p. 150)

REFERENCES

Ackoff, R. (1979) 'The Future of Operations Research Is Past'. *Journal of Operations Research Society,* **30**, 93–104.

Anderson, L. M. and Evertson, C. M. (1978) *Classroom Organization at the Beginning of School: Two Case Studies.* Paper presented to the American Association of Colleges for Teacher Education, Chicago, IL.

Argyris, C. and Schon, D. (1974) *Theory in Practice: Increasing Professional Effectiveness.* San Francisco, CA: Jossey-Bass Publishers.

Ben-Peretz, M. (1975) 'The Concept of Curriculum Potential'. *Curriculum Theory Network,* **5**(2), 151–9.

Buckley, P. K. and Cooper, J. M. (1978) *An Ethnographic Study of an Elementary School Teacher's Establishment and Maintenance of Group Norms.* Paper presented to the American Educational Research Association, March.

Carnahan, R. S. (1980) *The Effects of Teacher Planning on Classroom Processes,* Technical Report No. 541. Madison, WI: Wisconsin Research and Development Center for Individualized Schooling.

Clark, C. M. and Elmore, J. L. (1979) *Teacher Planning in the First Weeks of School,* Research Series No. 56. East Lansing, MI: Institute for Research on Teaching, Michigan State University.

Clark, C. M. and Elmore, J. L. (1981) *Transforming Curriculum in Mathematics, Science and Writing: A Case Study of Teacher Yearly Planning,* Research Series No. 99. East Lansing, MI: Institute for Research on Teaching, Michigan State University.

Clark, C. M. and Peterson, P. L. (1986) 'Teachers' Thought Processes'. In Wittrock, M. C. (ed.) *Handbook of Research on Teaching,* 3rd edition. New York: Macmillan.

Clark, C. M. and Yinger, R. J. (1977) 'Research on Teacher Thinking'. *Curriculum Inquiry,* **7**(4), 279–394.

Clark, C. M. and Yinger, R. J. (1979) *Three Studies of Teacher Planning,* Research Series No. 55. East Lansing, MI: Institute for Research on Teaching, Michigan State University.

Dahllof, U. and Lundgren, U. P. (1970) *Macro- and Micro Approaches Combined for Curriculum Process Analysis: A Swedish Education Field Project.* Goteborg, Sweden: Reports from the Institute of Education, University of Goteborg, mimeo.

Dewey, J. (1933) *How We Think.* New

York: Heath and Company.

Dewey, J. (1966) *Democracy and Education*. New York: Free Press.

Eisner, E. W. (1967) 'Educational Objectives: Help or Hindrance'. *School Review,* **75**, 250–60.

Gauthier, D. P. (1963) *Practical Reasoning: The Structure and Foundations of Prudential and Moral Arguments and Their Exemplification in Discourse*. London: Oxford University Press.

Goodlad, J. I. and Klein, M. F. (1970) *Behind the Classroom Door*. Worthington, OH: C. A. Jones.

Greene, M. (1984) 'How Do We Think About Our Craft?' *Teachers College Record,* **86**, 55–67.

Hill, J., Yinger, R. J., and Robbins, D. (1981) *Instructional Planning in a Developmental Preschool*. Paper presented at the annual meeting of the American Educational Research Association, Los Angeles, CA.

Jackson, P. W. (1968) *Life in Classrooms*. New York: Holt, Rinehart & Winston.

Joyce, B. (1978–9) 'Toward a Theory of Information Processing in Teaching'. *Educational Research Quarterly,* **3**(4), 73–7.

Joyce, B. R. and Harootunian, B. (1964) 'Teaching as Problem Solving'. *Journal of Teacher Education,* **15**, 420–7.

Joyce, B. R. and Weil, M. (1972) *Models of Teaching*. Englewood Cliffs, NJ: Prentice-Hall.

Kerr, D. H. (1981) 'The Structure of Quality in Teaching'. In Soltis, J. F. (ed.) *Philosophy and education*, Eightieth yearbook of the National Society of the Study of Education, Part I. Chicago, IL: University of Chicago Press.

McCutcheon, G. (1980) 'How Do Elementary School Teachers Plan? The Nature of Planning and Influences on It'. *The Elementary School Journal,* **81**, September, 4–23.

McLeod, M. A. (1981) *The Identification of Intended Learning Outcomes by Early Childhood Teachers: An Exploratory Study*. Unpublished doctoral dissertation, the University of Alberta.

Morine-Dershimer, G. (1979) *Teacher Plan and Classroom Reality: The South Bay Study, part IV*, Research Series No. 60. East Lansing, MI: Institute for Research on Teaching, Michigan State University.

Morine-Dershimer, G. and Vallance, E. (1976) *Teacher Planning*. Beginning Teacher Evaluation Study, Special Report C. San Francisco, CA: Far West Laboratory for Educational Research and Development.

National Institute of Education (1975) *Teaching as Clinical Information Processing*. Report of Panel 6, National Conference on Studies in Teaching. Washington, DC: National Institute of Education.

Newell, A. and Simon, H. A. (1972) *Human Problem Solving*. Englewood Cliffs, NJ: Prentice-Hall.

Peterson, P. L., Marx, R. W., and Clark, C. M. (1978) 'Teacher Planning, Teacher Behavior and Student Achievement'. *American Educational Research Journal,* **15**(3), 417–32.

Popham, J. W. and Baker, E. L. (1970) *Systematic Instruction*. Englewood Cliffs, NJ: Prentice-Hall.

Pylypiw, J. (1974) *A Description of Classroom Curriculum Development*. Unpublished doctoral dissertation, the University of Alberta.

Reid, W. A. (1979) 'Practical Reasoning and Curriculum Theory: In Search of a New Paradigm.' *Curriculum Inquiry,* **9**, 187–207.

Schon, D. (1983) *The Reflective Practitioner: How Professionals Think in Action*. New York: Basic Books.

Shavelson, R. J. and Stern, P. (1981) 'Research on Teachers' Pedagogical Thoughts, Judgments, Decisions, and Behavior'. *Review of Educational Research,* **51**(4), 455–98.

Shultz, J. and Florio, S. (1979) 'Stop and Freeze: The Negotiation of Social and Physical Space in a Kindergarten/First Grade Classroom'. *Anthropology and Education Quarterly,* **10**, 166–81.

Simon, H. A. (1981) *The Sciences of the Artificial*, 2nd edition. Cambridge, MA: MIT Press.

Smith, E. L. and Sendelbach, N. B. (1979) *Teacher Intentions for Science Instruction and Their Antecedants in Program Materials*. Paper presented to the American Educational Research Association, San Francisco, CA.

Taylor, P. H. (1970) *How Teachers Plan Their Courses*. Slough, Bucks: National Foundation for Education Research.

Tikunoff, W. J. and Ward, B. A. (1978) *A*

Naturalistic Study of the Initiation of Students into Three Classroom Social Systems, Report A-78–11. San Francisco, CA: Far West Laboratory for Educational Research and Development.

Tyler, R. W. (1950) *Basic Principles of Curriculum and Instruction.* Chicago, IL: University of Chicago Press.

Wiggins, D. (1978) 'Deliberation and Practical Reason'. In Raz, J. (ed.) *Practical Reasoning.* New York: Oxford University Press.

Yinger, R. J. (1977) *A Study of Teacher Planning: Description and Theory Development Using Ethnographic and Information Processing Methods.* Unpublished doctoral dissertation, Michigan State University.

Zahorik, J. A. (1970) 'The Effect of Planning on Teaching'. *Elementary School Journal,* **71**, 143–51.

Zahorik, J. A. (1975) 'Teachers' Planning Models'. *Educational Leadership,* **33**, 134–9.

4

'150 DIFFERENT WAYS' OF KNOWING: REPRESENTATIONS OF KNOWLEDGE IN TEACHING

Suzanne M. Wilson, Lee S. Shulman and Anna E. Richert

What do teachers need to know? Researchers have begun to investigate the professional knowledge base of teaching from a variety of perspectives, many of which are represented in the chapters of this volume. Some researchers explore the sources of teachers' understandings, contrasting knowledge gleaned from classroom experience with knowledge acquired through more formal modes of teacher preparation. Others are interested in the cognitive processes teachers use during the pre-active and interactive stages of instruction. Still others approach the study of teacher knowledge by focusing on the content of teachers' thoughts—their knowledge of learners, of pedagogy, of curricula.

Our interest is in the realm of teachers' subject matter knowledge and the role that it plays in teaching. In studying novice teachers, it is clear to us that teachers need more than a personal understanding of the subject matter they are expected to teach. They must also possess a specialized understanding of the subject matter, one that permits them to foster understanding in most of their students. Frank, a novice teacher, reflects on what it means to know biology for teaching:

> When you learn [biology] for teaching you have to know it a lot better I think ... When you learn it to teach, you have to be able to handle ... 150 different approaches to it because you have to be able to handle every different student's approach ... They're going to ask you questions from different areas and you're going to have to be able to approach it from their mind-set. So when you learn it as a teacher, you have to learn it in terms of how you're going to teach it and how it's going to affect the students and how they're going to be able to understand it.

But how can a teacher 'know' biology in 150 different ways? As Frank suggests, teachers may need to generate alternative approaches to the subject matter—analogies, illustrations, metaphors, examples—that take into consideration differences in student abilities, prior knowledge, and learning styles. To classroom teachers, such a suggestion is far from revolutionary. However, educational researchers and theorists have just begun to focus on the role that subject matter knowledge and its representations play in teaching. In this chapter we will first discuss previous research that is related to the influence of teacher knowledge on instruction. We will then present the preliminary results of our research program, a study that has been specifically designed to investigate the influence of subject matter knowledge on teaching.

OVERVIEW

Because the goals of instruction include the transmission of knowledge and understanding to students, the question of what type of subject matter knowledge is needed for teaching is a compelling one. Intuitively, one would think that the effectiveness of any teaching is dependent, to some extent, on what the teacher knows about the subject matter to be taught. However, while a personal understanding of the subject matter may be necessary, it is not a sufficient condition for being able to teach. Teachers must find ways to communicate knowledge to others. In a sense, they must have two types of subject matter knowledge: knowledge of the subject field, both *writ large* and in its particulars, and knowledge of how to help their students come to understand the field.

Little is known about how teachers understand or need to understand their subject matter. Personal accounts such as Frank's suggest that it is dangerous to assume that subject matter expertise is enough. In most teacher education programs, pre-service teachers are required to take courses in disciplines related to the subject(s) they will teach in schools. Social studies teachers take traditional courses in history, geography, anthropology, government, sociology, economics, and other social sciences. Science teachers take classes in biology, chemistry, physics, and other physical or natural sciences. While these courses are considered essential to the education of teachers, seldom are explicit connections made between the coursework specific to teacher education and the coursework in content areas. Consequently, subject matter and pedagogy are treated as separate domains.

But are subject matter and pedagogy independent? Is it enough that a prospective teacher have knowledge of a content area and knowledge of pedagogical principles? Is pedagogy a set of generic principles that can be applied to any discipline? Is there a subject-specific aspect of pedagogy? Do teachers need to have a pedagogical understanding of the subject matter that may vary across disciplines?

RESEARCH ON TEACHER KNOWLEDGE

Within the realm of cognitive psychology, 'knowledge base' is a term usually associated with cognitive science. It refers to the set of rules, definitions, and strategies needed by a computer to perform as an expert would in a given task environment. That set of rules is usually rather specific to a particular domain or task. It is the secret of an 'expert system's' expertise. In teaching, the knowledge base is the body of understanding, knowledge, skills, and dispositions that a teacher needs to perform effectively in a given teaching situation, e.g. teaching mathematics to a class of 10 year olds in an inner-city school or teaching English literature to a class of high school seniors in an elite private school.

Discussion of what teachers need to know, as well as the manner in which such knowledge should be learned and used in the service of effective teaching, has been an important topic for educational scholars, primarily philosophers. These include John Dewey (1902, 1904), Israel Scheffler (1965), Thomas Green (1971), Gary Fenstermacher (1978), and B. O. Smith (1980). Dewey (1902) explains the difference between a scientist's understanding of the subject matter and the specialized understanding of that same material required for teaching:

> Every study or subject thus has two aspects: one for the scientist as a scientist; the other for the teacher as a teacher. These two aspects are in no sense opposed or conflicting. But neither are they immediately identical. For the scientist, the subject matter represents simply a given body of truth to be employed in locating new problems, instituting new researches, and carrying them through to a verified outcome. To him the subject matter of science is self-contained. He refers various portions of it to each other; he connects new facts with it. He is not, as a scientist, called upon to travel outside its particular bounds; if he does, it is only to get more facts of the same general sort. The problem of the teacher is a different one. As a teacher he is not concerned with adding new facts to the science he teaches, in propounding new hypotheses or in verifying them. He is concerned with the subject matter of the science as representing a given stage and phase of development of experience. His problem is that of inducing a vital and personal experiencing. Hence, what concerns him, as teacher, is the ways in which that subject may become a part of experience; what there is in the child's present that is usable with reference to it; how such elements are to be used; how his own knowledge of the subject matter may assist in interpreting the child's needs and doings, and determine the medium in which the child should be properly directed. He is concerned not with subject matter as such, but with the subject matter as a related factor in the total and growing experience. Thus to see it is to psychologize it. (pp. 285–6)

While Dewey and other philosophers claim that teaching requires knowledge that goes beyond subject matter knowledge *per se*, educational researchers have failed to provide a theoretically or empirically based conceptualization of the professional knowledge base of teaching. Instead, research on teaching has concentrated on what effective teachers need to do, with the types of performance associated with their effectiveness. Researchers have been much less interested in what sorts of knowledge or understanding are needed to make desirable performance possible. Paraphrasing the linguists, performance has taken precedence over competence.

Teacher knowledge and student performance

Some of the earliest research on teaching, labeled 'presage-product' research by Dunkin and Biddle (1974), sought to estimate specific relationships between teacher characteristics and student outcomes. Among the teacher characteristics examined were measures of teacher knowledge. However, studies that correlated teacher knowledge with student achievement failed to yield consistent, significant findings. This inconsistency is counter-intuitive. Since one of the goals of education is the communication and development of subject matter knowledge, it seems reasonable to assume that teachers must know something about the content of their courses. Why, then, has research in this tradition failed to find consistent relationships between what teachers know and what students learn?

One reason why these investigations have not been fruitful is the inconsistency with which teacher knowledge has been operationally defined (Byrne 1983). Researchers have defined teacher knowledge in a variety of ways, ranging from the number of courses taken in college to teachers' scores on standardized tests such as the Scholastic Aptitude Test. In the absence of any adequate conceptual analyses, it is unclear whether these measures are valid proxies for a common underlying construct of teacher knowledge. The shared assumption underlying this research is that a teacher's knowledge of the subject matter can be treated as a list-like collection of individual propositions readily sampled and measured by standardized tests. Thus researchers ask how much a teacher knows (how many such propositions) and not how that knowledge is organized, justified, or validated. Both the independent and dependent variables of these studies are limited by the same narrow operationism: teacher knowledge and student knowledge have been typically defined by what the achievement tests measure. Consequently, research done in this tradition has failed to provide insight into the character of the knowledge held by students and teachers and the ways in which that knowledge is developed, enriched, and used in classrooms.

Research on teacher thinking

The research of scholars working within alternative traditions in research on teaching, however, holds more promise for understanding the roles of knowledge in teaching. Researchers in the area of teacher thinking, for example, have found that teachers think about a variety of issues during the pre-active and interactive stages of teaching: teachers are constantly making decisions and they draw on a rich store of knowledge when they are engaged in planning and instruction. In reviewing this body of research, Clark and Peterson (1986) explain:

> First, the research shows that thinking plays an important part in teaching ... Teachers do plan in a rich variety of ways, and these plans have real consequences in the classroom. Teachers do have thoughts and make decisions frequently (one every two minutes) during interactive teaching. Teachers do have theories and belief systems that influence their perceptions, plans, and actions. This literature has given us the opportunity to broaden our appreciation for what teaching is by adding rich descriptions of the mental activities of teachers to the existing body of work that describes the visible behavior of teachers. (p. 292)

Since research on teacher thinking has focused primarily on generic cognitive processes that transcend the particularities of the subject matter, this body of research tells us little about the role played by subject matter understanding in teachers' thoughts. Mrs Warfel, when planning for her fifth-period American literature class, does not think about teaching generically. Instead, she thinks about teaching *Moby Dick* or *The Color Purple* to a particular group of students, who learn in particular ways at a particular time of the day. While one can infer from studies of teacher thinking that teachers have knowledge of their students, of their curriculum, of the learning process that is used to make decisions, it remains unclear what teachers know about their subject matter and how they choose to represent that subject matter during instruction. In their review of the literature on teachers' thoughts, judgements, and decision-making, Shavelson and Stern (1981) noted that:

> Very little attention has been paid to how knowledge of a subject-matter is integrated into teachers' instructional planning and the conduct of teaching. Nevertheless, the structure of the subject matter and the *manner* in which it is taught is extremely important to what students learn and their attitudes toward learning and the subject matter. (p. 491)

We have called this gap in the literature the 'missing paradigm' in research on teaching.

> In their necessary simplification of the complexities of classroom teaching, investigators ignored one central aspect of classroom life: the content of instruction, the subject matter ... Occasionally subject matter entered into the research as a context variable, a control characteristic for subdividing data sets in terms of content categories ... But no one focused on the subject matter content itself. No one asked how subject matter was transformed from the knowledge of the teacher into the content of instruction. Nor did they ask how particular formulations of that content related to what students came to know or misconstrue. (Shulman 1986, p. 8)

The new research on teacher knowledge

Recently researchers have become interested in several aspects of teacher knowledge. Some have looked primarily at 'practical' or commonsense knowledge (Amarel and Chittenden 1982; Angus 1984; Clandinin 1985; Elbaz 1983). By emphasizing the practical, and to some extent, idiosyncratic knowledge that teachers use, these researchers present a truncated conceptualization of teacher knowledge. Teachers have theoretical, as well as practical, knowledge of the subject matter that informs and is informed by their teaching; any portrait of teacher knowledge should include both aspects.

The work of Leinhardt and her associates at Pittsburgh's Learning Research and Development Center provides a more comprehensive analysis of subject matter knowledge for teaching. Working within the information-processing paradigm, Leinhardt and Smith (1985) have used the expert–novice contrast to examine the knowledge that teaching requires. They argue that teaching draws upon two bodies of knowledge: knowledge of lesson structure and knowledge of subject matter.

Leinhardt and Smith define lesson structure knowledge as 'the skills needed to plan and run a lesson smoothly, to pass easily from one segment to another, and to explain material clearly' (p. 247). Lesson structure knowledge is general for subject areas such as arithmetic. However, subject matter knowledge is topic-specific and involves, for elementary school mathematics teachers, knowledge of 'the concepts, algorithmic operations, the connections among different algorithmic procedures, the subset of the number system being drawn upon, the understanding of classes of student errors, and curriculum presentation' (p. 247). For Leinhardt and Smith, complete systems of subject matter knowledge for teaching include 'multiple representations, understanding of basic arithmetic principles such as the identity function, and multiple linkages across concepts that are used in any one aspect of arithmetic' (p. 269).

In another study of teacher knowledge, Hashweh (1985) examined the influence of subject matter expertise on the pedagogical reasoning of experienced teachers. Hashweh found that prior subject matter knowledge affected teachers' transformation of the curriculum, in terms of both the modifications that were made of the textbook materials and the representations that teachers used in their explanations of concepts and principles. Knowledgeable teachers rejected the textbook's organization of material when it did not match their own understanding. Teachers who had more subject matter knowledge were also more likely to notice misleading or poorly articulated themes. In addition, teachers with a richer understanding of the content were more likely 'to detect student misconceptions, to utilize opportunities to "digress" into other discipline-related avenues, to deal effectively with general class difficulties, and to correctly interpret students' insightful comments' (p. 305).

Hashweh also noted that all of the teachers used representations to teach particular topics. However, he observed a qualitative difference in the representations generated by knowledgeable versus unknowledgeable teachers.

> The two groups of teachers generated almost an equal number of representations in planning to teach each of the two topics. An analysis of the discussion and use of these representations revealed, however, that the representations reflected the different understandings of the topics that the two groups had. The representations used by the unknowledgeable teachers reflected their surface knowledge of the topic. Their representations were often inappropriate. Sometimes they were misleading because they reflected [the teachers'] preconceptions and knowledge inaccuracies. The representations used by the knowledgeable teachers reflected their deeper understanding of the topic, which usually involved invoking basic concepts, principles, themes, or conceptual schemes from the disciplines. (pp. 245–6)

Hashweh also found that knowledgeable teachers were capable of generating more non-topic disciplinary representations. That is, they used more representations that related a specific topic to other topics within the discipline. Less knowledgeable teachers did not make those intra-disciplinary connections for students.

In conceptualizing teacher knowledge and explanation as systems of representations and relationships, Leinhardt, Smith, and Hashweh recognize the importance of investigating the ways in which an individual's knowledge of the subject matter is organized. Resnick (1983) claims that 'to understand something is to know relationships. Human knowledge is stored in clusters and organized into schemata that people use both to interpret familiar situations and to reason about new ones' (pp. 477–8). Cognitive psychologists, including Marton (1986), Norman (1980), and Gardner (1986), have demonstrated that human beings have ways of translating their experiences into internal representations. In *The Mind's New Science*, Gardner writes:

> To my mind, the major accomplishment of cognitive science has been the clear demonstration of the validity of positing a level of mental representation: a set of constructs that can be invoked for the explanation of cognitive phenomena, ranging from visual perception to story comprehension. (p. 383)

These researchers have long argued that the ability to *represent* the subject matter is an important aspect of an individual's subject matter knowledge. If teachers want to develop understanding in their students, they must be concerned with the representations students develop in their effort to comprehend the content of instruction. To facilitate the development of powerful, appropriate representations, teachers need to evaluate their own understanding of the subject matter. Then they must generate representations that take into account their understanding, as well as knowledge that is already held by their students.

Byrne (1983) describes the implications of cognitive psychology for conceptualizations of teacher knowledge when he explains:

> Where the term 'knowledge' has been used in relation to the teachers' subject-knowledge, this knowledge has two aspects which concern us. On the one hand, there is subject-knowledge in the sense in which this is normally understood ... A teacher should certainly possess a certain minimum facility with, and understanding of, the subject to be taught. However, there is another aspect of the teacher's subject-knowledge which is also important ... This concerns a teacher's capacity for representing the knowledge to be taught ... Teachers should have a good knowledge of the representational possibilities of the subject which are relevant to the particular types of pupils to whom they will teach this subject. (p. 18)

Successful teachers cannot simply have an intuitive or personal understanding of a particular concept, principle, or theory. Rather, in order to foster understanding, they must themselves understand ways of *representing* the concept for students. They must have knowledge of the ways of transforming the content for the purposes of teaching. In Dewey's terms, they must 'psychologize' the subject matter. In order to transform or psychologize the subject matter, teachers must have a knowledge of the subject matter that includes a personal understanding of the content as well as knowledge of ways to communicate that understanding, to foster the development of subject matter knowledge in the minds of students.

The Stanford studies on knowledge growth in teaching (Shulman et al 1983; Shulman 1985a, b; Richert et al 1986) have investigated the subject matter knowledge held by novice teachers. The project raises questions about the ways in which a new teacher's understanding of the subject matter influences and is influenced by the act of teaching. Instead of looking for generic teaching skills that transcend the particularities of specific subjects or topics, our project focuses on what teachers know about their subject matter, where and when they acquired that knowledge, how and why that knowledge is transformed during teaching or teacher education, and how knowledge is used in classroom instruction.

Our 21 teacher collaborators for the first year of the study were young professionals starting their careers as secondary school teachers in the areas of social studies, mathematics, English, and biology. During the first year of the study, they were enrolled in several teacher education programs in California. In the second year of the study we continued to interview and observe 12 of these teachers into their first year of full-time teaching. By looking at individuals who are engaged in the complex process of learning to teach, we are attempting to map the transition from 'expert learner' to 'novice teacher' (Baxter et al 1985; Grossman et al 1985; Gudmundsdottir et al 1985; Shulman 1985b; Steinberg et al 1985; Richert et al 1986).

We began our data collection with attempts to understand what knowledge and beliefs they held about their subject matter and about teaching prior to their teacher education. The first stage of our research was directed at developing intellectual biographies of our teachers in order to provide us with this baseline information. What knowledge did they have about teaching prior to entering their teacher education program? What knowledge of the subject matter did they have as a result of their previous education, undergraduate and otherwise?

Through a series of semi-structured interviews, we developed intellectual histories of our informants (Clift and Angus 1985). In this first set of interviews, we asked our informants about their conceptions of the subject matter and about pedagogy. In the area of subject matter knowledge, we were particularly interested in ascertaining our teachers' knowledge of the substantive and syntactic structures of their discipline (Schwab 1964). We used a variety of tasks to evaluate their knowledge of concepts, ideas, and facts within the content area, their knowledge of the relationships between those concepts and facts, and their knowledge of the methods with which new information and ideas are brought into the field. For example, we examined biology teachers' knowledge of topics they were required to teach, such as genetics and photosynthesis. In addition, we asked them to explain the relationships among such topics. Finally, we have also explored their understanding of the role that scientific inquiry plays in the field of biology.

Although a portrait of the knowledge held by each teacher was an important starting point, the nature of our research, in tracing the *growth* of knowledge, makes the formulation of complete intellectual biographies an ongoing concern. We started our data collection with transcript-guided interviews in which we asked our subjects to retell the story of their undergraduate education, highlighting the courses and experiences that had the greatest impact on their intellectual development. While the transcripts of these interviews provide us with exciting and stimulating insights into our teachers, we found that these interviews gave us self-reports of what our teachers *thought* they knew about a particular field. While we were still unsure of the actual content of their knowledge, we were reluctant to jeopardize our relationship with the teachers by asking them to take achievement tests. Therefore, we have continued to experiment with ways of assessing both the breadth and depth of the changing subject matter knowledge of our informants. These methods include free association and card sort tasks in which our subjects are asked to respond to a series of words that represent key concepts, principles, or ideas in their subject matter. Biology teachers tell us everything they know about DNA, genes, and mutation. Social studies teachers tell us everything they know about the stock market crash of 1929, the Hawley-Smoot tariff, and the Tennessee Valley Authority. Another method involves the analysis of a piece of text—English teachers are asked to analyze a poem or a short story; history teachers are asked to reflect on an excerpt from Samuel Pepys' diaries or an account of the Civil War; math teachers are asked to critique a chapter from an algebra textbook.

In addition to the biographical and knowledge interviews, we conducted a series of 'planning–observation–reflection' cycles during which we talked with the teachers as they prepared to teach a particular piece of subject matter, focusing on what they knew about the content and what they wanted their students to learn about the content. We then observed the lessons as they were taught. Finally, after the observations were completed, we talked with our informants about their teaching in an effort to detect changes in their knowledge of the subject matter, of pedagogy, and of the perceived sources of those changes. These cycles are not unusual in the literature of teacher planning research. However, when conducted in the context of an ongoing longitudinal study of teachers and when guided by a complex conception of teacher knowledge (rather than a model of the planning process), they yield enormously rich data on the connections among teachers' comprehension of the content, their planning, their teaching, and their reflections.

Preliminary findings

As we observe and converse with our teacher collaborators we find that they *are* concerned with issues of subject matter. Fuller and Brown's (1975) research demonstrated that novice teachers' primary concerns during the first stage of their professional development are focused on survival, suggesting that little attention is devoted to matters of formal instruction or the conceptions of content. Our studies belie that claim. While young teachers are certainly preoccupied with their survival and with the management of the classroom, they unquestionably must think about content and will tell us about those matters if we but ask. In making the transition from student to pedagogue, novice teachers struggle with finding ways to explain the content of their disciplines to high school students. In their struggle to communicate understanding, they are forced to examine their personal understanding of the content. Subsequently, they generate representations of the subject matter that will facilitate the development of understanding in their students. These representations or *transformations* of subject matter take many forms—metaphors, analogies, illustrations, examples, in-class activities, and homework assignments.

For example, one of our teachers was required to teach Shakespeare's *Julius Caesar* to a group of ninth graders during the last weeks of school. Concerned with their level of interest, as well as their intellectual sophistication, Alan wanted to find a meaningful way to introduce *Caesar* to his students. After considering several alternative approaches to the play, he decided that an appropriate goal for teaching Shakespeare in this context was to emphasize the theme of moral conflict. However, because his students had little understanding of the nature of moral conflict, Alan anticipated having some difficulties teaching that theme. He describes how he decided to introduce the play:

> *Julius Caesar* is basically a play about internal conflicts, a moral decision for which there is really no wrong or right answer. If we kill this man, we might save our republic but we endanger ourselves. If we don't kill him, we could be endangered. One man's struggle with a moral decision, the consequences of his actions and how people turn against him. And so what I had them do was ... I gave them an artifical scenario. I said, 'You are the first officer on the Starship Enterprise. Captain Kirk has been getting out of hand. He's a good captain, he's been made Commander of the Fleet. But you, his closest friend, and your fellow officers have been noticing that he's been getting too risky, a little big-headed. You're afraid that he's going to endanger the Federation Fleet and might just seek glory in some farcical campaign.' And they really took off on that ... they said they found out there really wasn't a right answer. They argued back and forth. You couldn't just kill him because the whole fleet likes him. If you kill him, it's your head on the chopping block, too. But you also have a moral obligation to your country and you can't let him go on. What they finally came up with was that it's a pretty tough decision to make.

The next day in class, Alan introduced Julius Caesar as the Captain Kirk of the Roman Empire. He transformed his understanding of the play, as a piece of literature that deals with the issue of moral conflict, into an activity that would allow his students to experience the emotional and intellectual struggles that are involved in moral conflict.

Our transcripts of interviews and observations are full of such alternative representations and we are presently focusing on the process by which a teacher transforms the subject matter for teaching. We begin with the idea that a teacher holds a specific, favored representation of particular ideas for her own purposes. In the course of becoming a fine teacher, she further develops the capacity to introduce variations on the schema, alternative representations of the subject matter. These representations are alternative for both the teacher and the students: the teacher actively creates multiple representations; the learners, in turn, are stimulated to invent their own as they experience the representational activity of the teacher. We use the general term 'transformation' to designate the set of activities engaged by the teacher to move from her own comprehension of a matter, and the representations most useful for that understanding, to the variations of representation, narrative, example, or association likely to initiate understanding on the parts of students. As students are multiple, so representations must be various. As multiplicity of connections renders understanding more durable and rich, so the range of variations produced by the transformations is argued, in principle, to be a virtue. Hence, teachers should possess a 'representational repertoire' for the subject matter they teach. And, as the representational repertoire grows, it may enrich or extend the teacher's subject matter understanding *per se*.

Teachers draw upon many types of knowledge when they are making decisions about the content of their courses (see Figure 4.1 below). Teachers use their *content knowledge*—their understanding of the facts or concepts within a domain—as well as their grasp of the structures of the subject matter (Schwab 1964). Teachers must have knowledge of the substantive structures—the ways in which the fundamental principles of a discipline are organized. In addition, they must have knowledge of the syntactic

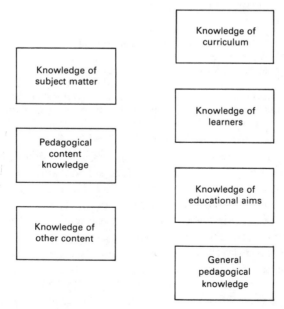

Figure 4.1 *Components of the professional knowledge base of teaching.*

structure of a discipline—the canons of evidence and proof that guide inquiry in the field. Teachers' *knowledge of educational aims, goals, and purposes* also contributes to pedagogical decisions. Frequently teachers use their *knowledge of other content* that is not within the scope of the discipline they are teaching. Teachers use *general pedagogical knowledge*—knowledge of pedagogical principles and techniques that is not bound by topic or subject matter. Teachers also have *knowledge of learners*, including knowledge of student characteristics and cognitions as well as knowledge of motivational and developmental aspects of how students learn. Finally, teachers frequently draw upon their *curricular knowledge*—their understanding of the programs and materials designed for the teaching of particular topics and subjects at a given level.

In creating the Captain Kirk exercise, Alan used several types of knowledge. Alan considered alternative purposes for the teaching of Shakespeare (knowledge of educational aims). In addition, he used his knowledge of *Julius Caesar* as a play about conflict (subject matter knowledge), his knowledge that the unknown should be taught in terms of the known (general pedagogical knowledge), his knowledge of the television series *Star Trek* (knowledge of other content), and his knowledge that students know about Captain Kirk and are concerned about the issues of loyalty, friendship, bonds, promises, parental authority, and group solidarity (knowledge of learners).

Pedagogical content knowledge

Our preliminary findings suggest that novice teachers, as they prepare to teach their content as well as during actual instruction, develop a new type of subject matter knowledge that is enriched and enhanced by other types of knowledge—knowledge of the learner, knowledge of the curriculum, knowledge of the context, knowledge of pedagogy. We call this form of knowledge *pedagogical content knowledge*. It is a form of content knowledge that

> ... embodies the aspects of content most germane to its teachability. Within the category of pedagogical content knowledge I include, for the most regularly taught topics in one's subject area, the most useful forms of representation of those ideas, the most powerful analogies, illustrations, examples, explanations, and demonstrations—in a word, the ways of representing and formulating the subject that make it comprehensible to others ... [It] also includes an understanding of what makes the learning of specific topics easy or difficult: the conceptions and preconceptions that students of different ages and backgrounds bring with them to the learning. (Shulman 1986, p. 9)

Alan, in thinking about how to teach *Julius Caesar*, generated one representation of the play. Given another set of students, another school, another semester, he may generate an alternative transformation of the play. He may, for example, select a transformation that emphasizes Shakespeare's use of the language. In another class, he may transform *Julius Caesar* in a way that showcases the historical aspects of the play. As a result of planning to teach, as well as their experiences during instruction, our novice teachers begin to develop this special understanding of the content for the purposes of teaching. We have watched them as they move from a personal understanding of the material to an understanding of the material enriched by new knowledge they have gained from such sources as their teacher education coursework and their field experiences (Grossman and Richert 1986).

But pedagogical content knowledge is not simply a repertoire of multiple representations of the subject matter. It is characterized by a way of thinking that facilitates the generation of these transformations, the development of *pedagogical reasoning*. As Feiman-Nemser and Buchmann (1985) explain:

> Teaching means helping people learn worthwhile things. It is a moral activity that requires thought about ends, means, and their consequences. Since teaching is concerned with learning, it also requires thinking about how to build bridges between one's own understanding and that of one's students. There is a difference between going through the motions of teaching (e.g., checking seatwork and talking at the blackboard) and connecting these activities to what students are learning over time ... Ends–means thinking and attention to student learning are central to pedagogical thinking. While teachers cannot directly observe learning, they can learn to detect the signs of understanding and confusion, of feigned interest and genuine absorption. Thus pedagogical thinking is strategic, imaginative, and grounded in knowledge of self, children, and subject matter. (pp. 1–2)

An extended example of the struggle of one English teacher serves to illustrate the complexity of this special kind of teacher thinking. George was asked to explain how he would choose to teach the idea of 'theme' to his students. He responded:

> Well, the first thing I'll do is ask them to address this question in a journal: 'In fiction or short stories, what is a theme?' I'm not sure how they'll respond but we'll talk about it and that will get me a little better understanding of where they are. Probably right in there I'll have them read the first two or three short stories ... I'll try to trace a theme, sort of an in-class discussion. So, in other words, I'm going to do with the class, orally, what I'm going to have them do later on paper. Coincidental with that, I'm going to try to get this great Mozart piece ... it's a simple piano concerto, it's an example of what counterpoint is in music. How it is repeated by different instruments, echoed, and how it's changed a little bit.

In thinking about how to teach 'theme' for the first time, George plans to use a pedagogical technique, the 'freewrite', to get an idea of what his students' preconceptions are. Then he decides to model thematic analysis as a way of teaching his students about theme. To complement the activity, he decides to use a piece of music as another illustration of what a theme is. George was troubled by his responses in our initial interview. He thought he had rambled. He sensed that he did not have a clear notion of how he was going to handle the issue of 'theme' in his class. So he sat down and wrote the following entry in his journal:

> A theme is an idea or thought that a story explores or treats. A single story may explore or treat several themes to varying degrees of depth. To be able to trace a theme in a story is to be able to recognize it at different parts of a story and to be able to compare what is said about that theme in each appearance. How is it different in each circumstance? How is it similar? After a theme is introduced, it is the repetition and variation on the theme later on that gives it meaning. A composer does the same thing with theme in music and with the use of counterpoints. Thinking of stories now where counterpoint might be visible. The Bible has many. Jacob deceives his father, Isaac, in the dark into giving him Esau's birthright. Later, on the night Jacob is to wed Rachel, Rachel's father puts Leah in the tent in the dark. Jacob has been fooled by the same means he fooled others. And here two themes emerge: blindness and deception.
>
> I'm trying to think of an everyday example of this so as to 'get into it' with the students ... What things are repeated in your life—but are never the same each time? Seasons, school, sunrises, meals, etc. ... For example: A baseball game has a pattern that we can anticipate—9, 3-out innings. However, it is how that pattern is varied in each of its nine repetitions that gives a game meaning, that tells us who wins or loses. We know that a school year has a planned pattern of 2 semesters and four grading periods. But it is the

variation within that pattern that gives the school year meaning for you or for me. What is in those semesters, those quarters? The people, the classes.

In this journal entry, we see George introduce a definition of theme. Throughout his undergraduate education, he had been required to do thematic analyses in his literature courses. Yet he had never been required to define the concept of theme. Until he had to *teach* theme, his intuitive understanding of theme, as reflected in his use of the analogy to musical counterpoint, had been sufficient. In thinking about communicating his understanding to his subjects, however, he struggled with explicating that intuition, bringing his tacit knowledge of theme and thematic analysis to the surface. After he has defined theme, he goes on to examine ways that he might communicate this notion to his students. He thinks about things that repeat in their lives in an effort to bring the strange—theme—into a more familiar realm—baseball or school. (We apologize to our readers from outside the United States who may find that references to baseball leave them out in left field.)

After he taught the concept of theme to his sophomore English class, George was asked what he knew about the concept of theme after the experience of teaching it. He recounts:

> What frustrated me with the lesson from Tuesday was the inability on my own part to connect the repetition and pattern of a theme, even as it appeared in 2 or 3 forms in the parable. The image I tried to use was of the innings in a baseball game. I was trying to show that themes are general ideas that take on new meanings when placed in specific character and setting circumstances of a story. In other words, treating a theme in a story is looking at something old in a new way. Just like we know that a baseball game has 9 innings and 27 outs, we know how we see a theme as it appears generically—whether it be honesty, jealousy, loneliness, or whatever. What gives the game and the theme meaning, however, is how it worked out in the game itself, in the story itself.

George 'understood' the concept of theme prior to teaching it. In preparation for teaching, however, he searched for a way to relate the concept to the lives of tenth-grade boys. He chose baseball, a sport he had played in college and coached at his high school. George *transformed* his understanding of theme (the form of which he related to music and Biblical text) into a form that he thought would be more meaningful for his students (baseball). In this way, his conception of student understanding broadened his understanding of content and consequently his pedagogical choices.

What George discovered, however, was that his initial choice of metaphor was unsuccessful; his students had difficulty understanding how the concept of theme was related to the innings of a baseball game. In addition, they did not understand how to find a theme in text, George's major goal in the lesson. As a result of his initial failure, George transformed the content again, this time focusing on the trail of a wounded animal. In the course of doing so he adds a new representation of the material to his repertoire, making his pedagogical content knowledge richer and fuller. He explains:

> Anyway, my frustrations led me to look for a better image, a better metaphor that I could give the guys for tracing and understanding theme. What I came up with was the trailing of a wounded animal by a hunter. Here the hunter discards all or most of the information the scene before him presents. He concentrates only on that which pertains to the animal he is searching for. Now some of the clues might be from the animal itself—blood or hair—just as the word or words of a theme might appear outright in any given passage. But also a hunter must see the broken grass, the hoofprint, the things that are indicators. A story can deal with a theme indirectly also. By association, juxtaposition, and other evidence. So we read a story through again, looking for that theme, searching for that game. This is the kind of reading

that opens a story up because, if the theme being traced is a major one, the close reading makes one realize the interconnectedness of the whole story. After looking long enough, one begins to see how every part of a story or novel is related in some way or another to that theme.

Through the process of planning, teaching, adapting the instruction, and reflecting on classroom experiences, George slowly acquires new types of knowledge. He knows more about teaching the concept of theme; he has a more refined understanding of the use of analogies for instruction; he knows more about some difficulties students have with this concept. George's struggle with making the subject matter meaningful to his students is only one of many examples that we continue to find in our interview and observational data. We have countless instances of teachers trying to transform their knowledge of the subject matter for the purposes of teaching. Frank, a biology teacher, describes the process of learning through experience:

Interviewer: You learn through preparing to teach it? And teaching it?
Frank: Then evaluating it. Then re-preparing it. And re-teaching it. And re-evaluating it. And you keep on going in this cycle.
Interviewer: What makes you learn more?
Frank: Well, first I evaluate what I know. I read the materials and I say, 'Well, I stumbled over these words, I couldn't pronounce these words, I wasn't quite sure on this concept, I got the Hill reaction mixed up with, you know, the light and dark cycles, I couldn't remember the two names where the parts ...' You know, just like that. And then you go back. So right there you evaluate and do it there. Another thing you do is you take the test papers when they come in, and the labs when they come in, and you see where they [the students] missed it and you think back. 'Well, how did I explain this? Did I explain it wrong or did I just fail to explain it? Now here's another thing I have to re-do.' So you get it basically in two ways: you get it from your own evaluation and then you get it from your students' work.
Interviewer: And then?
Frank: You re-do it. And then the next year you teach it. And I would bet from year to year things improve geometrically. Well, there's a huge jump between the first and second year. Then a fairly decent step between the second and third year, and the third and fourth there's not much.
Interviewer: A big jump in terms of what?
Frank: ... Your own comprehension of the subject matter and your ability to teach the subject matter. Yeah, those two things.

Our novice teachers are learning to think pedagogically about the subject matter. We believe that pedagogical reasoning is as important to successful teaching as observable performance. Just as 'process-product' research has depended on observable performances to gain insight into behaviors that are more or less effective in classroom teaching, we use the pedagogical reasoning of teachers as an avenue toward understanding the knowledge base of teaching.

FUTURE DIRECTIONS

We believe that the transformation of subject matter knowledge is at the heart of teaching in secondary schools.[1] The subject matter knowledge of the individual, furthermore, plays a major role in this process. It is also clear that our novice teachers are constantly acquiring new knowledge that contributes to the transformation of content. Currently, our energies are directed at answering two major questions:

1. What do we mean by transformation of subject matter for teaching? What are the components of the transformation process? How does the teacher's knowledge of subject matter influence the process of transformation? What are the aspects of knowledge, skill, or aptitude that might be involved?
2. What are the logical components of the professional knowledge base of teaching? What forms of knowledge contribute to the choices that teachers make? What are the relationships between these types of knowledge? How is knowledge of learners and context related to knowledge of the curriculum? How is pedagogical content knowledge related to knowledge of subject matter?

We are developing two theoretical frameworks: one for the components of the professional knowledge base (Grossman 1986; Shulman 1986; Wilson 1986) and a second for the process of pedagogical reasoning with transformation at its heart (Shulman and Sykes 1986). These emergent frameworks serve as the foci for our current work.

The first of these frameworks is a logical model of the components of the professional knowledge base for teaching (see Figure 4.1). We are developing this model from the perspective that teachers require a body of professional knowledge that encompasses both pedagogy and subject matter. *General pedagogical knowledge* includes knowledge of theories and principles of teaching and learning, knowledge of learners, and knowledge of principles and techniques of classroom behavior and management. *Subject matter knowledge* includes both the substantive and syntactic structures of the discipline. The substantive structures include the ideas, facts, and concepts of the field, as well as the relationships among those ideas, facts, and concepts. The syntactic structures involve knowledge of the ways in which the discipline creates and evaluates new knowledge.

In addition to general pedagogical and subject matter knowledge, our model includes *pedagogical content knowledge*. This knowledge includes an understanding of what it means to teach a particular topic as well as knowledge of the principles and techniques required to do so. Framed by a conceptualization of subject matter for teaching, teachers hold knowledge about how to teach the subject, how learners learn the subject (what are subject-specific difficulties in learning, what are the developmental capabilities of students for acquiring particular concepts, what are common misconceptions), how curricular materials are organized in the subject area, and how particular topics are best included in the curriculum. Influenced by both subject matter and pedagogical knowledge, pedagogical content knowledge emerges and grows as teachers transform their content knowledge for the purposes of teaching. How these kinds of knowledge relate to one another remains a mystery to us. As Figure 4.1 reveals, they are just boxes floating on a page. In our future work we intend to explicate the distinctions between different types and forms of knowledge, as well as the relationships between these entities.

The second model portrays the process of pedagogical reasoning and action through six common aspects of the teaching act: comprehension, transformation, instruction, evaluation, reflection, and new comprehension (see Figure 4.2).

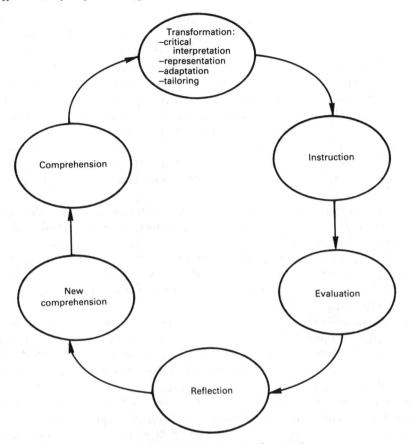

Figure 4.2 *Model of pedagogical reasoning.*

Pedagogical reasoning begins with **comprehension**. Teachers must critically understand a set of ideas, a piece of content, in terms of both its substantive and syntactic structure. History teachers should understand the causes of the American Civil War. English teachers should be able to do analyses of the themes and characters in *To Kill a Mockingbird*. Teachers should also understand the relationships between that piece of content and other ideas within the same content as well as ideas in related domains. Math teachers should understand the relationships between fractions and decimals. English teachers need to have some knowledge of the Bible in order to understand the symbolism in *Moby Dick*.

The **transformation** process involves four subprocesses: critical interpretation, representation, adaptation, and tailoring. *Critical interpretation* for preparation involves reviewing instructional materials in the light of one's own understanding of the subject matter. Are there any errors in the text? Has the interpretation of Franklin Roosevelt's New Deal legislation changed since the textbook was written? Once the materials for instruction have been critically examined, a teacher considers alternative ways of *representing* the subject matter. George used analogies of a baseball game and a hunter to explain the concept of theme. Alan chose to represent Julius Caesar as the Captain Kirk of the Roman Empire. Ideally, teachers should possess a *representational* *repertoire* that consists of the metaphors, analogies, illustrations, activities, assignments, and examples that teachers use to transform the content for instruction.

Adaptation involves fitting the transformation to the characteristics of students in general. Student characteristics that might influence the ways in which material is represented include student misconceptions or misunderstandings about the material, student ability, gender, and motivations. When preparing a lesson on light, science teachers might think about the preconceptions that students may have about light that will interfere with their learning. Math teachers preparing to teach fractions might consider students' prior knowledge of coins and how best to use that prior knowledge in developing a more sophisticated understanding of the material. *Tailoring* refers to adapting the material to the specific students in one class rather than to the student population in general.

Together, interpretation, representation, adaptation, and tailoring produce a plan, a set of strategies for teaching a lesson, a unit, or a course. **Instruction** is the observable performance of the teacher. It involves all the well-documented features of effective direct instruction, including management, grouping, pacing, co-ordination of learning activities, explanation, questioning, and discussion. It is during the process of instruction that the corpus of research on teacher knowledge intersects with the literature on teaching effectiveness.

Evaluation occurs both during and after instruction. Teachers check for understanding and misunderstanding in their students as part of teaching. In addition, they deploy a variety of more formal modes of evaluation like unit tests and end-of-semester examinations. Furthermore, teachers evaluate their own teaching through the process of **reflection**. Reflection is the process of learning from experience. It is what a teacher does as he or she looks back at the teaching and learning that has occurred and reconstructs the events, the emotions, and the accomplishments. Finally, we come full circle, arriving where we began with **new comprehension**. But this comprehension is enriched; it is a new understanding that has been enhanced with increased awareness of the purposes of instruction, the subject matter of instruction, and the participants—teacher and students. George has an enriched understanding of theme after his experiences teaching the concept. While new comprehension is certainly not discernible after each episode or unit of teaching, we have seen many such instances of new comprehension in our research. At times, this enriched understanding may grow slowly by accretion. Alternatively, a single experience may promote a quantum leap. In many cases, however, no changes occur for long periods of time. We do not understand why. It is worth knowing.

In all the processes involved in transformation, subject matter knowledge provides the focal point. Beyond subject matter knowledge, however, the teacher draws on knowledge of learners, pedagogical content knowledge, knowledge of context, knowledge of educational aims, and knowledge of other disciplines. It is the enrichment and testing of this model, as well as the model of the components of teacher knowledge, that guides our current endeavors.

In the spirit of qualitative inquiry, we are using these theoretical models to alter our data collection strategies for the remainder of our research. Through the use of these new strategies, we hope to accomplish two goals. First, we want to build our conceptualization of the knowledge base for teaching. We are interested in understanding the components of that model with special interest in the nature of pedagogical content knowledge. Since our focus is on subject matter knowledge, furthermore, our particular emphasis is on learning about the role that subject matter knowledge plays in instruction. How do teachers use their knowledge of the content for teaching? We can approach this question from a variety of perspectives, designing our future methods to reflect the questions being asked. For example, we can compare two teachers who differ in their knowledge of the subject matter as they prepare to teach the same material. Or we can do within-subject comparisons by asking teachers to prepare and teach two lessons—one involving content that they know intimately, one involving content they have never encountered (Hashweh 1985). As we analyze our interview and observational data, we can investigate the ways in which subject matter knowledge interacts with other types of knowledge in the pre-active, interactive, and reflective stages of teaching.

Our second goal is to test the validity of our model of pedagogical reasoning. Does the transformation of a teacher's content knowledge for the purposes of teaching correspond to the processes posited in our model? We do not expect to see evidence of each process every time a teacher prepares to teach a given text. However, we are not only interested in the possibility that teachers *actually* engage in each of these stages; we are also open to the possibility that teachers possess the *capacity* to engage in any stage but only do so when it is appropriate, convenient, or required for a given instructional task.

The role that teachers' subject matter knowledge plays in teaching is complex. We have begun to explore the nature of that role in secondary school teaching. Subject matter knowledge may play a fundamentally different part in elementary school teaching. There is no easy answer to our initial question, 'What do teachers need to know?' We are, however, learning about the nature of teacher knowledge. It seems only fitting that we allow Frank, whose words opened this chapter, also to close this paper with his thoughts on what it means to have subject matter knowledge for teaching:

> *Frank*: I think there are very few teachers who go into teaching who really know enough. It takes them a couple of years before they know more.
> *Interviewer*: What do you need to know enough?
> *Frank*: I don't think even people with an undergraduate degree have enough [subject matter knowledge] ... They've studied it all but it's just not really available to them. The resources aren't within them. Mostly they're like myself—they have to go back and find it. Fortunately for them, they have a lot of resources where they know where to go. ... To really know something you have to study it more than once. You have to take more than one class in it ... To know it well enough to teach it you need to have studied it numerous times and, I don't know who says it, but 'There's no better way to learn something than to teach it.' You know, when you teach something and you tell somebody something five times a day, or five classes a day, you tell them this one thing—then you know it. You can recite it in your sleep.

NOTE

1. We have studied only secondary school teachers and trainees in our research. When reporting the findings of research to elementary teacher educators, we have received two apparently

contradictory reactions. Some of our colleagues suggest that elementary teachers treat students and their characteristics as the starting point of instruction, rather than focusing on considerations of content, its comprehension, and transformation. Other elementary educators assert the opposite. They argue that the content perspective is as important for the teaching of younger children, but tends to be overlooked or inappropriately subordinated to socialization goals.

We suspect that both views are valid. Most elementary school teachers probably devote their initial attention to students and their characteristics. But they *should* attend much more seriously than they do (or, at times, are capable of doing) to the comprehension and representation of the content they teach.

ACKNOWLEDGEMENTS

The research reported in this chapter was sponsored by a grant from the Spencer Foundation to Stanford University for the 'Knowledge Growth in a Profession' project. The chapter is, in part, based on an earlier paper by Richert et al. The authors wish to thank Cathy Ringstaff and Pam Grossman for their contributions to this chapter.

REFERENCES

Amarel, M. and Chittenden, E. A. (1982) *A Conceptual Study of Knowledge Use in Schools*. Princeton, NJ: Educational Testing Service.

Angus, M. J. (1984) *The Mediation and Supplementation of Theoretical Knowledge about Teaching*. Unpublished doctoral dissertation, Stanford University, Stanford, CA.

Baxter, J., Richert, A., and Saylor, C. (1985) *Content and Process of Biology*. Paper presented at the Annual Meeting of the American Educational Research Association, Chicago, IL, April.

Byrne, C. J. (1983) *Teacher Knowledge and Teacher Effectiveness: A Literature Review, Theoretical Analysis and Discussion of Research Strategy*. Paper presented at the 14th Annual Convention of the Northeastern Educational Research Association, Ellenville, NY, October.

Clandinin, D. J. (1985) 'Personal Practical Knowledge: A Study of Teachers' Classroom Images'. *Curriculum Inquiry*, 15(4), 361–85.

Clark, C. and Peterson, P. (1986) 'Teachers' Thought Processes'. In Wittrock, M. C. (ed.) *Handbook of Research on Teaching*,

3rd edition, pp. 255–96. New York: Macmillan.

Clift, R. T. and Angus, M. (1985) *Creating a Methodology*. Paper presented at the Annual Meeting of the American Educational Research Association, Chicago, IL, April.

Dewey, J. (1902) 'The Child and the Curriculum'. In Boydston, J. A. (ed.) *John Dewey: The Middle Works, 1899–1924, Volume 2: 1902–1903*, pp. 273–91. Carbondale, IL: Southern Illinois University Press.

Dewey, J. (1904) 'The Relation of Theory to Practice in Education'. In McMurry, C. A. (ed.) *The Relation of Theory to Practice in the Education of Teachers, Third Handbook of the National Society for the Scientific Study of Education, Part 1*. Bloomington, IL: Public School Publishing.

Dunkin, M. J. and Biddle, B. J. (1974) *The Study of Teaching*. New York: Holt, Reinhart and Winston.

Elbaz, F. (1983) *Teacher Thinking: A Study of Practical Knowledge*. New York: Nichols Publishing Company.

Feiman-Nemser, S. and Buchmann, M.

(1985) *The First Year of Teacher Preparation: Transition to Pedagogical Thinking?* Research Series No. 156. East Lansing, MI: Institute for Research on Teaching, Michigan State University.

Fenstermacher, G. (1978) 'A Philosophical Consideration of Recent Research on Teacher Effectiveness'. In Shulman, L. S. (ed.) *Review of Research in Education, Volume 6*, pp. 157–85. Itasca, IL: F. E. Peacock.

Fuller, F. F. and Brown, O. (1975) 'Becoming a Teacher'. In Ryan, K. (ed.) *Teacher Education: Seventy-Fourth Yearbook of the National Society for the Study of Education, Part 2,* pp. 25–52. Chicago, IL: University of Chicago Press.

Gardner, H. (1986) *The Mind's New Science: A History of Cognitive Revolution.* New York: Basic Books.

Green, T. F. (1971) *The Activities of Teaching.* New York: McGraw-Hill.

Grossman, P. (1986) *The Influence of Teacher Education on Subject-Specific Pedagogical Knowledge of English.* Unpublished manuscript, School of Education, Stanford University, Stanford, CA.

Grossman, P., Reynolds, A., Ringstaff, C., and Sykes, G. (1985) *English Major to English Teacher.* Paper presented at the Annual Meeting of the American Educational Research Association, Chicago, IL, April.

Grossman, P. and Richert, A. R. (1986) *Unacknowledged Knowledge Growth: A Re-examination of the Effect of Teacher Education.* Paper presented at the Annual Meeting of the American Education Research Association, San Francisco, CA, April.

Gudmundsdottir, S., Carey, N., and Wilson, S. M. (1985) *Role of Prior Subject Matter Knowledge in Learning to Teach Social Studies.* Paper presented at the Annual Meeting of the American Educational Research Association, Chicago, IL, April.

Hashweh, M. Z. (1985) *An Exploratory Study of Teacher Knowledge and Teaching: The Effects of Science Teachers' Knowledge of Subject-Matter and Their Conceptions of Learning on Their Teaching.* Unpublished doctoral dissertation, Stanford University, Stanford, CA.

Leinhardt, G. and Smith, D. A. (1985) 'Expertise in Mathematics Instruction: Subject Matter Knowledge'. *Journal of Educational Psychology* **77**, 247–71.

Marton, F. (1986) *Towards a Pedagogy of Content.* University of Gothenburg, Sweden.

Norman, D. A. (1980) 'What Goes on in the Mind of the Learner'. In McKeachie, W. J. (ed.) *New Directions for Teaching and Learning: Learning, Cognition and College Teaching, Volume 2.* San Francisco, CA: Jossey-Bass.

Resnick, L. B. (1983) 'Mathematics and Science Learning: A New Conception'. *Science,* **220**, 477–78.

Richert, A. R., Wilson, S. M., and Marks, R. (1986) *Knowledge Growth in Teaching: Research in Progress on Beginning Secondary Teachers.* Paper presented at the Annual Meeting of the American Educational Research Association, San Francisco, CA, April.

Scheffler, I. (1965) *Conditions of Knowledge: An Introduction to Epistemology and Education.* Chicago, IL: University of Chicago Press.

Schwab, J. J. (1964) 'The Structures of the Disciplines: Meanings and Significances'. In Ford, G. W. and Pugno, L. (eds) *The Structure of Knowledge and the Curriculum.* Chicago, IL: Rand McNally.

Shavelson, R. J. and Stern, P. (1981) 'Research on Teachers' Pedagogical Thoughts, Judgments, Decisions and Behavior'. *Review of Educational Research,* **51**(4), 455–98.

Shulman, L. S. (1985a) 'Paradigms and Research Programs for the Study of Teaching. A Contemporary Perspective'. In Wittrock, M. C. (ed.) *Handbook of Research on Teaching,* 3rd edition, pp. 3–36. New York: Macmillan.

Shulman, L. S. (1985b) *The Study of Knowledge in Teaching.* Paper presented at the Annual Meeting of the American Educational Research Association, Chicago, IL, April.

Shulman, L. S. (1986) 'Those Who Understand: Knowledge Growth in Teaching'. *Educational Researcher,* **15**(2), 4–14.

Shulman, L. S. and Sykes, G. (1986) *A National Board for Teaching?: In Search of a Bold Standard.* Paper commissioned for the Task Force on Teaching as a Profession, Carnegie Forum on Education and the Economy, March.

Shulman, L. S., Sykes, G., and Phillips, D. C. (1983) *Knowledge Growth in a Profes-*

sion: *The Development of Knowledge in Teaching*. Proposal submitted to the Spencer Foundation. School of Education, Stanford University, CA.

Smith, B. O. (1980) *A Design for a School of Pedagogy*. Washington, DC: US Department of Education.

Steinberg, R., Haymore, J., and Marks, R. (1985) *Teachers' Knowledge and Structuring Content in Mathematics*. Paper presented at the Annual Meeting of the American Educational Research Association, Chicago, IL, April.

Wilson, S. M. (1986) *Subject Matter Knowledge for Teaching: An Expert–Novice Study of Social Studies Teachers*. Unpublished manuscript. School of Education, Stanford University, Stanford, CA.

5

TEACHERS' ASSESSMENTS OF STUDENTS' DIFFICULTIES AND PROGRESS IN UNDERSTANDING IN THE CLASSROOM

Rainer Bromme

This chapter describes teachers' perceptions and explanations of their students' understanding in the classroom situation. We begin with the assumption that students' understanding and learning of subject matter in the classroom form an important object of teacher activity: one could almost say that it is the core of the teacher's real task. As well as providing a review of our own and other studies, inferences will be drawn about how teachers' knowledge is in fact organized. We hypothesize that teachers' practical knowledge consists not so much of an abundance of facts that one knows and takes into account as a teacher, but of the relations and connections between those facts. This hypothesis could be formulated in another way: the essence of practical knowledge concerns the relations between factual situations, persons, and objects. Although this may appear somewhat obvious, it has not previously been acknowledged by researchers, who have often been more concerned with sorting teachers' thoughts into different categories. One essential achievement of teachers, namely the production of mental relationships, thus does not fall into the researchers' field of vision. We therefore aim to demonstrate that the researcher's categories have other boundaries than the teachers' cognitive units. In practical knowledge, the world of the classroom is not categorized in terms of the variables traditionally used by researchers.

RESEARCH ON TEACHERS' VIEWS ABOUT STUDENTS' UNDERSTANDING

Although the encouragement of students' understanding is probably the most important task of the teacher, there have been very few investigations of teachers' perception and interpretation of understanding in the classroom. There are, however, many studies on teachers' general perceptions of students (e.g. Hofer 1981; Brophy and Evertson 1981). Although these studies differ in some details, they demonstrate that the students were perceived according to traits and behaviours that were functional for the teachers' tasks (Cooper 1979).

The validity of teachers' judgements has also been investigated. Teachers' judgements have been found to be relatively valid in terms of both independent observations and predictive validity. However, judgements were valid only when the teachers had the opportunity to get to know the students they were to judge, and when asked to judge concrete performance or behaviour. In other cases, stereotypes were applied that were less valid (Wang 1973; Pedulla et al 1980; Leinhardt 1983; Natriello and Dornbusch 1983).

Why do so few investigations focus upon teachers' understanding of their students in the classroom? In the early days of research into teachers' views of their students, it was assumed that teachers' concepts of their students were situationally invariant. As long as one supposed a stable number of cognitive categories by which students are perceived (for a long time, a total of three to five categories was considered empirically proven), there was no need to describe situation-specific teacher perspectives on their students. Since then, it has been shown that the fixed number of student types is possibly an artefact of the data analysis procedure (factor or cluster analysis; e.g. Oldenbürger 1986), and that the differentiation of the teacher's view of students depends on the situation in which students are perceived (e.g. Morine-Dershimer 1978/9).

Both methodological and cognitive psychological reasons support the idea that one should investigate teachers' situation-specific views of students. Hofer (1986) refers in this context to the schema concept. The assumption that the actions of teachers are structured by means of schemata implies a situation-specific differentiation of the teachers' perception of students. The basic ideas of the schema construct are that knowledge of a situation enables one to perceive similarities between situations, and that this knowledge can differ in detail. To have a schema at one's disposal means that one has these different degrees of knowledge available that can be activated according to the situation.

Our own empirical study of teachers' recall of learning progress and problems in understanding (see below) aims to investigate teachers' situation-specific views of their students by choosing one type of situation—classroom instruction in mathematical tasks. In order to analyse teachers' situation-specific views, we made two specifications of the situation. We investigated the teacher's recall of students in the *classroom* (and not in any other situation) and regarding their *understanding* (and no other behaviour).

Empirical investigations of teachers' views of understanding in the classroom

Studies of teachers' interactive decision-making are of particular interest for our research, because they focus on teachers' thinking in the classroom and are therefore concerned with the first specification. However, since they attempt a general comprehensive description of teachers' interactive thinking, they omit specific reference to teachers' thinking about students' understanding. One exception to this will be mentioned later.

The available studies suggest that the student and his or her activities in the classroom occupy a large space in teachers' thinking during the lesson. A review of the content analyses from six studies using video-stimulated recall (VSR) reveals an amazingly high level of agreement (Clark and Peterson 1986). According to these studies, 40–50 per cent of all considerations are related to students, and about 20–30 per cent are related to the instructional process. The subject matter is mentioned only 5–14 per cent of the time, and in some of the studies it is not even granted a special category. Most of the references concerning students are related either to their learning process or to their behaviour in the classroom (e.g. McNair and Joyce 1979).

It is quite remarkable that 'subject matter' is so rarely mentioned as a cue that precedes decisions, as the students' learning process is concerned with the content. This also surprises us because we have found different results in two studies in which we investigated teachers' *retrospective* explanations for their students' mastering of tasks. A large part of the teachers' explanations concerned operations and knowledge of the subject matter. One could almost say that the structure of the subject matter permeated the teachers' thinking about their students (Bromme and Juhl 1984; Bromme and Dobslaw 1986a). Although these studies were not concerned with considerations during the lesson, they raise the question whether the subject matter is really so seldom present in teachers' thinking in the lesson as suggested by the studies on interactive decision-making.

The distinctions made in the studies of interactive decision-making between thoughts about students, thoughts about the subject matter, and thoughts about the learning process may possibly contribute to the fact that teachers' considerations of understanding apparently occur so rarely. Thus Clark and Peterson (1986, p. 269) note that the teacher's statement 'I thought after I explained it to her, I didn't make that very clear' was rated as an utterance concerning instructional process, while, in contrast, the statement 'I was thinking they don't understand what they are doing' was labelled as an item concerning the student. However, one can interpret both statements as indicators of a situation that is concerned with understanding, in which the teacher considers the relation between subject matter and student.

This interpretation is also relevant when one considers the cues teachers attend to in making decisions. A study by Fogarty et al (1983) differentiates student cues in terms of deficient responses, initiations (i.e. unrequested student activities), mistakes, and unsuitable level of attention. Unfortunately it is not clear whether the first two cues relate only to the subject matter. Nevertheless, the relatively high frequency of mistakes as cues for the choice of teachers' actions is again an indicator that non-routine action is particularly related to the students' difficulties with the subject matter.

We know from these studies that students' cues are frequently mentioned as antecedents of teachers' decisions, but what does this signify? The meaning of these findings is blurred owing to the previously mentioned problem that little attention has been paid to learning and understanding in the classroom. Therefore, what is observed in students in the classroom, which students are observed, and in what way these observations take into account learning and understanding remain open questions.

The study by Shroyer (1981), however, presents a few provisional answers. This study will be reviewed in more detail as it is one of the few investigations that have explicitly investigated teachers' perceptions of the process of understanding.

Shroyer investigated whether mathematics teachers regard the problems and difficulties of their students during classroom interaction as being sufficiently problematic to act upon them. She also investigated whether teachers utilize sudden unexpected insights from their students. This research question is notable, since it recognizes the way of coping with problems and students' insights as being a part of the teacher's work. By using learning episodes and student mistakes to uncover cognitions, Shroyer avoids breaking up verbal data into distinct content categories of student and subject matter.

Shroyer videotaped two mathematics lessons given by each of three fourth- to sixth-grade teachers, and coded them in order to assess 'student occlusions', i.e. situations in which either a false or unrequested student contribution pointed out a problem or in which an unexpected insight occurred. In the three teachers' lessons, there were (in each block of two lessons) between 49 and 217 such situations. After the lesson, a stimulated recall session was held. The teachers were asked to '... recall thoughts, feelings, or decisions that occurred while teaching the mathematics lesson' (p. 50). If the teachers themselves offered no comment, the researcher cautiously probed for teachers' recall of thoughts during 'student occlusions' and teachers' 'elective actions'. Shroyer then investigated how many 'student occlusions' were also viewed by teachers as being problematic for their teaching; i.e. whether the teachers recalled these situations during the lesson as causing them cognitive difficulty or emotional discomfort. Only an average of 3 per cent of student errors or sudden insights were regarded by teachers as being problematic for their teaching. The author states that this somewhat underestimates the real number because the student errors mentioned by teachers were noted as examples of pervasive teaching problems. Nevertheless, the proportion of all student errors and insights that gave rise to further thinking was surprisingly small. The study did not clearly state how many of the observer-coded errors were perceived by the teachers, but showed that only a small percentage of 'student cues' led to deliberate decisions on further actions.

This leads us to ask what is the nature of the students' cues that have been reported in other studies as being so important for teachers' interactive decision-making. It is also unclear how many student problems are so important that they are remembered by teachers at all.

AN EMPIRICAL STUDY OF TEACHERS' RECALL ON STUDENTS' UNDERSTANDING IN MATHEMATICS TEACHING

Our study was concerned with the following questions:

- How many and what problems and progress in students' understanding are remembered by teachers if they are interviewed immediately after the lesson?

If it should emerge that there is little memory of instances of understanding and of problems, then we must ask:

- Who or what is in the focus of the recall?

Data collection

The study is based on interviews carried out subsequent to classroom observations. In this section, we will first describe the data collection in detail, and then explain why we conducted interviews rather than following, for example, a VSR design.

As part of a larger project on the teaching of probability in secondary schools, we observed the teaching behaviour of mathematics teachers and interviewed them after the lessons. In the classroom observation, student participation was recorded and field notes were taken on the course of the lesson. All teachers taught the same subject matter, namely an introductory course on probability. For this, they were given curriculum material developed by the project team. This consisted of a system of mathematical tasks, out of which the teachers could freely select the tasks of their choice.

The interviews were carried out in the teachers' next free lesson or, at the latest, before their lunch break. At the beginning of the interviews, the tasks that had been used in the lesson and the lesson phases (individual work, group work, discussion of homework, etc.) were entered on a sheet of paper in their order of occurrence. Then questions were presented on teaching goals and the desired motivational effect of the methods the teacher had chosen. After the course of the lesson had been called into memory by these questions, the questions relevant to our investigation were presented, namely:

- Do you remember any subject-oriented learning progress made by individual students or groups of students, i.e. single questions or comments that made it clear to you that the student or students had learnt or understood something? (Question on *progress* in understanding)
- Do you remember any subject-oriented mistakes or misunderstandings from individual students or groups of students, i.e. single questions or comments that made it clear to you that the student or students had made a mistake or misunderstood something? (Question on *problems* in understanding)

Additionally, answers to a third question were included in the analysis:

- Were there deviations and differences from your plan, and why? (Question on the *plan* of the lesson)

The interview was constructed so that the teacher had the opportunity to recall the course of the lesson. The accompanying questions attempted to ensure that observations on students' understanding would not be held back because teachers found the communication of other matters to be more important. The interviewer's classroom observation and the tape-recording that was made of the lesson prevented any intentionally fictional reports from being given. The teachers we interviewed had to assume that all the events they reported might also have been observed by the interviewer. Classroom observation by the interviewer was also important as it produced a shared background experience that made it unnecessary for the teachers to describe the setting of the events they had noticed. It is a rule of conversation that only that which cannot be presupposed by the listener is communicated (Grice 1975). Therefore we could also analyse the verbal structure of the reports without them being buried in descriptions of the settings.

Although the interview was designed so that recall of individual students' understanding was encouraged as much as possible, we did not use lists of names in our questioning, as this would have destroyed the natural structure of the recall. We were much more interested in keeping the interview as freely structured as possible, so that we could then analyse the structure of the reports (What was recalled? What was the sequence of recall? How many students were recalled?).

Digression: A justification for the method of data collection

The method of data collection will be discussed in some detail as we did not use the VSR method that is normally applied in such studies (see Calderhead 1981). In carrying out an interview that was backed up only by a single written recording of the course of the lesson, we naturally did not obtain such a complete picture of the perceptions and considerations in the classroom as would have been provided by the joint viewing of a video-recording. However, it is likely that only those events would be recalled that were subjectively important for the teacher, and to which he or she paid conscious attention during the lesson. In our study, this has one advantage compared to the VSR design, namely that the teacher is unable to make new discoveries and interpretations of students' mistakes, based on the viewing of the videotape. This can occur without teachers having any conscious intent to deceive.

On the other hand, one must be aware that the semantic integration effect causes a blurring between the perceptions of understanding in the classroom and the teacher's existing knowledge. The semantic integration effect refers to the fact that new information is integrated into old knowledge, and that it is often no longer possible to separate the new information that was actually perceived (Bransford and Franks 1971). We must therefore assume that the teachers' reports can, in some circumstances, distort the actual events. However, it is assumed that this subjective structuring of observations on understanding that teachers perform is not an arbitrary process, but reflects the teachers' concepts of understanding. In this sense, the teachers' recall on their students presents us with information about the teachers themselves. In other words, the alteration of events through memory processes is not a hindrance to our investigation. Thus, with our method we obtain not the immediate perceptions of the teacher during the lesson, but an application of existing knowledge to the classroom situation. However, this is exactly what we wished to reveal with our questions.

For this purpose, it was also important that the interview was designed to produce the minimum amount of anxiety in order to avoid a distortion of the answers. The teachers had already met the interviewer on several previous occasions, and it was clearly pointed out that we were interested in the teachers' experiences and were not trying to tell the teachers what to do. In addition, the interviews were designed to allow the teacher considerable freedom in guiding the course of the conversation. With these methods, a confidential relationship with the teachers was achieved.

Subjects

Interviews with 19 teachers were analysed in this study. The teachers taught either fifth, sixth, or seventh grade (students aged 11–14 years) in one of five different comprehensive schools. The average length of professional experience was about eight years. All of the teachers volunteered for the study. Each teacher was observed and interviewed on at least four occasions, in addition to earlier 'warm up' observations. One lesson per teacher was chosen relatively early in the series, as at this stage the lesson content was most similar in all classes.

Data analysis

The answers to the questions were transcribed, and comments made by the teachers on other occasions during the interview that concerned the learning progress and problems in understanding of their students or class were also included in the analysis. For the content analysis, a system of categories was formed that was loosely based upon concepts from story or text understanding research.

These categories show similarities to the most important elements of stories (Thorndyke 1977). Our interviews had in fact required verbal presentations of short stories about understanding. As verbal protocols are texts, it is at least heuristically meaningful to relate the construction of the content analysis to the instruments from research into the production and understanding of texts (Bromme 1983).

In our study, we used the story structure of protagonist, event, and cause to provide us with an instrument to identify the relation of subject matter, students, and their activities. In other words, it is a first step aimed at overcoming the above criticized *a priori* separation of relations during the analysis of verbal data.

Description of the content analysis system

In the classification of the *protagonists*, we differentiated between specific named students, a specific exactly defined group of students (e.g. those sitting together at one table), and the entire class, or majority of the class (which is what teachers mean when they talk about the entire class). Additionally, many answers contained no reference to a protagonist and gave only non-specific descriptions of difficulties. A separate category was prepared for such answers.

The categories for *events* describe individual activities in the learning and application of concepts and procedures in probability, the construction of which is based on a rational task analysis of mathematical tasks. Operating with subject-related concepts requires either observable activities (for example, drawing a table for a tree diagram is difficult for the students) or mental inferences or insights (for example, comparing chances between different random generators is difficult for students). Eleven such subject-related categories were available which, after coding, were summarized under the two headings mathematical activities and mathematical insights. There were additionally some instances of organizational events (for example, the occurrence of administrative tasks).

A large proportion of the answers contained an element that could be regarded as the *cause* of the event. To cover causes in the analysis, a list was constructed that included the important variables of the instructional process taken from recent research models of teaching and learning; for example, variables that refer to student characteristics, the task, and the instructional quality. The concepts and skills in the lesson unit were listed in order to record the teachers' mentionings of the subject-related knowledge and abilities of their students as causes of understanding. These items were summarized according to their content before the quantitative analysis was performed.

Table 5.1 presents the revised list of all categories. All these categories about events and causes could be used to record cases of successful understanding or difficulties as well as deviations from the lesson plan. Rating was performed by a coder who was familiar with the content of the lesson unit. Each statement in which at least one cause or event was given was regarded as one coding unit. Then the protagonist for each unit was ascertained. Six interviews were selected at random and coded by a second rater in order to assess rater reliability. Agreement between raters was 79 per cent, which is sufficient for our descriptive purposes.

RESULTS OF THE INTERVIEW STUDY

Responses to questions

In reply to the question on the progress of understanding of individual students or groups of students, teachers recalled a total of 83 cases—an average of 4.4 per teacher per 45-minute lesson. The protagonists named in these cases were: named individual students (64 per cent), the entire class (23 per cent), and groups of students (13 per cent). Table 5.1 gives the frequencies for all teachers.

The question on problems of understanding produced 69 cases—an average of 3.6 per teacher. The protagonists were: individual named students (56 per cent), the entire class (28 per cent), and groups of students (16 per cent).

Teachers named 39 cases of deviation from the lesson plan. The protagonists named were: 62 per cent the entire class, 10 per cent named individual students, and 10 per cent groups of students. For the remainder, no protagonist was named and only the events were described.

The mentioning by name of individual students per teacher was on average only 3 for the question on progress in understanding (one teacher mentioned a maximum of 6 students). There were very few individual differences. For the question on problems in understanding, each teacher mentioned on average 2 students by name, with a maximum of 6 students by 2 teachers. Individual differences were larger in this question; 8 out of the 19 teachers mentioned no individual student by name.

Table 5.1 *Frequencies of protagonists, events, and causes for all teachers (N = 19)*

	Deviation from lesson plan		Interview questions Progress in understanding		Problems in understanding	
	Frequency	%	Frequency	%	Frequency	%
Protagonist						
Not specified	7	18	–	–	–	–
Group of students	4	10	11	13	11	16
Entire class	24	62	19	23	19	28
Named student	4	10	53	64	39	56
Total	39	100	83	100	69	100
Event						
No event (but cause mentioned)	5	13	27	30	22	32
Task not treated	4	10	–	–	–	–
Organizational event	6	15	–	–	–	–
Subject matter activities	12	31	28	35	32	46
Subject matter insights	12	31	28	35	15	22
Total	39	100	83	100	69	100
Cause						
No cause (but event mentioned)	10	26	39	47	29	42
Task difficulty	4	10	4	5	1	1
Students' knowledge and skills	–	–	8	10	6	9
Quality of teacher planning and knowledge	4	10	–	–	2	3
Pacing and course of the lesson	9	23	–	–	–	–
Instructional quality	8	20	9	11	9	13
Students' giftedness	–	–	6	7	5	7
Students' engagement	2	5	3	3	8	12
Self-confidence or anxiety of students	–	–	–	–	–	–
Motivation of students	1	3	13	16	5	7
Global characterization (good vs. bad student)	1	3	1	1	4	6
Total	39	100	83	100	69	100

Spearman rank correlations were calculated over the 19 teachers in order to determine whether there were interrelations between the frequencies of responses to the three questions. Teachers who named a lot of cases in the question on successful understanding also named a relatively high number in the question on problems. The correlation was: $r = 0.65$ ($p < 0.001$). However, the frequency of cases in both questions correlated negatively with the mentioning of deviations from the lesson plan. The correlation was $r = -0.41$ ($p < 0.05$) between the number of cases in the question on the lesson plan and the number of cases in the question on understanding problems. Thus our teachers differed according to whether they tended to remember most problems in connection with the general course of the lesson and its deviation from their plan, or remembered problems in connection with the questions on understanding progress and difficulties.

What events and causes are named?

Events. The most frequent events relating to *problems in understanding* concerned students' difficulties with observable subject matter activities. These were twice as frequently mentioned as events concerning insight into the subject matter. The observable activities that turned out to be a problem for the students were, for example, drawing a tree diagram for the possible results of dice throws, or listing the frequencies of various two dice combinations in tables.

The question on *understanding progress* gave a different result, in that subject matter insights were as frequently mentioned as observable activities. A subject matter insight event was, for example, the comparison between different random generators (dice vs. coin tossing). The most frequent *deviations from lesson plan* events were also students' activities and insights into the subject matter. In addition, organizational events or the fact that the task could not be treated were events that were recalled as deviations from the teacher's plan.

Causes. The most frequently stated cause of events involving *problems of understanding* was the quality of instruction followed by student engagement and students' knowledge and skills. In reply to the question on *understanding progress*, the most frequently named cause was students' motivation followed by teachers' instructional quality and students' knowledge and skill. The frequencies for instructional quality and students' knowledge and skill were similar in both questions. They differed with respect to student engagement, which was more frequently named as a cause of problems, and student motivation, which was more frequently named as a cause of understanding progress.

Responding to the question on *lesson planning*, the most frequently named cause was 'pacing and course of the lesson other than planned'. This category does not really describe anything more than the actual question, namely the difference between the plan and the lesson. Nevertheless, this was how the question was answered. One might conclude from this that teachers experienced the lesson, its pacing, and its course as having an independent autonomous 'gestalt'. This 'independent momentum' that a lesson can develop is perceived as being the cause of a deviation from the lesson plan.

The instructional quality was also frequently mentioned, indicating that the teachers see themselves as being responsible for the deviation from the lesson plan.

In which events are either individual students or the entire class named as protagonist?

This question is of particular interest for progress and problems. Table 5.2 presents the events classified according to protagonist.

Table 5.2 *Frequencies of protagonist–event combinations*

	Event					
	No event (but cause mentioned)		Subject matter activities		Subject matter insights	
Protagonist	*Frequency*	*%*	*Frequency*	*%*	*Frequency*	*%*
Progress in understanding						
Not specified						
Group of students			7	25	4	14
Entire class	4	15	6	21	9	32
Named students	23	85	15	54	15	54
Total	27	100	28	100	28	100
Problems in understanding						
Not specified						
Group of students			5	16	6	40
Entire class	3	14	7	22	9	60
Named students	19	86	20	62		
Total	22	100	32	100	15	100

It is interesting to note that 86 per cent of the cases for which no event was given involved individual named students. In such cases, it was said that there had been a problem with student N that was due to cause a, without a problem event itself being stated. This rarely occurred for the entire class, and for groups of students a concrete event was remembered on each occasion. This finding was similar for both questions. There was, however, a difference between the questions with respect to the relation between subject matter insight and subject matter activities. It has already been pointed out above that the total number of subject matter insights was much lower for understanding problems than for progress. It is thus clear that in the few cases in which problems with subject matter insights were remembered, this always involved the entire class or groups of students, and not individual students.

In order to determine whether the tendency to name individual students was common to both questions, Spearman rank correlations were calculated for the numbers of students named. There was no significant correlation; i.e. teachers who, compared to their colleagues, tended to name relatively more individual students with problems in understanding, did not show the same behaviour with progress, and vice versa. In contrast, when the entire class was perceived as the protagonist, there was a significant correlation between the number of cases of progress and problems ($r = 0.47$ ($p < 0.05$)).

A closer look

The number of recalled cases of student problems and progress is surprisingly low. However, both detailed transcript analyses of some individual lessons (see Bromme and Steinbring 1986) and field notes from all lessons indicate that considerably more than an average of two individual students per lesson and teacher had problems in understanding. However, these were hardly mentioned by the teachers in their reports. This leads to a first impression that only a few observations were important enough to be remembered by the teachers afterwards.

This is not to say that nothing at all was remembered. Instead, the teachers recalled the problems and progress of the class as a whole. This was most marked in relation to problems. Observations can be found for all teachers for the protagonist 'the class', but there were eight teachers who did not name a single individual student as having a problem.

The structure of the reports also supports the view that the concrete observations were predominantly based on the class as protagonist. Thus, causes without events were more frequently introduced with the individual student as protagonist than with the class as protagonist (see Table 5.2). One interpretation of this is that answers about students were often the result of 'theorizing', whereas answers about 'the class' referred to observed events (see Calderhead 1984, p. 58).

There were, of course, other namings of individual students, such as, for example, comments on stable features (e.g. immigrant students' language difficulties) or observations on individual students who were named as examples for global judgements. When naming individual students, some teachers gave only global judgements that were related to the engagement or performance.

It would seem that our study has produced a disappointing picture of teachers' memory for individual student's understanding that is similar to Shroyer's (1981). However, it also contains indications that something completely different was in the focus of recall (and, as we infer, in the focus of teachers' awareness during instruction), namely the entire class and the instructional flow. This alters the impression of apparent blindness toward the learning process in the classroom. In the following, we will clearly point out what the teacher's attention was focused on in the classroom, using examples and quotations from the teachers' answers. We will have to dispense with a quantitative analysis, as the number of reports per teacher in which the class is the centre of recall was low. A more interpretative description is necessary in order to account for the emphasis given to the class as a protagonist in teachers' interviews. This cannot be inferred merely from the frequencies of the categories.

There were always only one or two episodes in the lesson that contained problems and progress. However, these were the episodes in which a new step in the presentation of the curriculum took place. In this respect, they were key episodes from the teacher's perspective. This inference is supported by the sequence of the recall of problems and progress. In most reports, the subject-related activities of the entire class were described first. Then, individual students were mentioned whose comments had indicated that the class had not yet understood something, or articulated the insight that was desired for the entire class. The position of episodes in the course of the lesson was determined by the subject-related course of the lesson discussion, and not by the time of their occurrence.

Three teachers could even recall long verbal dialogues. One teacher began his account with a question from a student, and was then able to reconstruct the subsequent answers. He commented, 'This answer helped a great deal'. The remembered situation occurred at the point where it was necessary to understand the new and really difficult task in the lesson. Sometimes only a single word was remembered: 'Frank gave a key word at the beginning that indicated that he had made great progress'. This answer illustrates how our question on the progress of individual students was often answered. Starting with such lesson episodes, comments were made on individual students that were oriented toward the subject content of the episode. Occasionally other students were also listed at this point. Memories of progress were more closely related to single situations featuring the contributions of individual students. In contrast, problems were not linked to the comments of individual students in this way. In such cases, the problem was described in subject-related terms, and was less frequently related to the utterances of individual students. For example: 'The main difficulty in chance comparisons was that the students had to compare fractions'. 'The greatest difficulty was with the comparison of tables [on the results of dice throws]'.

In summary, we can note that student contributions were remembered when they had a strategic value. By strategic value, we mean that they occurred at the moment when the lesson 'had got stuck' (as one teacher expressed it) from the teacher's perspective, or where the actual transition from old to new knowledge was supposed to occur.

Both the pacing of teaching in classes of this age group and the methodological construction of the lessons permitted very few such transitions from old to new knowledge. Each class had only a few such 'peaks'. This also explains why all the teachers reported only between one and three episodes in which the class was the protagonist. The episodes may have occurred more frequently during the 45-minute lesson, but they were arranged in memory not according to the time of their occurrence, but according to content, and in this respect only a few cases were concerned with problems in understanding and success.

Differences between teachers: quality of teaching and professional experience

Observer ratings of the teachers' instructional quality was available from another part of the research project (Bromme and Dobslaw 1986b). A factor analysis of these ratings produced two relatively independent instructional quality factors. Factor I covered subject-matter-related and student-related engagement, and Factor II described the degree of content-related and organizational structuring of the course of the lesson. The teachers' individual factor scores were correlated with the number of cases in which the different types of protagonist were named. No correlation could be found for Factor I (engagement). Factor II correlated with the naming of the entire class as the protagonist in progress ($r = 0.40$ ($p < 0.05$)), but did not correlate with the recall for individual students in the classroom. The reverse held true for problems in understanding. There was a correlation of $r = 0.41$ ($p < 0.05$) between the Factor II score ranking and the naming of individual students.

Therefore, when teachers actively structured their lessons, they remembered more progress in understanding by the entire class and more problems of individual students compared to colleagues who did not guide their class so firmly. However, this does not mean that a more structured class is actually more effective. In the instructional quality study mentioned above, we found indications that a higher degree of structure was accompanied by a lower increase in learning for the particular subject of probability.

There was no relation between professional experience and the recall of classroom events that concern progress and problems in understanding.

After their fourth year, students in West Germany change to another school. Therefore sixth- and seventh-grade teachers have known their students longer than fifth-grade teachers. So we tested whether there was a relation between this and the degree and extent of recall for students' progress and problems in understanding. However, Kruskal-Wallis one-way analyses of variance with grades five, six, and seven as groups did not show any significant relation.

There was, however, a relation between a teacher's function as class teacher and the number of cases of individual students' problems in understanding. A Mann–Whitney U-test showed that class teachers named significantly more individual students with problems in understanding than did teachers working with a class for which they were not the class teacher ($U = 15, p < 0.05$).

During classroom interactions, a notional 'collective student' was assembled from the many and varied contributions of individuals.[1] All teachers showed good recall for the problems and difficulties of this 'collective student' but only about half of them did so for any of the individual students' problems. In the next section, the results will be discussed within the framework of the demands that are placed on teachers in the classroom.

STUDENTS' UNDERSTANDING AND LEARNING IN THE CLASSROOM AS A DEMAND ON THE TEACHER

As we are interested in the perception and explanation of students' understanding as part of the teachers' task, we must investigate the nature of the tasks that teachers have to master. In doing this, we assume that teachers' actions and perceptions are shaped by the tasks with which they are confronted in the classroom (Doyle 1979, 1980; Bromme and Brophy 1986).

The term 'task' is more precisely defined in industrial psychology, but some conceptual differences may be applied to the work of teachers, and are useful for the interpretation of our data. In industrial psychology, a differentiation is made between the objective task content and its subjective reconstruction by the actor (Hackmann 1969). The task content influences which actions are used to master the task. (The diagnosis of student mistakes, for example, demands different actions than the diagnosis of illnesses.) Task content, however, only defines the space of action possibilities, as it can be interpreted and carried out differently. The task content is also dependent on the 'nature' of persons, processes, or objects that have to be worked on in order to master the task. As a teacher's activity is an interaction between teacher and different students, constrained by the communication of subject matter and the medium of the lesson, the 'nature' of the task content is not constant. However, some aspects of the nature of the teacher's task can be described.

We assume here that one important aim of the classroom work of both teachers and students (though, of course, not the only one) consists in conveying or gaining knowledge and developing understanding. If one accepts this assumption, it becomes clear that the students' own psychological processes of learning and understanding contribute to the task demand facing the teacher (Doyle 1983).

Although the teaching process cannot be directly derived from the learning process, the processes and conditions of understanding largely determine the task demand that the teacher has to master. We will now proceed to outline some recent findings from the psychology of the acquisition of knowledge.

1. Students already have preconceptions of what a new concept could mean for at least the majority of subjects dealt with in the classroom. Thus learning and understanding do not mean the passive filling up of a container, but rather mean a restructuring of knowledge that is already present (Romberg and Carpenter 1986; Davis 1984). These findings from studies with students agree with the psychological pure research on understanding and retention, which also points out the importance of existing knowledge structures for the understanding of new information (Rumelhart and Ortony 1977). However, this finding leads to the 'learning paradox': how can new knowledge arise through the application of old knowledge? This is not just a theoretical problem for researchers, but also represents a practical task for the teacher (Bereiter 1985). In mathematics lessons, it occurs as a practical problem in the sense that students are not aware that their old knowledge is mathematical knowledge; it is not organized according to the curriculum. Students have everyday concepts of 'number', 'equal', or 'probability' that the teacher is not able simply to exchange for the mathematical meaning of these concepts. Therefore teaching requires not only the imparting of mathematical skills and concepts, but also the conveying of a mathematical meta-knowledge. It is this that enables students to understand the mathematical nature of concepts such as 'number', 'probability', etc.

2. The integration with old knowledge and the restructuring of old insights in the light of new information are not just a concern of psychology. They are also a consequence of the logical relationships of knowledge. To give an example, the meaning of the concept of irrational numbers is related to the concept of the rational number, which, in turn, is related to the concept of the natural number. The meaning of the concept 'number' alters according to the type of number under consideration. However, the meaning of the types of number that have already been understood also changes when one learns about new types of numbers. Knowledge has to be considered in this way in other subject matter areas too. In other words, the meaning of a concept depends on its relations with other concepts.

   Thus, not only the psychological process of understanding but also the structure of knowledge imply that the understanding of new knowledge involves a restructuring of the old. This is why operations with knowledge are sometimes described with concepts of the content itself without recourse to psychological concepts about the operations.

   Teachers may also possibly reflect on students' understanding in terms of subject matter content. Thus, one cannot deduce that teachers only reflect on understanding by studying their thoughts about the students; their thoughts on understanding could also be hidden within considerations and perceptions of the subject matter of the lesson. For example, ideas on an appropriate sequencing of mathematical topics (do we need to introduce fractions before dealing with probability) may be expressed by teachers as considerations about the 'logic' of the content, but are influenced by their experience with students' difficulties in understanding (it is possible to introduce some elementary concepts of probability without presupposing a knowledge of fractions).

3. The understanding of subject matter requires activity, i.e. it is more easily achieved by self-contained working on tasks than by simply listening to instruction. This fact of knowledge acquisition has also altered the view of the role of the teacher. While in earlier research on teaching a direct effect of the teacher on learning was assumed or investigated, the teacher is currently viewed as only indirectly influencing students' learning, and as directly influencing only activities in the classroom (Harnischfeger and Wiley 1977; Denham and Liebermann 1980). By stimulating these activities, and directing students to suitable tasks, teachers can provide learning opportunities but neither learning nor understanding. Learning and understanding occur only as a result of students' own activities, while the educational environment supports this process (Bereiter 1985).

4. The previous basic findings on understanding render it plausible that, when students have difficulties and make mistakes, they do not simply stop learning, but they construct their own, sometimes creative and sometimes false, solution strategies. This is particularly well proven in mathematics instruction, but is also true for other subjects (for mathematics, see Brousseau et al 1986; for biology, see Eaton et al 1983).

   Their own constructions of meaning sometimes enable the students to solve the required tasks even when they have not understood the subject matter in the way intended by the teacher or the curriculum. These independent constructions do not have to hinder understanding. They are simultaneously a prerequisite for the intended knowledge to be appropriately acquired. Students' subjective constructions and interpretations of lesson subject matter are not accidents. They do not only occur as students' errors, but rather their development in the mind of the student is a first step in the process of understanding. This is why incorrect answers from students are not *per se* obstructions to the course of the lesson, but constitute an essential object of the teacher's work.

These findings from cognitive psychology describe some of the demands that have to be mastered by teachers. It is necessary to bear them in mind if one wants to explain teachers' thoughts on their students' understanding. However, the process of knowledge acquisition in students only constrains and does not determine the teaching method.

Therefore we must ask which teaching method was prevalent in our study. Our data are concerned with lessons in which an open dialogue was carried out involving the entire class. This procedure was interrupted by phases of group and individual work. However, most of the time, the lesson followed the pattern of a 'questioning developing classroom discourse' (Voigt 1985). This method of instruction is widely used and takes up most of the instruction time between the fifth and tenth grades in West German schools, as pointed out in studies by Hopf (1980) and Hage et al (1985).

With this pattern of working on new knowledge, the teacher attempts to cultivate a student verbalization of the new knowledge through the use of suitable tasks and questions. Thus, the students do not just have to fulfil a learning role. To the extent that they participate, they take over—for themselves and the others in the class—a part of the presentation of the subject matter. This can develop so far that the teacher avoids explaining the new knowledge herself, and regards a lesson as having been effective only when at least some of the students have verbalized the new knowledge.[2]

EXPLANATION OF THE FINDINGS

The basic results on the nature of students' understanding and the teacher's instructional methods provide a sufficient description of the 'nature' of the teacher's task to enable us to explain our findings.

The teachers remembered events from the phases of the lesson in which the new knowledge was introduced, and in which this introduction was prepared. No teacher reported observations on group work or the discussion of homework. It can be assumed that these peak phases demand a great deal of attention from the teacher, and that he or she is then least able to rely on routines. In these phases, the entire potential structure of knowledge of the unit in question (potential because it must—at least partially—be reactivated in the mind of the student) has to be re-established in order to introduce the new knowledge. At the same time conceptual conflicts must be generated that can function as connection points for the new knowledge. The introduction of the new knowledge then places further attention demands on the teacher.

In our study on the instruction of probability, a particular difficulty lay in coping with the relation between formalization and non-mathematical reality in probability. For example, for the students, this was the question whether chance can be subjected to calculation. Of course, such didactic problems vary within a subject and from subject to subject. The amount of attention they demand of a teacher is essentially dependent on experience with the subject matter and the position of the subject within the whole curriculum. Nevertheless, this example has been mentioned in order to illustrate that teachers do not simply deliver the subject matter with an instructional procedure without having to think about it, but must concentrate part of their attention on the problems involved in its unfolding. Thus, not only the reactivation of the potential structure of old knowledge, but also the presentation of the new, demand attention that cannot simultaneously be directed at the learning processes of individual students. Nevertheless, the presentation is aimed at the learning process of the individual student. Apart from this, the possibility of noticing individual students' problems depends on the teacher's familiarity with the students.

Some student comments were very precisely recalled as *understanding progress*, as they were part of the subject matter presentation. The progress of these students was recalled because it presented the intended understanding and served as a model for the other students.

Some student comments were very precisely recalled as *problems in understanding*, as they formulated the incorrect constructions of meaning and misunderstandings that were the object of the lesson discussion. Teachers need an instructional presentation of these incorrect constructions in order to cope with the task of taking students' preconceptions into account. It is ineffective and sometimes impossible for teachers to anticipate all misunderstandings when planning their lessons. Therefore, by letting students explicate their understanding, the problems can be dealt with in the classroom. A teacher can take into account the students' incorrect constructions of meaning without diagnosing them as individual students' problems in understanding; they are the problems of the 'collective student'. Naturally, these problems were only a small proportion of the problems in understanding that actually occurred during the lesson.

A second type of problem was also recalled. Incorrect answers based on a lack of knowledge or misunderstandings that did not belong to the subject matter planned for the lesson endanger the course of further work on the new knowledge. This could be seen in our study by, for example, the calculation of fractions, which is not, in itself, a part of teaching probability, but is necessary for some of the tasks. Problems in understanding were then problems in the sense of the teacher's difficulties in guiding the instructional flow. Thus, whether the students' problems in understanding disturbed the instructional flow, or whether they were turned into the object of explanation and thus eliminated, depends on the flexibility and the breadth of the teacher's professional knowledge.

TOWARD A MODEL OF TEACHERS' THINKING ABOUT STUDENTS AND CONTENT: SOME THEORETICAL IMPLICATIONS

In this section we will sketch the consequences for models of teachers' instructional activity. Such models have been formulated by, for example, Peterson and Clark (1978) and Shavelson and Stern (1981). These authors describe instructional activity as a succession of routines in which the teacher's attention is directed at whether the students' behaviour remains within a framework of specific limits. Conscious decisions become necessary only if the students' behaviour crosses the threshold of tolerable deviations. 'Student cues' are regarded as being decisive for the teacher's judgement of the actual state of the instructional flow.

Clark and Peterson (1986) have pointed out that, in empirical studies on interactive decision-making, student cues certainly provide more than one-half of the triggers for conscious decisions. However, there are studies in which it becomes clear that, for example, the available time, the instructional material, or other factors influence the teacher's decision (see Shavelson et al 1977). Finally, the teacher's behaviour is not just a reaction to deviations that are already present; it is also directed by the anticipation of possible and desired developments (Hofer 1986).

Therefore, Clark and Peterson (1986) question this model, and propose that one should wait for further empirical findings before developing it further. In our opinion, a further empirical gathering of other possible cues that could likewise determine the action of teachers is not alone sufficient to solve the above-mentioned dilemma in the model. It would be more fruitful to abandon the search for isolated cues that are differentiated according to the traditional concepts of psychological research (i.e. person vs. subject matter vs. instruction). The cognitive units of teachers in the classroom would appear to have other boundaries. Subject matter activities and insights are important units in teachers' thinking that cover both persons and context. The boundaries of the teacher's cognitive units are not constant, but differ according to the work task for which they are required. Thus, one is more likely to find a cognitive unit 'individual student' in a task in which students must be judged (e.g. marking), than in the shaping of the instructional flow.

Our study has also provided indications for a cognitive unit that is often overlooked—the collective student. Teachers apparently have pictures of the class that are not the sum of their impressions of individual students. It is not yet known when it is more the teachers' view of the collective student or more their view of the individual student that influences their decisions. In any case, it must be realized that the interaction between the teacher and the class is not simply the sum of one-to-one interactions.

The theoretical dilemma described by Clark and Peterson (1986) is also due to the concept of instructional flow. This flow metaphor has its strengths and its weaknesses. Its strength lies in the emphasis on the *gestalt* quality of the course of the lesson. The teacher perceives the course of the lesson as a whole and this provides the backdrop against which individual student comments are recalled. The weak side of the metaphor lies in the fact that it does not capture the structuring effect of the teacher's plans and knowledge about the lesson (or, as Leinhardt 1983 calls it, 'agenda'). The course of the lesson appears as something constant that flows of its own momentum. In reality, however, teachers do not just watch over a flow, but generate it by presenting the students with subject-related goals and activities. Teachers and students have different roles in the classroom, even when the students retain much freedom in their contribution to the shaping of the course of the lesson.

The metaphor of instructional flow thus hides the fact that there are 'peaks' in the lesson, to which the teacher's attention is directed, and which are particularly important for the students' progress in learning. In our study, the teachers particularly recalled the phases of working on new knowledge. Hömberg (1982) has shown that mathematics teachers are especially good at recalling the length of phases in which they themselves were actively involved with the subject matter, while they were not so good at estimating the length of other phases. Lessons are experienced not as a steady flow of instruction, but as a succession of episodes of differing importance for the participants.

Students have different functions within the framework of the shaping of the lesson. They participate not only by individually understanding and acquiring knowledge, but also by presenting the subject matter and its possible interpretations. Thus, a model of instructional activity in which cues are identified that determine the action of the teacher must also take into account the different functions of students.

Students' verbalized misunderstandings serve as a subject of instructional discussion about the students' own construction of meaning. This has important consequences for models of teacher thinking. In the early days of research into teachers' cognitive processes, the teacher was still regarded as a diagnostician, analogous to a medical doctor (NIE 1975; Clark 1986). However, when the students' constructions of meaning are no longer deviations from actual learning processes, this becomes a false view. The problems in understanding must now much rather be understood as the material from which the teacher shapes the lesson, and on which the participants in the classroom work. This needs to be taken into account in both the formation of models and in the empirical investigation of teachers' thinking.

In summary, it can be stated that the concept of instructional flow requires modification. It is necessary to allow for the different roles that the teachers and students occupy, and for the development of the subject matter within the instructional flow. Additionally, teachers' cognitive units have been shown to be a key question. Our data suggest that it is not only the individual students, but also the reactivation of old knowledge and the development of new knowledge within the instructional flow that stand in the focus of the teacher's memory.

NOTES

1. Of course, the collective student's contributions are a combination of the answers and questions of individual students, and therefore they may also contribute to the teacher's picture of the individual student. It must also be recognized that not all students participate to the same extent, and they also do not all receive the same amount of attention. Therefore, all students are not equally important for the forming of the 'collective student'.
2. The pattern of a 'questioning–developing classroom discourse' can have various negative effects. One danger is that only a few good students, who are regarded by the teacher as being sufficiently competent, actually take part in this shared shaping of the lesson. Another danger is that the scope of possible answers is narrowed to the one answer that is expected by the teacher (Voigt 1985). It can also lead to problems when the students can only guess from the teacher's questions what the lesson is actually about, instead of being clearly told what they have to do and what they have to learn (Brophy et al 1983). These criticisms have been known for a long time. Nevertheless, the pattern is very widely used in schools. This makes us wonder whether there are not also positive effects that have contributed to the persistence of this pattern. One possible positive effect could be that the misunderstandings of students are best articulated by students themselves, and thus become an object of the classroom dialogue. Another possible effect could be that the contributions of good students describe the 'zone of proximal development' for the other students.

ACKNOWLEDGEMENTS

This study was supported by the VW Foundation (Project LEDIS). I am grateful to Wolfgang Barz, Gudrun Dobslaw, and Claudia Krüger for their help with the data collection and coding, and to Jonathan Harrow for translating the text into English.

REFERENCES

Bereiter, L. (1985) 'Toward a Solution of the Learning Paradox'. *Review of Educational Research*, **15**, 201–26.

Bransford, J. D. and Franks, J. J. (1971) 'The Abstraction of Linguistic Ideas'. *Cognitive Psychology*, **2**, 331–50.

Bromme, R. (1983) '"Understanding Texts" as Heuristics for the Analysis of Thinking Aloud Protocols'. *Communication and Cognition, 16*, 215–31.

Bromme, R. (1986) 'Der Lehrer als Experte—Skizze eines Forschungsansatzes'.

In Neber, H. (ed.) *Angewandte Problem-lösepsychologie*. Münster: Aschendorf.

Bromme, R. and Brophy, J. E. (1986) 'Teachers' Cognitive Activities'. In Christiansen, B., Howson, G., and Otte, M. (eds) *Perspectives on Mathematics Education*, pp. 99–139. Dordrecht, Netherlands: Reidel.

Bromme, R. and Dobslaw, G. (1986a) 'Teachers' Instructional Quality and Their Explanation of Students' Understanding'. In Ben-Peretz, M., Bromme, R., and Halkes, R. (eds) *Advances in Research on Teacher Thinking*. Lisse, Netherlands: Swets & Zeitlinger.

Bromme, R. and Dobslaw, G. (1986b) 'Zu einigen Variablen der Instruktionsqualität im Mathematikunterricht. Ergebnisse und Probleme einer empirischen Untersuchung zum Stochastikunterricht'. In Steiner, H.-G. (ed.) *Grundfragen der Entwicklung mathematischer Fähigkeiten*, pp. 261–80. Cologne: Aulis.

Bromme, R. and Juhl, K. (1984) *Students' Understanding of Tasks in the View of Mathematics Teachers*. Occasional Paper, IDM, Bielefeld: University of Bielefeld, IDM.

Bromme, R. and Steinbring, H. (1986) *Was ist Klarheit im Mathematikunterricht? Eine Untersuchung zum Umgang mit Aufgaben in leistungsheterogenen Klassen*. Occasional Paper, IDM, Bielefeld: University of Bielefeld, IDM.

Brophy, J. E. and Evertson, C. M. (1981) *Student Characteristics and Teaching*. New York: Longman.

Brophy, J. E., Rohrkemper, M., Rashid, H., and Goldberger, M. (1983) 'Relation between Teachers' Presentation of Classroom Tasks and Students' Engagement in Those Tasks'. *Journal of Educational Psychology*, **75**, 544–52.

Brousseau, G., Davis, R. B., and Werner, T. (1986) 'Observing Students at Work'. In Christiansen, B., Howson, G., and Otte, M. (eds) *Perspectives on Mathematics Education*, pp. 205–41. Dordrecht, Netherlands: Reidel.

Calderhead, J. (1981) 'Stimulated Recall: A Method for Research on Teaching'. *British Journal of Educational Psychology*, **51**, 211–17.

Calderhead, J. (1984) *Teachers' Classroom Decision Making*. London: Holt, Rinehart & Winston.

Clark, C. M. (1986) 'Ten Years of Conceptual Development in Research on Teacher Thinking'. In Ben-Peretz, M., Bromme, R., and Halkes, R. (eds) *Advances in Research on Teacher Thinking*. Lisse, Netherlands: Swets & Zeitlinger.

Clark, C. M. and Peterson, P. L. (1986) 'Teachers' Thought Processes'. In Wittrock, M. C. (ed.) *Handbook of Research on Teaching*, 3rd edition, pp. 255–98. New York: Macmillan.

Cooper, H. M. (1979) 'Pygmalion Grows up: A Model for Teacher Expectation, Communication and Performance Influence'. *Review of Educational Research*, **49**, 389–410.

Davis, R. B. (1984) *Learning Mathematics: The Cognitive Science Approach to Mathematics Education*. London: Croom-Helm.

Denham, L. and Liebermann, A. (eds) (1980) *Time to Learn. A Review of the Beginning Teacher Evaluation Study*. California Commission for Teacher Preparation and Licensing.

Doyle, W. (1979) *The Task of Teaching and Learning in Classrooms*. R & D Rep. No. 4103. Austin, TX: University of Texas, Research and Development Center for Teacher Education.

Doyle, W. (1980) 'Classroom Effects'. *Theory into Practice*, **18**, 138–44.

Doyle, W. (1983) 'Academic Work'. *Review of Educational Research*, **53**, 159–99.

Eaton, J. F., Anderson, C. W., and Smith, E. (1983) *Students' Misconceptions Interfere with Learning: Case Studies of Fifth Grade Students*. IRT Research Series, No. 128, East Lansing, MI: Michigan State University.

Fogarty, J., Wang, M., and Creek, R. (1983) 'A Descriptive Study of Experienced and Novice Teachers' Interactive Instructional Thoughts and Actions'. *Journal of Educational Research*, **77**, 22–32.

Grice, H. P. (1975) 'Logic and Conversation'. In Cole, P. and Morgan, J. L. (eds) *Syntax and Semantics, Vol. 3: Speech Acts*, pp. 41–58. New York: Seminar Press, 41–58.

Hage, K. et al. (1985) *Das Methodenrepertoire von Lehrern*. Opladen: Leske.

Hackman, J. R. (1969) 'Toward Understanding of the Role of Tasks in Behavioral Research'. *Acta Psychologica*, **31**, 97–128.

Harnischfeger, A. and Wiley, D. E. (1977) 'Kernkonzepte des Schullernens'. *Zeitschrift für Entwicklungspsychologie und Pädagogische Psychologie*, **9**, 207–30.

Hofer, M. (1981) 'Schülergruppierungen in Urteil und Verhalten des Lehrers'. In Hofer, M. (ed.) *Informationsverarbeitung und Entscheidungsverhalten von Lehrern*, pp. 192–222, Munich: Urban u. Schwarzenberg.

Hofer, M. (1986) *Sozialpsychologie erzieherischen Handelns*. Göttingen: Hogrefe.

Hopf, D. (1980) *Mathematikunterricht. Eine empirische Untersuchung zur Didaktik und Unterrichtsmethode in der 7. Klasse des Gymnasiums*. Stuttgart: Klett-Cotta.

Hömberg, E. (1982) *Wahrnehmung und Steuerung der Zeitdauer von Unterrichtsprozessen—Anforderungen an die Lehrertätigkeit im Mathematikunterricht*. Dissertation: University of Bremen.

Leinhardt, G. (1983) *Expert and Novice Knowledge of Individual Students' Achievement*. Paper presented at the American Educational Research Association Conference, New York, 1982.

McNair, K. and Joyce, B. (1979) *Teachers' Thoughts while Teaching: The South Bay Study, Part II*. Research Series No. 58, Institute for Research on Teaching. East Lansing, MI: Michigan State University.

Morine-Dershimer, G. (1978/9) 'How Teachers "See" Their Pupils'. *Educational Research Quarterly*, **3**, 43–65.

NIE (1975) *Teaching as Clinical Information Processing*. Report of Panel 6, National Conference on Studies in Teaching, Washington, DC: National Institute of Education.

Natriello, G. and Dornbusch, S. M. (1983) 'Bringing Behavior back in: The Effects of Students' Characteristics and Behavior on the Classroom Behavior of Teachers'. *American Educational Research Journal*, **20**, 29–43.

Oldenbürger, H. (1986) 'Does a Tendency to Group Pupils or Attributes Exist within Teachers' Cognitions/Judgements?' In Ben-Peretz, M., Bromme, R., and Halkes,

R. (eds) *Advances in Research on Teacher Thinking*. Lisse, Netherlands: Swets & Zeitlinger.

Pedulla, J. J., Airasian, P. W. and Madams, G. F. (1980) 'Do Teacher Ratings and Standardized Test Results of Students Yield the Same Information'. *American Educational Research Journal*, **17**, 303–7.

Peterson, P. L. and Clark, C. M. (1978) 'Teachers' Reports of their Cognitive Processes during Teaching'. *American Educational Research Journal*, **15**, 555–65.

Romberg, T. A. and Carpenter, T. P. (1986) 'Research on Teaching and Learning Mathematics: Two Disciplines of Scientific Inquiry'. In Wittrock, M. (ed.) *Handbook of Research on Teaching*, 3rd edition, pp. 850–74. New York: Macmillan.

Rumelhart, D. and Ortony, A. (1977) 'The Representation of Knowledge in Memory'. In Anderson, R. C., Spiro, R. J., and Montague, W. E. (eds) *Schooling and the Acquisition of Knowledge*, pp. 99–136. Hillsdale, NJ: Lawrence Erlbaum.

Shavelson, R. J., Atwood, N. K., and Borko, H. (1977) 'Experiments on Some Factors Contributing to Teachers' Pedagogical Decisions'. *Cambridge Journal of Education*, **7**, 51–70.

Shavelson, R. J. and Stern, P. (1981) 'Research on Teachers' Pedagogical Thoughts, Judgments, Decisions, and Behavior'. *Review of Educational Research*, **51**(4), 455–98

Shroyer, J. C. (1981) *Critical Moments in the Teaching of Mathematics: What Makes Teaching Difficult?* Dissertation, Michigan State University, East Lansing.

Thorndyke, P. W. (1977) 'Cognitive Structures in Comprehension and Memory of Narrative Discourse'. *Cognitive Psychology*, **15**, 437–46.

Voigt, J. (1985) 'Patterns and Routines in Classroom Interaction'. *Recherches en Didactique des Mathématiques*, **6**, 69–118.

Wang, M. C. (1973) 'The Accuracy of Teachers' Predictions of Children's Learning Performance'. *Journal of Educational Research*, **66**, 462–5.

6

TEACHERS' KNOWLEDGE STRUCTURES AND COMPREHENSION PROCESSES

Kathy Carter and Walter Doyle

Studies of teacher thinking have generally focused on the *processes* of planning and decision-making (Clark and Peterson 1986). In contrast, the research program described in this chapter emphasizes the *knowledge structures* that underlie teachers' cognitions. The program is based on the twofold premise that (a) teachers' thinking is knowledge driven and (b) this knowledge is organized in large measure by the tasks teachers encounter in classroom environments. That is, teachers' planning and decision-making are governed by what they know about teaching, learning, and curriculum, and about the manifestations of these phenomena in classroom events. To understand teachers' thinking, then, it is necessary to describe the tasks teachers face in classrooms and explicate the knowledge structures that underlie the interpretation and accomplishment of these tasks.

The ultimate goal of research within this framework is to make explicit the implicit knowledge that teachers use in responding as they do in classrooms. In contrast to studies that emphasize planning or decision-making, the focus of inquiry here is on teacher *comprehension*, i.e. on how teachers use their knowledge to 'make sense' of or come to understand classroom events and their actions with respect to these events. Research of this nature is vigorously *theoretical* in the sense that efforts are made to model teachers' knowledge structures and interpretive processes. At the same time, the inquiry is strongly *empirical* in that extensive observations and analyses of classroom data are used to track how teachers accomplish tasks in actual classroom settings. Finally, the motivation for research is explicitly *practical* in that an effort is made to define knowledge teachers and teacher educators can use to understand and communicate about teaching.

Two strands of research are summarized in this chapter. The first strand has focused on knowledge associated with the achievement of social order in classrooms (Carter 1985, 1986; Doyle 1986a). The second strand has emphasized the management of academic work in classrooms (Doyle 1983; Doyle and Carter 1984). A description of these two strands constitutes the central core of the chapter. To provide an intellectual context, these descriptions are preceded by a brief statement of the conceptual and methodological foundations of both research programs. The chapter ends with a discussion of the state of knowledge in this area, directions for further inquiry, and implications of this research for designing pre-service and in-service teacher education programs.

CONCEPTUAL AND METHODOLOGICAL FOUNDATIONS

This section is designed to orient the reader to the conceptual framework of the research program and to the basic research strategies used to study teaching in classrooms. Particular attention is given to the concepts of 'task' and 'comprehension' since they are fundamental to the approach being described.

The concept of task

Classroom tasks provide a window into the cognitive world of teaching. The concept of 'task' calls attention to three basic dimensions of action–situation relationships: (a) a goal state or end product to be achieved; (b) a problem space or set of conditions and resources available to research the goal state; and (c) the operations involved in assembling and using available resources.

Broadly speaking, teachers face two inter-related tasks in classrooms: (a) establishing and maintaining social order; and (b) representing and enacting the curriculum. Teachers must, in other words, organize groups of students, establish rules and procedures, elicit students' co-operation in classroom activities, and sustain order for designated blocks of time across several months. At the same time, teachers must create work for students that conveys the curriculum, explain the intellectual processes involved in doing the work, and provide assistance and feedback as students carry out and complete assignments. The tasks of social order and curriculum enactment are accomplished interactively, i.e. the order and curriculum enactment are jointly constituted by teachers *and* students (see Erickson and Shultz 1981). This interactive property of task accomplishment, combined with the inherent complexity of the classroom environment (see Doyle 1986a), makes teaching in classrooms an extraordinarily difficult enterprise.

Knowledge and comprehension

As noted earlier, the central focus of the present research program is on how teachers 'make sense of' or interpret classroom scenes. Interpretation, in turn, is viewed as a quest for order and intelligibility among the many possible patterns of sense that a classroom scene affords to a teacher. The sense that a teacher makes of a particular scene is a product of ordered prior knowledge of classroom scenes, awareness of particular features of a present scene, and cognitive processes that connect knowledge with current awareness.

Recent concepts in cognitive psychology are particularly well suited to the study of teachers' knowledge and how it is used to accomplish classroom tasks. A central premise of cognitive science is that comprehension is a *constructive* process (see Bransford and Franks 1976). Meaning does not result from reception or rehearsal of information. Rather, understanding involves an active construction of a cognitive representation of events or concepts and their relationships in a specific context. This constructive process is both interactive and sequential, involving information from the environment and from semantic memory (Rumelhart 1981). In comprehending prose, for example, a reader gradually builds a model of the semantic structure or meaning of a passage. Information from the environment makes contact with information from semantic memory to suggest a likely interpretation. This interpretation establishes expectations about what subsequent information will likely be. These expectations, in turn, guide processing of new information in working memory to confirm and update the initial interpretation.

Schemata play an especially important role in ordering knowledge and accounting for ambiguities in passages or situations (see Schank and Abelson 1977; Trabasso 1981). A schema is an ordered representation of objects, episodes, actions, or situations that contains slots or variables into which specific instances of experience in a particular context can be fitted. A schema provides, therefore, a framework for structuring and interpreting experience. Moreover, passages or episodes are seldom fully specified. A schema furnishes a structure for 'filling in the gaps', i.e. for making inferences to complete the picture of associations and causality among events or episodes. Thus, in reading the sentence 'Michael entered a restaurant', a reader can use a restaurant schema to infer what is likely to happen.

From this perspective, teachers' knowledge of classrooms consists of schema or scripts that permit them to interpret instances of behavior and predict the likely configuration of events in a particular context. To understand teachers' knowledge, then, it is necessary to map the schema they use to comprehend classroom events and processes.

Studying teachers' knowledge structures

Access to teachers' schemata is seldom direct. It is unlikely, in other words, that teachers can readily provide an analytical description of their classroom knowledge and how it is used to comprehend classroom events (see Ericcson and Simon 1980).

In the research program described in this chapter, an indirect strategy was used to delineate knowledge structures and comprehension processes (see Doyle 1979a, b). In this strategy, thinking is inferred from an analysis of teachers' preoccupations and actions in accomplishing classroom tasks. To conduct such an analysis it is necessary first to *model the task* and then to *describe how the task was accomplished*, including such matters as what the teacher attended to, talked about, and did in the task environment. Information about the task itself and how it was accomplished is obtained from extended classroom observations, often conducted on a daily basis over several weeks. From an analysis of this observational data it is possible to *construct a cognitive model* that accounts for the teacher's pattern of action in accomplishing the task. It is possible to claim that the model resulting from such an analysis accounts for the actions exhibited in accomplishing the task. But the model is not a record of the teacher's conscious thoughts. Furthermore, it is not uniquely determined. More than one model might fit the data. The choice of a model depends upon the quality of its fit with the data and its utility in building an understanding of classroom knowledge.

TEACHER COMPREHENSION OF CLASSROOM MANAGEMENT

Some progress has recently been made in delineating the knowledge structures that underlie classroom management (Doyle 1986a) and in constructing models of teacher comprehension of management events and processes (Carter 1985, 1986). This research is summarized in this section.

Classroom management as a teaching task

Classroom management provides a particularly useful context in which to study teachers' knowledge. In the first place, teachers think a great deal about management issues (Clark and Yinger 1979) and many of their decisions are driven by management considerations (see Carter and Doyle 1984). At the same time, management is rooted in cognitive structures and skills that enable teachers to interpret classroom events and recognize when to act to influence immediate circumstances. An analysis of management choices, then, is likely to lead directly to information about teacher thinking. Finally, considerable knowledge about classroom management has accumulated recently (see Doyle 1986a). As a result, a reasonably complete model of the management task in classrooms is available. Such a task model is essential to begin an exploration of teacher comprehension.

A task model of classroom management has the following components. The management task can be defined primarily as a problem of gaining and maintaining co-operation in activities that fill the available time and serve educative purposes (Doyle 1986a). From this perspective, the *activity* is a fundamental unit of classroom life. An activity is 'a bounded segment of classroom time characterized by an identifiable focal content or concern and a pattern or program of action' (Gump 1982). The program of action embedded in an activity is especially important because (a) it defines the nature of order at a given time; and (b) it pulls teachers and students along specific pathways. The program of action, in other words, provides slots and sequences for participants' behavior and defines the direction, momentum, and energy of classroom events. Recent studies indicate that types of activities are significantly related to the behavior of teachers and students, in particular, the level of student involvement in work (see Berliner 1983; Ross 1984). Order in a classroom, in other words, rests on the activities a teacher creates and sustains.

Analyzing teacher comprehension

Carter (1985, 1986) has constructed comprehension models to account for how junior high school English teachers, who differed on indicators of management success, established and maintained programs of action in their classes. For these studies, detailed narrative descriptions of class sessions conducted across the school year were used to map the way order was achieved under different circumstances.

Four levels of analysis were identified to move systematically from running accounts of classroom behavior contained in the narrative records to progressively more general propositions about what teachers do to establish order in classrooms and what teachers are likely to know about classrooms, and how this knowledge is organized for use in accomplishing lessons. The first level of description involved transforming the narrative records into activity units or segments and describing the character of these units. Once all class sessions for a single teacher were analyzed, a second-level analysis consisting of a general description of how management was accomplished in the class across the year was written. This analysis provided a history of a particular classroom group for the school year. The basic analytical unit was still the activity, but the focus shifted to questions of how the segments were managed over longer periods of time and how one meeting influenced and was influenced by other meetings.

The third-level analysis was designed to transform second-level propositions about how individual teachers solved the problem of order in classrooms into more general statements about common patterns associated with teachers' management of the demands of the classroom environment. These statements were designed to provide a reasonably complete picture of the character of classroom activities. Because success in management and in instruction was a known quality of the teachers in this study, it was also possible to make statements at this level about the patterns of activity management associated with a 'successful' case compared with patterns discovered for the less successful manager.

At the final level of analysis, an attempt was made to transform statements about common patterns of activity management into propositions about how the teachers in this study thought about or understood classroom events and their management. At this level, attention shifted from the features of classrooms and the performance of teachers to the structure of knowledge implied by descriptions of what a teacher reacted to or dwelled upon in solving the problem of class order. These models are viewed as representations of teachers' comprehension of classroom events and their management.

Contrasting cases of two teachers will illustrate the character of the findings from this research. Teacher 32 was relatively successful in establishing smooth-running classes and in promoting the academic achievement of the students. Much of what Teacher 32 did to manage her classes appeared to reflect a conception of her role as *a driver navigating a complex and often treacherous route*. Her emphasis, in other words, was on sustaining activities and steering around obstacles rather than confronting them directly. One day, for instance, Teacher 32 struggled to get a discussion moving.

Rather than rebuke the students for their sluggishness, the teacher abruptly switched the topic to students' preferences for hamburgers. A lively discussion followed during which students rehearsed procedures for conducting a class discussion. When the teacher returned to the official curriculum, the activity flowed smoothly. Because she emphasized movement and navigation, Teacher 32 appeared reluctant to reprimand individual students when that action might disrupt the flow of activity in the class. She preferred, rather, to incorporate students' comments into the lesson and to speak to misbehaving students privately at the end of the class.

Teacher 18, in contrast, had difficulty in maintaining classroom order, and students in her classes made only minimal academic progress. Most of Teacher 18's management efforts consisted of reprimands directed to individual students, as if the problem of order were solved by policing, confronting, and then attempting to 'win out' over students. Such actions in solving the problem of classroom order reflect a conception of her role as *a defender of a territory or a commodity*. This metaphor captures her emphasis on reprimands, authority, and supervisory power to control inappropriate and disruptive behavior. Given this perspective, Teacher 18 reacted to nearly all student misbehavior regardless of the immediate circumstances. At times, however, her attempts to defend order stopped the flow of an activity. This failure to recognize the key role of activity flow in management seemed to have been a major factor in limiting Teacher 18's success.

It is interesting to speculate that the two teachers in this study would react quite differently to the same information about classroom management. Teacher 32 and Teacher 18 differed especially in the extent to which they were willing to reprimand inappropriate comments publicly. If both teachers were to attend an in-service session on classroom management practices, it is reasonable to expect that Teacher 18 would be predisposed to listen for information about how to reprimand and Teacher 32 would ignore such information. Staff development, in other words, would very likely have different effects on these two teachers.

MANAGING THE CURRICULUM

A second strand of classroom research relevant to teacher thinking has focused on curriculum representation and enactment in the form of the academic work students are required to accomplish in science, English, and mathematics classes (see Doyle 1983; Doyle and Carter 1984; Doyle et al 1985). This section contains a summary of curriculum-focussed studies, with special attention to work in junior and senior high school English classes.

The character of academic work in classrooms

Methodologically, studies of academic work have involved several weeks of daily observations focused on assignments. The information gathered has included descriptions of teacher and student actions related to assignments in the classes, copies of all texts and handouts, and copies of students' work after the teacher has graded it. Finally, teachers and students were interviewed to explore how they talked about the work they did in the classes.

English classes proved to be especially fruitful for studies of academic work. In the first place, they contained multiple strands of work. Spelling and vocabulary work typically relied heavily on memorization of words, definitions, and illustrative sentences. Such assignments were usually quite familiar to students because of consistency and uniformity across years, and they were routinized early in the school year. Moreover, these assignments were typically enacted with considerable ease and efficiency in classrooms. Grammar usually required memorizing rules and applying them to specially constructed instances that highlighted the particular rule or rules under consideration.

Composition or writing can cover a wide range of work types. Free forms such as journal writing and 'loop' writing were often recurring events but the products were seldom inspected by the teacher. In one class, the teacher began every class day with approximately seven minutes of journal writing and looked at the journals twice during a six-week grading period. Paragraphs or essays were often specified by type (descriptive, persuasive, analytical) and by format or structure (topic sentence followed by three supporting sentences and a closing sentence). Writing was also accompanied by related work such as exercises on topic sentences or revising and sessions for peer editing or brainstorming.

Connections across assignments varied with teachers. In some instances, stories from literature books or ideas from journals were used as sources of topics for writing assignments, or students were required to include particular grammatical forms or vocabulary words in essays.

This description suggests that curriculum content can be represented in classrooms in a variety of fundamentally different ways. For example, writing can consist of having students combine short sentences to form more complex expressions or having them struggle to express their own interpretation of a story or an incident. Similarly, problem-solving might involve applying a standard and predictable computational procedure to a set of 20 arithmetic problems or deciding which mathematical language adequately represents a scientific process in an experiment. Clearly a list of topics a teacher intends to cover in class gives only minimal information about the actual curriculum in use in the class. To understand the curriculum as enacted in classrooms, it is necessary to examine the work a teacher requires students to accomplish with content.

Teachers' thinking about the curriculum

Descriptions of academic work have been written largely from the perspective of students and the cognitive processes they use in meeting work demands in classrooms. Yet, these descriptions provide insight into the teaching task of curriculum representation and enactment (see Doyle 1986b) and, thus, furnish a basis for examining teachers' thinking about curriculum. In particular, the descriptions suggest that teachers are sensitive to the pressures different types of academic work place on activity flow in classrooms and on students' willingness to co-operate in classroom activities. Teachers respond to these pressures by manipulating work demands and accountability in a variety of subtle ways. In the following sections, examples of how teachers manipulate work systems are presented. These examples illustrate aspects of teachers' understanding of the curriculum events in classroom environments.

Enactment configurations and credit economies

Two general themes have become apparent in the research on assignments and work systems. The first of these centres on the enactment configurations associated with different types of work, and the second centres on credit economies in class.

An early study of academic work (Doyle and Carter 1984) suggested that assignments with different cognitive and procedural complexity for students were enacted in very different ways in the classroom and that these differences had consequences for both classroom management and the nature of the work students accomplished. In particular, familiar, routinized, and simple work was accomplished with ease. Explanations were clear and precise, students' misunderstandings were minimal, and work began quickly and proceeded efficiently. Moreover, there was a reasonably high congruence between the announced work and the final products students handed in, and the teacher's criteria for evaluating products were consistently and often rigorously applied.

Complex assignments in which students encountered novel information and were required to make decisions about content in order to generate products were considerably more difficult to enact. Explanations were longer and more labored, students frequently failed to grasp key points, and work sessions were punctuated with frequent student questions and delays, if not overt attempts to negotiate requirements. Moreover, products seldom matched the specifications given by the teacher, and grading criteria were often loosely applied. Finally, and importantly, assignments drifted, i.e. the announced work and the work students actually accomplished were often quite different. In particular, product specifications became more explicit over time and the scope of students' decisions about content became more narrow.

A second interesting feature of classroom work began to emerge in this early study: the teacher created an artificial economy of surplus credit in the class by awarding students bonus points equal to the score of the local professional football team if the team won its game that week. The teacher mentioned these bonus points explicitly whenever writing assignments were given and warned students not to waste their points on such mundane assignments as vocabulary or grammar.

Subsequent studies in junior and senior high school science, English, and mathematics classes produced information consistent for the most part with these findings (see Doyle et al 1985). When higher-order assignments were given—and they were seldom given—they often appeared fragile and several forces operated to make them more predictable and less demanding for students (and probably for teachers also). Although open negotiation to reduce work demands was not common, high error rates and low completion rates for complex assignments appeared to motivate teachers to simplify work demands. In addition, an economy of surplus credit, generated by bonus points and the like, seemed to operate in every class. Grading criteria for complex, decision-based work, such as writing, were frequently applied loosely, and this potential inflation of grades was balanced by applying criteria more rigorously for simple, routine work such as spelling and grammar. One gets the impression that surplus credit in its various forms served as a primary motivator to entice students to accomplish complex assignments.

In sum, the curriculum as represented and enacted in classrooms often seems to be a crater-filled lunar landscape in which students encounter gaps of various magnitudes. Small gaps, such as words in blanks in grammar exercises, are easily crossed. Large gaps, such as writing assignments, are more difficult to cross and students frequently hesitate at the rim. Teachers, in turn, often respond to such hesitations by either throwing a net under the gap, in the form of bonus points or easy grading, or providing posts along the way to reduce the length of any one leap. Teachers make these adjustments in order to preserve activity flow, which research on classroom management tells us is essential for sustaining order in classrooms. In the process of helping students across large craters, teachers sometimes reconstruct the work they would have students accomplish and, thus, redefine the classroom curriculum.

Familiarizing work

As noted above, familiarity often results in a smooth-running work system. Teachers sometimes create familiarity by maintaining similarities in features of assignments across occasions in which students work with a particular content strand. This process of familiarizing, in turn, appears to reduce substantially the amount of intellectual effort students must expend to accomplish assignments. For example, an eighth-grade English teacher in one study (see Doyle et al 1985) administered a pronoun test that required students to (a) recognize personal pronouns in a paragraph; (b) select the proper form of 'its' or 'it's' to complete sentences; (c) choose the correct form of personal pronouns to fill blanks in sentences; (d) write sentences with personal pronouns defined by their position on a pronoun chart; and (e) fill in all the blanks in a pronoun chart. The test appeared to demand a considerable mastery of pronouns. At the same time, there was a high congruence between the exercises students completed prior to the test and the sections of the test itself. For instance, the students had many opportunities to practice identifying pronouns in paragraphs, selecting pronoun forms to fill blanks in sentences, and putting pronouns into cells on the pronoun chart. Although the exact items from previous exercises were not repeated on the test, it is likely that the test environment was quite familiar to students and that recall and application were greatly simplified by this familiarity.

Classrooms as production systems

Many of the classes observed in studies of academic work were designed for efficient production, that is, a great deal of student work was accomplished with a high degree of involvement from nearly all students. These high-production classes were often organized around routinized work patterns, such as warm-ups in math classes and recurring journal writing segments and spelling assignments in English classes. In addition, work was typically defined quite explicitly and students were given a great deal of guided practice with problem types.

Tasks in production classes are often highly familiar, and students are seldom required to assemble information or processes in ways that have not been demonstrated to them in advance. Content is divided into small chunks, instruction is step-wise, progress through the curriculum is rapid and efficient. In addition, there is often little differential weighting of credit for different assignments. All assignments are equal, and final term grades are calculated by averaging grades on individual assignments. Finally, assignments in production classes are often interchangeable. That is, while there may be a broad sequence (e.g. addition before multiplication, or fractions before decimals), the ordering of work for a day or a week is somewhat arbitrary. Decisions about order are based, it appears, on management considerations, personal preferences, or need, rather than on a logical or semantic thread that ties the separate assignments together.

In an eighth-grade science class, production was high but concept development across the term did not seem to follow a clear logical progression (see Doyle et al 1985). Students completed 30 assignments related to aspects of the circulatory and digestive systems, and engagement was high throughout the term. Typical assignments required students to read a passage and answer questions, do laboratory activities and record procedures and findings, or identify structures.

Activities in the class ran very smoothly, and students were quite productive. The work itself, however, had three distinctive characteristics. First, virtually all assignments were accomplished within one or two class periods and each counted as only a very minor portion of the grade for the six weeks. Second, all assignments were self-contained, that is, the information necessary to complete the work was given within the materials handed out so that integration or assembly across assignments was unnecessary. Moreover, the teacher did not overtly tie lectures to laboratory or worksheets assignments. Finally, the ordering of assignments was arbitrary. Units did not begin with an introduction and lead to a logical culmination. Rather, work covering parts of the unit was assigned before the introductory lecture, and textbook summaries of units were scheduled after several discrete assignments were already completed. All the information was there and often repeated, but assignments were treated as independent and interchangeable pieces.

The teacher's decisions in this class often appeared to be driven by the logic of classroom management (that is, keeping students engaged in work) rather than by the logic of the content. Assignments appeared to be scheduled on the basis of how work segments fitted into the time frames of class sessions or how topics appealed to students rather than how they were meaningfully connected. The students did a great deal of science-like work—labs, worksheets, textbook readings, etc.—but it was not clear that any overall meaning was built into the system. It is interesting to note that students were apparently not bothered by a lack of content progression or integration. Their contentment could have resulted from the fact that there was an inherent logic to the work system: work was explicit, predictable, and easy to accomplish.

There is some evidence available from this research program and those of other investigators (see Anderson 1983; Davis 1983; Eaton et al 1984; Erlwanger 1975) that production and understanding are not necessarily connected. Students practice computational algorithms or follow procedures for carrying out experiments with plants or light but fail to understand the mathematical or scientific principles that underlie the exercises. They can tell someone how to get an answer to a problem but not what the problem means. Moreover, they often retain or form misconceptions of these principles. Such outcomes obviously have long-term consequences for school learning and achievement. If skills are isolated from the semantic context of academic content and treated as interchangeable parts in the daily scheduling of lessons, then meaning is likely to be lost and students will not acquire flexibility and fluency in subject domains.

There is an important message here for teacher evaluation. If the criteria for judging teaching place an overriding emphasis on clarity, engagement, and order, it is possible that teachers will avoid ambiguous tasks because of their impact on the classroom efficiency and productivity. Teachers will be forced, in other words, to smooth out the work system in advance, emphasize only skills and guided practice, and avoid tasks that require students to struggle with meaning. In such management-driven classes, it is possible that meaningfulness and higher-level processing of subject matter will be pushed aside. Evaluation must be sensitive to the overall purposes of instruction in a particular class and to the effects of different types of academic work on classroom processes.

IMPLICATIONS

In this final section some of the theoretical and practical implications of research on teachers' knowledge and comprehension are illustrated. Particular attention is given to the contributions of this line of inquiry to an understanding of the proximal task of teaching in classrooms and to the design of curriculum for teacher education.

Learning as an epiphenomenon in classrooms

An analysis of teachers' thinking about classroom order and curriculum enactment would seem to have important implications for understanding an issue that often surfaces—indeed, is often taken for granted—in discussions of classroom research, viz. the relation of classroom processes to student learning. In particular, the analysis suggests that, from a teacher's perspective, learning is an epiphenomenon in classrooms, something that accompanies classroom events and is affected by them, but that has little immediate or direct role in the daily processes of classroom life. From a task perspective, the real stuff of classrooms is defined by products, performance, and accountability. Teachers define work for students, students interpret this work and accomplish it, and teachers judge the acceptability of the products turned in. Learning occurs behind the scenes of academic work and is affected indirectly by the information-processing requirements of a teacher's assignments. But learning itself is unobservable and thus too elusive a target for teachers' thinking about classroom events and processes.

This is not to say that teachers are not or should not be concerned about what students learn. Rather, the point emphasizes that learning in classrooms is embedded in a complex matrix of events and forces that must be managed first if students are to be brought into contact with the curriculum and thus afforded an opportunity to learn.

The issue of how classroom work connects to student learning is a central problem for further inquiry in research on teaching. An adequate treatment theory for classroom teaching, i.e. a set of propositions that explains how teaching effects occur, has not yet been constructed. Research on classroom work thus far has at least shown that, in attempting to affect student learning, teachers need to think primarily about the work they structure for students and about the factors that influence the enactment of that work in classrooms.

Curriculum for teacher education

Curriculum in teacher education has traditionally been defined in technical and experiential terms. That is, preparation focuses on the technical skills of teaching and relies heavily on field experience and an apprenticeship with a 'master' teacher. The teacher education student in this framework is viewed largely as a passive recipient to be certified as competent in an established tradition of thought and practice. Finally, evaluation is based on the demonstration of specific competencies and on the judgements of experienced school practitioners.

Recently teacher education reformers have emphasized that truly professional teacher preparation should foster reflective capacities of observation, analysis, interpretation, and decision-making (see Zeichner 1983; Zumwalt 1982). Professionally trained teachers, in other words, should first and foremost be able to inquire into teaching and think critically about their work. The knowledge base for the preparation of reflective professionals includes the craft knowledge of skilled practitioners and propositional knowledge from classroom research and from the social and behavioral sciences. Within this framework, research and theory produce not rules or prescriptions for classroom application but rather knowledge and methods of inquiry useful in deliberating about teaching problems and practices. Along similar lines, teaching skills are seem as an important part of teacher education, but they must be embedded in a conceptual framework that enables teachers to decide when to use different skills. In addition, competencies in teaching are defined to include inquiry skills as well as classroom behaviors.

Research on teachers' knowledge and comprehension is especially compatible with this cognitive view of the substance of teacher education. By illuminating the intellectual frameworks and cognitive operations teachers use to interpret classroom scenes, this research provides a language with which practicing teachers and teacher educators can communicate about teaching and design laboratory and field experiences that contribute to the acquisition of appropriate knowledge structures and interpretive processes by beginning teachers. In this sense, the research program described in this chapter is essential to the knowledge base of teacher education.

CONCLUSION

The preliminary analyses summarized in this chapter represent an important foundation for inquiry into teachers' classroom knowledge and comprehension processes. In particular, they provide a language for formulating research questions and interpreting data about teachers' knowledge and understanding. But these analyses are only a beginning. Considerably more needs to be learned about the ways in which teachers recognize and interpret classroom events, order their thinking about the salience of particular incidents, predict the configuration of events over time, or reason about specific action–situation connections in classrooms. Research is also needed on how teachers' knowledge is accumulated as they go about solving problems posed by classroom environments.

In the long run, information about teachers' knowledge structures and comprehension processes would seem to be essential for understanding the decisions teachers make and the plans they formulate. Moreover, a better picture of how teachers comprehend the events that unfold in classroom environments would seem to provide a valuable intellectual context for understanding the character and outcomes of initial teacher preparation and staff development programs.

REFERENCES

Anderson, L. M. (1983) 'The Environment of Instruction: The Function of Seatwork in a Commercially Developed Curriculum'. In Duffy, G., Roehler, L., and Mason, J. (eds) *Comprehension Instruction: Perspective and Suggestions*. New York: Longman.

Berliner, D. C. (1983) 'Developing Conceptions of Classroom Environments: Some Light on the T in Classroom Studies of ATI'. *Educational Psychologist*, **18**, 1–13.

Bransford, J. D. and Franks, J. J. (1976) 'Toward a Framework for Understanding Learning'. In Bowers, G. H. (ed.) *The Psychology of Learning and Motivation: Advances in Research and Theory*, Vol. 10. New York: Academic Press.

Carter, K. (1985) *Teacher Comprehension of Classroom Processes: An Emerging Direction in Classroom Management Research*. Paper presented at the annual meeting of the American Educational Research Association, Chicago, IL.

Carter, K. (1986) *Classroom Management as Cognitive Problem Solving: Toward Teacher Comprehension in Teacher Education*. Paper presented at the annual meeting of the American Educational Research Association, San Francisco, CA.

Carter, K. and Doyle, W. (1984) 'Variations in Academic Tasks in High and Average Ability Classes'. In Lomas, L. (ed.) *Classroom Research*. Victoria, Australia: Deakin University Press.

Clark, C. M. and Peterson, P. L. (1986) 'Teachers' Thought Processes'. In Wittrock, M. C. (ed.) *Handbook of Research on Teaching*, 3rd edition. New York: Macmillan.

Clark, C. M. and Yinger, R. J. (1979) 'Teachers' Thinking'. In Peterson, P. L. and Walberg, H. J. (eds) *Research on Teaching*. Berkeley, CA: McCutchan.

Davis, R. B. (1983) 'Diagnosis and Evaluation in Mathematics Instruction: Making Contact with Students' Mental Representations'. In Smith, D. C. (ed.) *Essential Knowledge for Beginning Educators*. Washington, DC: American Association of Colleges for Teacher Education.

Doyle, W. (1979a) 'Making Managerial Decisions in Classrooms'. In Duke, D. L. (ed.) *Classroom Management*, 78th Yearbook of the National Society for the Study of Education, Part 2. Chicago, IL: University of Chicago Press.

Doyle, W. (1979b) *The Tasks of Teaching and Learning in Classrooms*, R & D Rep. No. 4103. Austin, TX: University of Texas, Research and Development Center for Teacher Education.

Doyle, W. (1983) 'Academic Work'. *Review of Educational Research*, **53**, 159–99.

Doyle, W. (1986a) 'Classroom Organization and Management'. In Wittrock, M. C.

(ed.) *Handbook of Research on Teaching*, 3rd edition. New York: Macmillan.

Doyle, W. (1986b) 'Content Representation in Teachers' Definitions of Academic Work'. *Journal of Curriculum Studies*, **18**, 365–80.

Doyle, W. and Carter, K. (1984) 'Academic Tasks in Classrooms'. *Curriculum Inquiry*, **14**, 129–49.

Doyle, W., Sanford, J. P., Schmidt French, B. S., Emmer, E. T., and Clements, B. S. (1985) *Patterns of Academic Work in Junior High School Science, English, and Mathematics Classes: A Final Report*, R & D Rep. 6190. Austin, TX: University of Texas, Research and Development Center for Teacher Education.

Eaton, J. F., Anderson, C. W., and Smith, E. L. (1984) 'Students' Misconceptions Interfere with Science Learning: Case Studies of Fifth-Grade Students'. *Elementary School Journal*, **84**, 365–79.

Ericcson, K. A. and Simon, H. A. (1980) 'Verbal Reports as Data'. *Psychological Review*, **87**, 215–51.

Erickson, F. and Shultz, J. (1981) 'When Is a Context? Some Issues and Methods in the Analysis of Social Competence'. In Green, J. L. and Wallat, C. (eds) *Ethnography and Language in Educational Settings*. Norwood, NJ: Ablex.

Erlwanger, S. H. (1975) 'Case Studies of Children's Conceptions of Mathematics—Part I'. *Journal of Children's Mathematical Behavior*, **1**, 157–283.

Gump, P. V. (1982) 'School Settings and Their Keeping'. In Duke, D. L. (ed.) *Helping Teachers Manage Classrooms*. Alexandria, VA: Association for Supervision and Curriculum Development.

Ross, R. P. (1984) 'Classroom Segments: The Structuring of School Time'. In Anderson, L. W. (ed.) *Time and School Learning: Theory, Research and Practice*. London: Croom Helm.

Rumelhart, D. E. (1981) 'Schemata: The Building Blocks of Cognition'. In Guthrie, J. T. (ed.) *Comprehension and Teaching: Research Reviews*. Newark, DE: International Reading Association.

Schank, R. C. and Abelson, R. P. (1977) *Scripts, Plans, Goals, and Understanding: An Inquiry into Human Knowledge Structures*. Hillsdale, NJ: Lawrence Erlbaum Associates.

Trabasso, T. (1981) 'On the Making of Inferences during Reading and Their Assessment'. In Guthrie, J. T. (ed). *Comprehension and Teaching: Research Reviews*. Newark, DE: International Reading Association.

Zeichner, K. M. (1983) 'Alternative Paradigms of Teacher Education'. *Journal of Teacher Education*, **34**(3), 3–9.

Zumwalt, K. K. (1982) 'Research on Teaching: Policy Implication for Teacher Education'. In Lieberman, A. and McLaughlin, M. W. (eds) *Policy Making in Education*, 81st Yearbook of the National Society for the Study of Education, Part 1. Chicago, IL: University of Chicago Press.

7

'KNOTS' IN TEACHERS' THINKING

Angelika C. Wagner

INTRODUCTION

In everyday school life, teachers' thought processes tend to be much more descriptive, more emotional, more contradictory and less straightforward than many current studies of teachers' thinking have led us to believe. This was the first major finding of our six-year in-depth study of what teachers (and students) actually think about during class, using the method of stimulated recall, in which teachers retrospectively think aloud as they view a video replay of their classroom lesson. We found that teachers' thinking quite often seemed to go around in circles, posing questions without resolving them, 'jumping' from one issue to another, considering goals and strategies without ever putting them into practice, with no apparent realization of the many contradictions in the content of teachers' thought. Some of these thought processes also revealed considerable emotional involvement—teachers got angry about students, were over-awed by their colleagues, sometimes identified with one of the students or had a strong desire to reach certain goals and were disappointed when they were not achieved.

We looked particularly at the inter-relationship between teachers' cognitive and affective processes, especially those leading to internal conflicts. The basic premise of this chapter is that many of the affective processes, like anger, anxiety, desire, attachment, and aggression, result from teachers' attempts, in vain, to resolve dilemmas. Moreover, our analysis of these dilemmas (which we have termed 'knots') shows that they can be understood in terms of consciousness mis-applying the TOTE model (Miller et al 1960).

Research on teachers' affects

Most of the research on teachers' affects has focused on concerns and anxieties (see

161

Kearney and Sinclair 1978), and this aspect of teachers' affect has attracted increasing attention over recent years. Coates and Thoresen (1976), in an overview of studies dating back to the 1930s, present evidence that between 33 per cent (Peck 1933), 37.5 per cent (National Educational Association 1939) and 78 per cent (National Educational Association 1967) of teachers studied were working under considerable or at least moderate strain and tension. It has been claimed that single female teachers seem to suffer more anxiety than married females (Powell and Ferraro 1960) and that black student teachers are initially more anxious than white student teachers (Carter 1970).

More recent studies by Möbius (1972) in East Germany and Raether (1982) in West Berlin report similar findings. Weidenmann (1978), Brück (1978) and Winkel (1979), based on case studies, come to the same conclusions: teachers are under considerable stress. Though there is conflicting evidence as to whether or not this stress is greater for teachers than for other professional groups, most studies agree that stress is a significant factor of everyday school life.

Teachers can also experience more positive affects, for example identification, desire and attachments. Jackson (1968), for instance, in his study of primary school teachers, noted 'the intensity of the teacher's emotional investment in her work' and 'the signs of emotional ties to her students and other aspects of her environment' (p. 147). However, there has been little systematic research on the significance of these features of teaching.

SELF-IMPERATED CONFLICTS IN TEACHERS' THINKING: THE 'KNOT' MODEL

Anxiety, anger, and stress, as well as attachment, desire, and identification, can be viewed as having one factor in common—they imply an imperative demand that something '*must*' or '*must not*' occur. Cognitions that have acquired this character of a subjectively felt '*must*' or '*must not*' we term self-imperated cognitions. The *perceived violation* of self-imperated cognitions gives rise to the affective conflicts that we have termed 'self-imperated conflicts' or 'knots'.

Theoretical background of the 'knot' model

In our research on teachers' knots, we have been influenced by a variety of theories in cognitive psychology, clinical psychology, and psychotherapy. Most notable of these are double bind theories (Bateson 1973; Watzlawick et al 1974), studies on paradoxes (Hofstädter 1979), action theory (Miller et al 1960), rational-emotive therapy (Ellis, 1978), cognitive behaviour therapy (Mahoney 1974; Lazarus 1968; Meichenbaum 1977), psychoanalytic theories of defence mechanisms (Freud 1964), and on client-centred views of the fully self-actualized person and the process of focusing

(Gendlin 1981), as well as literature concerning fragmentation, wholeness and the 'I' (Bohm 1980).

Empirical basis of the 'knot' model

The basis for developing the theoretical model presented below was our study of what teachers and students were thinking about during class, carried out at the Paedagogische Hochschule in Reutlingen. This study involved seven sixth-grade classrooms. The teachers and their students were first interviewed in depth on their subjective views of school life. Then two lessons in each classroom were videotaped; and afterwards the videotapes were presented to the teacher and the students separately, who were asked to recall what 'had been going through their minds during class'. Finally, these extended interviews were analysed sentence-by-sentence to ascertain the underlying structure of conflicting thought processes.

Analysis and types of 'knots'

Everyday examples of 'knots'

In teachers' stimulated recall protocols, they frequently voiced conflicts like these:

> For heaven's sake—I forgot, again, to check the students' homework. I really *should* have done that, but I forgot! I never like to do it, anyway, it seems such a waste of time—and yet, I really *ought* to remember!

> Our principal *ought* to realize that he cannot talk to us like that—as if we were little children; he *must* learn to treat us like adults.

> Tomorrow's lesson *must* not be as chaotic as today's, but I am afraid it will be!

> I *must* call upon all students who wish to speak up and I also *must* finish this lesson on time and there is no way of doing both right now!

> That darned projector is out of order again—it really *should* work after it has been repaired twice!

Mrs A, one of the teachers interviewed, said:

> It always makes me so angry that I don't make such a presentation more lively and exciting; one could make this much more interesting, and I always talk so boringly and always in the same flat tone of voice, it's just horrible. ... Sometimes I think I am going to train myself and practice being more stimulating. I have seen very active teachers who do this really well but I would feel like a complete fool doing this. I would feel like a phoney!

Characteristic symptoms of being caught in a 'knot'

In taking a closer look at this type of conflict, most or all of the following characteristics can usually be found:

- *Thinking goes around in circles without finding a solution*, at least as long as the situation as it is perceived does not change.

Mrs A, the teacher cited above who was angry about her 'boring' way of lecturing to the class, actually spent quite some time ruminating about this problem. Her interview ran along the following lines.

> 'I was boring ... I must not be boring ... but I was boring ... but I must not be ...', etc.

Mrs A subjectively feels that there is no way out of her dilemma: either she remains a boring lecturer—which is awful in her eyes—or she becomes 'a phoney'—which is equally awful.

- *Tension is being created*, the tension of an unresolved conflict in consciousness. This tension often shows up in the way the teachers talk and behave.
- *The tension is usually experienced as either anger, anxiety, hurt, aggression or depression.* In our example, Mrs A said of herself: 'This always makes me so angry.'
- *This tension influences outward behaviour, which becomes more tense, hurried, and rigid.* The videotape showed Mrs A in lecturing to be less relaxed and less spontaneous than usual; she ignored one or two attempts by students to speak up, and her gestures indicated nervousness.
- *The more the individual tries to resist this inner conflict, the worse it gets.* These conflicts often develop a dynamic of their own. In trying to get rid of them, the teacher experiences the conflict to increase and tension to mount; it feels as if it is 'getting worse and worse'.
- *The individual feels the conflict to be unresolvable.*
- *The conflict actually cannot be resolved*, at least as long as the situation—as it is perceived—remains unchanged and as long as the teacher keeps thinking along the same lines.

Some of these conflicts are quite short-lived because the perceived situation changes within a few minutes; for example, students who were acting up ('he *must* not do that') often do calm down again after a while. Other conflicts can last for years; for example, the anger and hurt of one of our teachers who felt herself to have been treated unjustly by her principal who once reported her to the superintendent's office; she kept repeating to herself: 'he did that to me—he *should not* have done that!'

Analysis of 'knots'

First of all, it seems important to distinguish between the perception of what actually happened in a situation and the reaction of consciousness to it. Of course, everyday school life is full of hazards: principals do sometimes treat teachers unfairly, students do act up in class, projectors break down, and teachers forget to check their students' homework. These external events may then give rise to affective responses. However, strictly speaking these events are not the *cause* of these feelings, as cognitive behaviour therapists have pointed out (e.g. Ellis 1978): the immediate cause of the internal conflict is the way consciousness reacts to its perception of the situation-at-hand.

Oversimplifying it a little, consciousness can deal with external events by

(a) either simply *perceiving* them *as they are*[1] in their complexity, including what it itself has set up as the wished-for state of affairs,
(b) or demanding (or imperating) that things *should* be in a certain way and by refusing to acknowledge that they may be different from what they are *supposed* to be.

These two different ways of dealing with what is being perceived find their analogy in language, where we distinguish between:

- speaking in the **indicative** mode, i.e. 'stating a thing as a fact, not as conception, wish, command etc. of speaker' (The Concise Oxford Dictionary, 1976).
- speaking in the **imperative** mode, i.e. 'expressing command…, request or exhortation; demanding obedience; that must be done or performed; urgent; of the nature of a duty; obligatory.'

This distinction can also be applied to the way teachers deal internally with what they would like to happen. The wished-for state of affairs can either, in the indicative mode, simply be stated, for example, 'I would prefer to be able to give more exciting lectures'. Or it can become an imperative demand, something consciousness imperatively demands of itself, for example, 'I really *must* become able to give more exciting lectures!'.

In both modes, the surface information is the same: a wished-for state of affairs, i.e. 'being able to give more exciting lectures'. However, in the first example, this is simply stated as such. In the second example, the command 'I really *must*…!' carries the implicit assumption that the desired outcome *must* be attained, that somehow it is forbidden *not* to become an exciting lecturer.

The consequences of these two different modes become most readily apparent when the teacher goes on giving boring lectures. If she remains in the indicative mode, then she will probably realize that again her lecturing was not as exciting as she wanted it to be, and this will leave her free to enquire why this happened. If, on the other hand, she imperatively demands of herself, 'I *must* not be boring!', then she will probably react to this new event with anger or anxiety.

Six types of self-imperated conflicts or 'knots'

Basically, 'knots' arise from self-imperated cognitions being in conflict with *something else*. What this something else is can vary considerably. During the course of our research study, we have come to distinguish six different types of 'knots'. These are not mutually exclusive, however; any 'knot' can be a combination of two or more of these basic types.

Type I: Reality knot. The most simple type of knot arises when self-imperated cognitions are in conflict with perceived current events.

> *For example*: A teacher keeps thinking 'Johnny *must* sit down and be quiet' while Johnny stands up and runs through the classroom.

These knots usually get resolved fairly easily because the external situation is changing continually, e.g. Johnny does sit down after a while.

Type II: Past events knot. The second type of conflict arises when the memory of past events collides with self-imperated cognitions.

> *For example*: 'That student was rude to me yesterday. He *should* not have been!'

Since past events usually cannot be changed anymore, this knot is more difficult to resolve.
Nietzsche (1910) describes one 'solution' of a past events knot quite aptly:

> '"I have done that," my memory says. "I *cannot* have done that," says my pride and remains merciless. Finally my memory gives in.'

Type III: Anticipation knot. Just as memories of past events can collide with self-imperated cognitions, so can images about what the future may bring. Since there are few limits to imagination, the possible number of Type III knots is quite large. Teachers can worry about everything and anything in life.

> *For example*: 'It may happen that my colleagues will think little of me—that *must* never happen!'

Type IV: Imperative dilemma knot. This type of knot implies two self-imperated cognitions that, in a given situation, are in conflict with each other. The example of Mrs A at the beginning of this chapter was of this type. Her two imperatives 'I *must* not speak boringly' and 'I *must* not become phoney' were in conflict with each other. In her view, either she kept on 'being boring' or she would have to become a 'phoney', so there was no way out.

Type V: Counter-imperative dilemma knot. Taking it a step further, sometimes teachers self-imperate two opposing things, for instance:

> 'I *must* not be afraid of this coming exam'

> 'I *must* be afraid of this coming exam or else I will not study for it.'

These two self-imperated thoughts flatly contradict each other in every situation; there is no way somebody can be at the same time both afraid and not-afraid.

Type VI: Paradoxical imperatives. Some self-imperated cognitions cannot be obeyed under any circumstances precisely *because* consciousness imperates itself to do something. For instance, in a tense situation, a teacher may imperate herself, 'Now I *must* act completely spontaneously.' However, the very moment she imperatively demands spontaneity of herself, she cannot act spontaneously anymore.

Bateson (1973) and Watzlawick et al (1974) have studied these paradoxes in human interaction in great detail, calling them 'double binds'. In their analysis, such double binds usually involve two people. However, individuals can also put themselves into such a double bind by imperatively demanding something of themselves that becomes impossible precisely because they are imperating themselves to do it.

Phenomenological aspects of self-imperated cognitions

On a **cognitive** level, self-imperated cognitions are thoughts equivalent to statements with an exclamation mark, e.g. 'I *must* ...!', 'It *must not* happen that ...!' 'They really *must* ...!' or 'One *ought* to ...!'.

On an **emotional** level, self-imperated cognitions are coupled with a sense of urgency, of distress, of frustration, of fright 'lest Y happens' or of desire 'lest Y does not happen'.

On a **connotative** level, self-imperated cognitions are commands of consciousness addressed to itself or to others. One might compare this to the orders that authoritarian teachers give to their students: in voicing them, they clearly imply that the students *must* obey them. Even if in everyday life the self-imposed injunctions are blocked by opposite injunctions—e.g. 'I *must* prepare my lessons thoroughly!' and 'I *must* not work myself into the ground!' – the quality of this being a self-imposed injunction usually persists (possibly resulting in feelings of guilt).

Sometimes there can be a chain of such self-imperated cognitions; for example, 'I *must* be able to solve this problem' because 'I *must* always do the right thing', because 'if I don't do the right thing, I am a failure, and I *must* not be a failure', because 'if I am a failure, life may not be worth living and life *must* be worth living'. Even though teachers are not usually very aware of such a chain of self-imperated cognitions, they often act 'as if their life depended upon it' and get quite agitated if something happens that they perceive as a violation of their self-imperated cognition.

At the level of **action**, self-imperated cognitions result in characteristic ways of behaviour: behaviour tends to become inflexible, strained, uncreative and rather rigidly fixed upon the present goal.

On the **content** level, self-imperated cognitions may contain socially undesirable behaviours as well as idiosyncratic ones. At the same time, it is possible to take social norms into consideration and to act in accordance with them without imperating oneself that one *must* do that. For instance, it is quite possible to perceive that it is customary to give homework to students without continually imperating oneself 'I *must* give the students homework!'.

A formal model of self-imperated conflicts

In order to clarify what has been said so far about consciousness dealing with externally perceived events in the imperative mode, we will take a look first at the TOTE

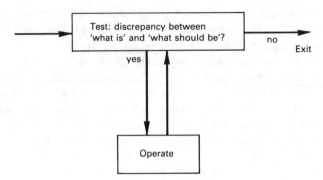

Figure 7.1 *Model of information processing and reacting in the indicative mode (TOTE model; see Miller et al 1960).*

(test–operate–test–exit) model by Miller et al (1960), which depicts dealing with events in the indicative mode (see Figure 7.1). According to this model, when we perceive a difference between 'what is' and 'what should be' we act to attempt to reduce the discrepancy, monitoring whether our actions are effective. Figure 7.2 shows the model of consciousness dealing with external events in the imperative mode. The models differ from each other in terms of the **reaction** of consciousness to what is already part of itself, the perception of a difference between what is and what should be.

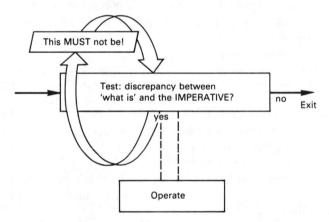

Figure 7.2 *Model of information processing and reacting in the imperative mode.*

A '**knot**' arises in consciousness if a discrepancy is detected between 'what is' and 'what *must* be', with consciousness reacting to this with the self-imposed injunction 'this discrepancy *must* not exist'. Because the discrepancy is already there, as part of consciousness itself, thinking does indeed go around in circles without finding an exit—as long as the perceived situation does not change, and as long as consciousness keeps imperating itself that this discrepancy *must* not be. Hence, tension arises, with thinking quite futilely attempting to solve a problem it has created itself by continuing to imperate itself that 'This *must* not be!' (see Figure 7.3).

If one tries to talk teachers out of self-imperating one often finds them quite resistant to change. A typical answer is, 'Well, but still it would feel awful, if …'. The underlying

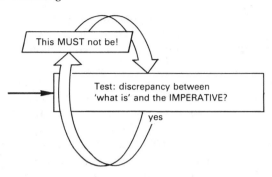

Figure 7.3 *Model of a 'knot'.*

sense of 'awfulness', of 'catastrophizing' as Ellis (1978) calls it, is closely associated with the cognition of 'what is to be avoided'. In counselling, this feeling of 'awfulness' often unravels as a bodily felt sense of 'something terrible' happening—some ingrained experience which has become linked with certain cognitive contents, often associated with images or fantasies, for instance of being isolated, endangered, or violently destroyed. So, in the final analysis, it appears that, in the process of self-imperating, consciousness is trying to get rid of this feeling of awfulness without being able to—because it is already part of itself. In doing this, consciousness falsely assumes that 'I' is something basically different from and unrelated to 'that', i.e. the bodily felt sense of 'something terrible' (panic, anger, hurt). As long as the process of self-imperating continues, these self-imperated cognitions will collide with others and with each other.

THE RESEARCH STUDY: METHODS AND RESULTS

Seven teachers (five female, two male) and 52 students (26 male and 26 female) from seven different sixth-grade classrooms participated in the study. The median age of the students was 13 years; the teachers were between 24 and 29 years of age.

In each class, the teacher and eight students (four high achievers, four low achievers) were first interviewed in depth about their experiences in school. These interviews were carried out in an exploratory, client-centred manner in order to facilitate openness and trust between interviewer and interviewees. Then, on two different days, a 35-minute classroom period was videotaped. Later the same day, this videotape was replayed to the teacher and the students, separately, and they were asked to recall 'what had been going through their mind' at that point in class. The videotape was stopped at intervals of about 40 seconds.

Tapes of the in-depth interviews and of the 'retrospectively thinking aloud' sessions, as well as of the actual classroom periods, were then transcribed, resulting in several hundred pages of protocols. In a first analysis three different lessons were chosen for examination, resulting in three different accounts of classroom periods tracing the inter-relationships between students' and teachers' thinking, perception, and action.

Then, based on the theoretical model presented above, a systematic and detailed qualitative method of analysing the interview protocols sentence by sentence was developed. Each sentence was analysed according to the following six steps:

1. *Identifying 'thematically coherent sequences of cognitions' (TCSs)*. Each protocol was first divided into subsets of several sentences each. The criterion for subdividing the interview protocols (including those arising from stimulated recall) was the subject talking consecutively about the same topic. A change in the topic, therefore, meant the beginning of a new TCS. Overall, about 4,500 of such TCSs were identified; typically they comprised between one and ten sentences.
2. *Coding the topic of each TCS*. In order to find out what topics were addressed by the teachers and the students, each TCS was coded according to a list of 100 possible items.
3. *Categorizing each sentence*. Based on the knot model presented above, a detailed category system has been developed that allowed each sentence to be assigned to one of the following major categories: 'goals', 'test criterion', 'self-imperated cognition', 'operate', 'subjective theory'.
4. *Reconstructing the cognitive structure of each TCS*. For each TCS, a structural diagram was developed depicting the inter-relationships of goals, subjective theories and assumptions, self-imperated cognitions and 'operates'. This structural diagram made it possible to diagnose whether or not a conflict arising from the perceived violation of self-imperated cognitions was implied.
5. *Categorizing the type of knot*. The self-imperated conflicts were then coded as to their type (see above).
6. *Analysing the cognitive strategy employed in attempting to resolve the 'knot'*. Finally, whenever a knot appeared, the subject's attempts to 'resolve' these knots were categorized. A separate category system was developed and used for this purpose (see below).

Results

Frequency of knots in teachers' thinking

Knots appeared in just about every third interview segment (TCS). In 32.1 per cent of the TCSs analysed, there were indications that teachers' thinking had been caught in self-imperated conflicts. These conflicts were significantly more frequent in the in-depth interviews carried out at the beginning of the study than in the stimulated recall protocols (35 per cent as compared to 28 per cent). Since self-imperated conflicts are unresolved conflicts arising from the perceived violation of self-imperated cognitions, it might be expected that teachers verbalize these conflicts more often when they are interviewed in depth about what classroom life means to them than when they are expected to 'retrospectively think aloud' to actual classroom events.

Frequency of different types of knots

The most frequent types of knots were reality and past events knots (for practical purposes, the two categories were combined): 61 per cent of knots in the interviews and 47 per cent of knots during stimulated recall were of this kind. (Students had an even higher percentage of this kind of 'knot': 81 per cent and 69 per cent respectively.) The second most frequent type were anticipation knots: 21 per cent of all knots during the interview and 32 per cent of the knots during stimulated recall came from teachers anticipating possible violations of their self-imperated cognitions for the future. Finally, 18 per cent (interview) and 21 per cent (stimulated recall) of the knots encountered were of the imperative dilemma type. (See Table 7.1.)

Table 7.1 *Distribution of different types of 'knots' in stimulated recall and in-depth interview: students and teachers*

Type of self-imperated conflict	Teachers		Students	
	In-depth interview	*Stimulated recall*	*In-depth interview*	*Stimulated recall*
Reality and past events	61%	47%	81%	69%
Imperative dilemmas	18%	21%	11%	4%
Anticipation	21%	32%	8%	27%

Note: Paradoxical imperatives were so infrequent that they were excluded from analysis.

This means that just about one-fifth of the knots were of the most difficult type: self-imperated cognitions conflicting with each other in the teacher's mind. Incidentally, this is one of the major differences between students and teachers. Teachers' thinking got 'snarled' in these kinds of self-imperated dilemmas much more frequently than did students' thinking. One possible explanation for this result may be that teachers, during their professional training, have internalized many more 'professional' self-imperated cognitions than students. Some of the implications of this finding for teacher training are discussed later.

Content of teachers' knots

For the analysis of the concerns that teachers' thinking is most likely to get into knots about only the results of the stimulated recall data were included, since during the in-depth interviews teachers were asked to respond to a number of issues raised by the interviewer, and these data might not reflect teachers' 'normal' thinking. There were 62 issues that teachers talked about at least 12 times or more. Four contained significantly more knots than the others.

The most 'knotty' issues were:

'fellow teachers' (83%)
'principal' (81%)
'giving permission vs. forbidding students to do certain things' (70%).
'students paying attention vs. being absent-minded or distracted' (65%)

This appears to be a most surprising result. The teachers, who were selected for this study because, among other things, they practised a student-centred approach to teaching, worried most about their colleagues and the principal. This seems to indicate an area of teacher concerns that so far has been rather neglected in teacher training, i.e. the way they get along (or do not get along) with the school institution, their fellow teachers, and the principal. Second in line to this were concerns about students paying attention and about what they may allow their students to get away with and where they feel they have to put their foot down.

At the opposite end of the scale, there is only *one* issue teachers' thinking gets significantly less frequently 'knotted' about than others: the subject matter of their teaching—an area in which apparently those teachers felt fairly competent.

Cognitive strategies employed by teachers in attempting to 'resolve' knots

There are various ways teachers can attempt to solve their own knots, i.e. reduce the tension involved. As Uttendorfer-Marek (1984) shows, one can distinguish twelve different ways of circumventing such a knot in one's own mind:

- complaining about it (teachers: 17.9%; students: 41.0%)
- strengthening the self-imperated cognition (e.g. 'Well, it simply *must* be that …'—teachers: 2.9%; students: 2.6%)
- doing something to change the situation or at least think about what one might do (teachers: 15.9%; students: 5.7%)
- thinking up a new self-imperated cognition (e.g. 'well, that means that in the future I really *must* do …!'—teachers: 17.4%; students: 10.9%)
- resigning themselves (e.g. 'Well, I guess nothing can be done about that'—teachers: 4.3%; students: 5.5%)
- expressing their feelings of being hurt, angry, frustrated, bewildered (teachers: 9.7%; students: 11.0%)
- believing in a 'deus ex machina' (e.g. 'Well, finally it did turn out alright'—teachers: 9.2%; students 3.5%)
- formulating subjective theories explaining away the knot (teachers: 11.6%; students: 11.0%)
- evading by fantasizing ('What might happen if …'—teachers: 5.3%; students 7.7%)
- setting up an internal hierarchy of self-imperated cognitions (teachers: 5.8%; students, 1.1%).

So, teachers most frequently react to their knots by

- complaining
- thinking up a new self-imperated cognition
- thinking about what they might do
- theorizing the knot away.

A closer analysis showed that teachers appear to have individual preferences in dealing with knots; one of the teachers studied, for instance, quite often built up new 'subjective theories', whereas others preferred to complain or else to think up new strategies in order to avoid future self-imperated conflicts.

Relationship of self-imperated conflicts to actual teaching behaviour

Finally, the effects of teachers' knots on actual teaching behaviour were studied. Due to the small sample of teachers and lessons involved in the study, only tentative generalizations could be made.

The most striking finding was that those teachers who praised students most frequently tended to have more anticipation knots. It is possible that these teachers praised students not because of a genuine appreciation of what the students did but rather because they wanted to avoid the violation of their self-imperated cognitions in the future.

Another interesting finding was that teachers apparently had their own habitual way of reacting to self-imperated conflicts. For instance, one of the teachers studied usually reacted by becoming quite authoritarian; she either directed students to do X or Y or she resorted to asking narrowly framed questions. Another teacher, who usually displayed a fairly open and communicative style, when caught in a 'knot' resorted to ignoring students' comments by simply passing on to the next student.

Teachers occasionally reacted quite paradoxically. Mrs A, who frequently complained about a certain student's rather lengthy and obscure answers, nevertheless reacted to this student by making things even more complicated: she seemed to be driven to 'enlarge' upon this student's comments, thereby increasing the very confusion she complained about.

Summary of results

The major results of the present study were:

- teachers' thinking gets snarled in a 'knot' quite frequently; in about one-third of the interview segments studied there were indications of self-imperated conflicts;
- these unresolved conflicts were more frequent when teachers were interviewed about their experiences in teaching than when they were recalling what 'had been going through their mind' during class;
- the 'knottiest' problems for teachers were their colleagues and the principal followed by student attention and discipline; the least 'knotty' issue was the subject matter of the lesson;
- teachers experience imperative dilemma knots significantly more often than do students;
- these knots seem to affect their actual classroom behaviour by making it more stereotypical and less adequate to the situation-at-hand;
- teachers often react to knots by complaining, setting up new self-imperated cognitions, thinking up a new 'operate', or inventing new subjective theories—not, however, by stopping the process of self-imperating.

THE ENDING OF SELF-IMPERATED CONFLICTS

First, the question arises whether it is advisable for teachers to end self-imperated conflict at all. Some teacher educators have expressed concern that ending self-imperated conflicts may lead to teachers happily and complacently going on doing what they are not supposed to do—for instance, giving boring lectures, being late for class, or demurely accepting unfair treatment by their superiors. It is in such cases that teacher educators often resort to instilling self-imperated cognitions hoping that the unwanted behaviour will thus be changed. What they do, in fact, is to attempt to superimpose a new imperative cognition (e.g. 'You *must not ...*!') on top of an old, already present self-imperated conflict. However, this does *not* lead to the ending of already present self-imperated conflicts; it just adds to the confusion. The hypothesis presented here is that resolving the underlying 'knot' would solve the problem in a much more satisfactory way.

Ways of resolving knots

Looking at the origin of knots, two basic approaches to their resolution present themselves:

(a) either something is done to remove whatever conflicts with the self-imperated cognition involved;
(b) or the teacher stops self-imperating that 'X *must* happen' or that 'Y *must* not occur'.

Teachers usually focus on the first approach by:

*   *changing the situation*, e.g. by shouting at students until they stop misbehaving, or
*   *redefining their appraisal of the situation*, e.g. 'J. is not really acting up, he simply wants some attention and that is O.K.', or
*   *changing the rules so that the self-imperated cognition does not apply any more to the situation*, e.g. 'Not having prepared this lesson well does not mean I am a poor teacher; actually, really good teachers keep an open mind and wait for what the students may bring up'.

These, however, are indirect methods of getting rid of specific knots—they do not prevent the teacher from becoming entangled in the same knot at some future time.

Cognitive behaviour therapists typically use a number of these methods of indirectly resolving 'knots'. One of the problems encountered in using such an approach in teacher training is that the teachers need to become actually convinced of this new point of view. However, quite often, a residual doubt lingers on in the teachers' minds: 'So what if most teachers don't prepare every lesson well—still, I was not perfect and it is awful if I don't do my best!'

The most radical way of ending self-imperated conflicts (radical in the word's original meaning, i.e. going to the root of it) is stopping the process of self-imperating itself.

Distinguishing between the objective difficulty and the subjective feeling of awfulness. In counselling, it is important to point out the distinction between the factual situation—for instance, 'Yes, it may be disadvantageous to be alone and defenceless'— and the subjectively associated feeling that such an event would be 'awful'. In attempting to facilitate the resolution of knots, it is helpful to ask the client to separate these two levels by first simply focusing on the feeling of 'awfulness' and to stop—for a while—looking for a practical solution to the problem (they usually do not find one anyway because of being caught in the 'knot').

Focusing on the feeling of 'awfulness'. Gendlin (1981) calls this process of seeing holistically the core of the catastrophic feeling 'focusing' and describes it in his book in much detail. As yet, science knows very little about the physiological and bio-chemical processes involved, but, as therapeutic experience shows, it does work. The process can be understood to be somewhat analogous to the process of arousal: any arousal that is not being blocked runs its normal course: it first increases until it reaches its peak and, then, gradually subsides and disappears. For a teacher to stop imperating herself that she *must* reach a certain point at the end of the lecture period simply means facing what it might mean if she does not reach that point. At that stage, teachers often just laugh and say 'Well, this would not be such a problem' and then begin to deal realistically with the situation at hand, often finding an unexpected creative solution for it.

Ceasing the process of self-imperating. So, in a sense, dissolving a knot simply means stopping what one has done so far, i.e. stopping the attempt to push away the feeling/thought of 'awfulness' associated with the cognitive content of the self-imperated cognition—in other words, simply to stop imperating oneself that *that* (awful thing) *must* never happen. Ceasing the process of self-imperating does *not* necessarily mean giving up the content of the self-imperated cognition.

Ending the process of self-imperating leads to effortless changes in behaviour. The quality of the change in behaviour is the most distinctive feature of what happens when a 'knot' is resolved. One student teacher, who sought counselling because she had a block against writing and typing lesson plans, afterwards reported that she now had not only written and typed two lesson plans but had actually enjoyed doing so. It was not a problem for her anymore—she just did it, effortlessly and with an inner sense of freedom and delight. This change spread into other areas of her life because now she felt more energy and enjoyed her student teaching experience much more than before.

THE IMPLICATIONS FOR TEACHER TRAINING

Even a rather superficial perusal of books on teacher education shows that these often abound in imperative exhortations of the teachers-to-be. 'A good teacher *must* be friendly, fair, kind, knowledgeable, warm, honest' etc., etc. And these imperatives are usually strengthened during teacher training, in theoretical discussions as well as during student teaching. Sometimes it seems as if we, as teacher educators, do our best to pile on more and more imperatives.

For instance, in communication skills training, we typically tell them, 'You *must* not be an authoritarian teacher'. This is frequently followed later on by another imperative, 'You, of course, *must* sometimes be directive', in order to make up for the unwanted side-effects of students taking the first imperative 'too seriously' and carrying it 'too far'. No wonder that the teachers in our study got caught in significantly more conflicting imperatives (imperative dilemma knots) than their students did. The implications of our research then would be that, in teacher education, we should provide much more opportunity for students to become aware of their own processes of self-imperating and should facilitate their ending them.

We have explored ways of actually facilitating this process in workshop-type seminars, where there was space for students to explore the issue of self-imperating as well as to face their own anger, anxiety, attachments, and desires bound up in it.

Facilitating the ending of the process of self-imperating requires more, however, than an occasional workshop or seminar. It requires an intellectual exploration into the causes and consequences of this process of self-imperating as an important aspect of educational psychology itself. Teachers not only do this to themselves, they also tend to induce imperative cognitions in their students. The debate and research on authoritarian teaching behaviour have pointed out many of the negative side-effects of such an approach to teaching. However, the experience during the last ten years of teacher education in Germany has amply shown that it does not suffice for teachers simply to imperate themselves 'not to be authoritarian!' The same holds true for most other innovations in education, whether they be 'open education', 'teaching competence', or whatever.

IMPLICATIONS FOR FURTHER RESEARCH ON TEACHERS' THINKING

Much of what has been discussed as shortcomings in the process of teachers' thinking—e.g. the tendency to over-generalize, to ignore certain facts, to refuse to follow up certain hypotheses—may in fact be the result of self-imperated conflicts. A teacher who is caught in a knot, may quite aptly develop a subjective 'theory' that 'proves' that his or her self-imperated cognition has not been violated at all (e.g. 'I *must* be competent'—'what I did *was* competent behaviour because of ...'). Our data show a high significant positive correlation between the frequency of self-imperated cognitions and the frequency of espousing subjective theories.

So, for future research it might be advisable to study the content of teachers' thinking *in connection with the function* these thought processes may have in the process of getting rid of self-imperated conflicts. Discovering the central self-imperated conflict underlying a particular belief structure may help considerably in understanding why the teacher stubbornly clings to this belief even in face of contradictory evidence. It may also provide a new way of analysing subjective theories and processes of decision-making, by tracing them back to their origin, possibly a core self-imperated cognition.

This is not to say, of course, that *all* of teachers' thinking originates in such knots; however, as our data suggest, quite a bit of it may have become snarled because of such a knot. And this leads to a second point of consideration for the further study of teachers' thinking: '*How much thinking is necessary for 'good' teaching?*'

Current research on teachers' thinking tends to imply that the more teachers think the better their teaching behaviour will be—provided, of course, that they are thinking the right kind of 'theories'. This, in itself, is a doubtful proposition because even the most rational thinking is inherently limited (see Bohm 1980). In any event, there is more to teaching than just 'thinking right'—most notably the ability to perceive, holistically and non-judgementally, what is actually going on in the classroom and 'within' the teacher's own mind.

Ending the process of self-imperating may free the mind of certain warped cognitions because it then becomes unnecessary to circumvent the self-imperated conflicts by thinking up certain 'theories'. Ending the process of self-imperating will therefore free the mind to perceive more clearly 'what is'. Having an 'empty mind'—as a result of having ended the process of self-imperating—may be a fascinating starting point for doing many things, including teaching.

NOTE

1. The term perception is used here rather loosely, neglecting for the moment that in fact perception itself is a rather complex process.

REFERENCES

Bateson, G. (1973) *Steps Towards an Ecology of Mind (Ökologie des Geistes)*. St. Albans, Herts: Paladin.

Bohm, D. (1980) *Die implizierte Ordnung. Grundlagen eines dynamischen Holismus*. Munich: Dianus-Trikont.

Bruck, H. (1978) *Die Angst des Lehrers vor seinen Schülern*. Reinbek: Rowohlt.

Carter, V. L. (1970) *Anxieties of White and Negro Elementary and Secondary Student Teachers in Biracial Participation*. Doctoral dissertation, North Texas State University.

Coates, T. J. and Thoresen, C. E. (1976) 'Teacher Anxiety: A Review with Recommendations'. *Review of Educational Research*, **46**(2), Spring, 156–84.

Concise Oxford Dictionary of Current English (1976), 6th edition, Oxford: Clarendon Press.

Ellis, A. (1978) *Die rational-emotive Therapie*. Munich: Pfeiffer.

Freud, A. (1964) *Das Ich und die Abwehrmechanismen*. Frankfurt: Fischer Taschenbuch.

Gendlin, E. T. (1981) *Focusing*. Salzburg: Otto Müller Verlag.

Hofstädter, D. (1979) *Gödel, Escher, Bach*. Stuttgart: Klett-Cotta.

Jackson, P. W. (1968) *Life in Classrooms*. New York: Holt, Rinehart and Winston.

Kearney, G. and Sinclair, K. E. (1978) 'Teacher Concerns and Teacher Anxiety: A Neglected Topic of Classroom Research'. *Educational Research*, **48**(2), Spring, 273–90.

Lazarus, R. S. (1968) 'Emotions and Adaption: Conceptual and Empirical Relations'. In Arnold, W. J. (ed.) *Nebraska Symposium on Motivation*. University of Nebraska.

Mahoney, M. J. (1974) *Kognitive Verhaltenstherapie*. Munich: Pfeiffer.

Meichenbaum, D. (1977) *Kognitive Verhaltensmodifikation*. Munich: Urban und Schwarzenberg.

Miller, G. A., Galanter, E., and Pribram, K. H. (1960) *Plans and the Structure of Behavior.* New York: Holt, Rinehart & Winston.

Möbius, E. (1972) *Erfassung der Persönlichkeitsdimension. Extraversion, Introversion, Neurotische Tendenz sowie der vegetatischen Labilität bei Lehrern unter dem Aspekt neurosebegünstigender Einflüsse.* Unpublished dissertation, Leipzig.

National Educational Association (1939) 'The Teacher Looks at Teacher Load'. *NEA Research Bulletin,* 17(5).

National Educational Association (1967) The American Public School Teacher, 1965–66'. *NEA Research Reports,* R4, 3–57.

Nietzsche, F. (1910) *Jenseits von Gut und Böse.* Frankfurt: Insel Verlag.

Peck, L. (1933) 'A Study of the Adjustment Difficulties of a Group of Women Teachers'. *Journal of Educational Psychology,* 27, 401–16.

Powell, M. and Ferraro, C. O. (1960) 'Sources of Tension in Married and Single Women Teachers of Different Ages'. *Journal of Educational Psychology,* 51, 92–101.

Raether, W. (1982) *Das unbekannte Phänomen Lehrerangst. Vielfältige Ursachen – weitreichende Folgen.* Vienna: Herderverlag.

Uttendorfer-Marek, I. (1984) 'Kopitel 7'. In Wagner, A. C., Barz, M., Maier-Stormer, S., Uttendorfer-Marek, I., and Weidle, R. *Bewusstseinskonflicte im Schulalltag.* Weinheim, Basle: Beltz.

Watzlawick, P., Beavin, J. H., and Fisch, R. (1974) *Lösungen. Zur Theorie und Praxis menschlichen Handelns.* Bern: Hans Huber Verlag.

Weidenmann, B. (1978) *Lehrerangst.* Reinbek: Rowohlt.

Winkel, R. (1979) *Angst in der Schule – Ursachen, Erscheinungen und Bewaltigungs-möglichkeiten Schulischer und Sozialer Angste.* Essen: Neue Deutsche Schule Verlag.

8

CURRICULUM CHANGE AND THE CLASSROOM ORDER

John K. Olson and Sandra Eaton

Current approaches to school reform emphasize a closer coupling of curriculum plans and teacher behavior, but ignore dilemmas inherent in teaching which may place limits on efforts to manage teacher behavior. In this chapter we argue for reform through greater teacher awareness of the nature of their practice and the dilemmas they face in dealing with the diffuse demands of teaching. We argue for a close analysis of how teachers construe the classroom order as a basis for curriculum change and school reform.

Much of the literature on school change reflects a **systems approach** in which practice itself is controlled through 'scientific' methods, an approach Schon (1983) calls technical rationality. The teacher is seen as somehow deficient in relation to a more rational 'go ahead' system. The problem with this view of teachers is that it renders them less rational and scientific than the system, even though there is no apparent reason why the system should be taken as rational and the teacher not. Perhaps innovators in the system have good ideas; perhaps teachers do. The matter cannot be settled by simply assuming that the system's plans make more sense than those of teachers.

Change proposals after all are shifts in orientation—new sets of unclear meanings whose implications take time to emerge. Typifying teachers' reaction to innovation as lack of awareness of or resistance to change ignores the fact that teachers operate well-functioning routines which for them may solve many difficult problems and fails to appreciate the slow process of working out the implications of new visions of schooling. The systems approach underestimates the problems inherent in this process and overestimates the system's capacities to convey unambiguous messages down the line. Perhaps the major problem is that the systems approach tends to ignore the reasons why the present classroom order exists.

The other dominant conception of change—the **ecological**—takes into account the complex conditions in which teachers work. It is based on the idea that, if one properly appreciates the complex social/technical situation of the teacher's practice, one will be in a position to make good policies for change. The fullest expression of this view can be found in Lortie's classic *Schoolteacher* (1975), in Dreeben's *The Nature of Teaching* (1970), and in the work of others influenced by them.

In this conception the teachers' work world is considered to be special. There is a low degree of volunteerism in the teacher–student relationship; there are difficulties in extracting work from immature workers; and teacher endeavors are often in a group context. Dreeben, in his analysis of the technical priorities of the teacher's work, stresses the social dimensions of that work and the special problems faced when dealing with large numbers of children.

It may be the case, indeed we think it is, that teaching is much more complex and sophisticated than Lortie's analysis might suggest. To find out more about teacher practice and its rationale the researcher would have to talk to teachers and watch their teaching, and do this for some considerable time. Ecologists have tended not to do this and have, we think, underestimated the technical capacity of teachers by assessing practice against idealizations of the classroom order based on sociology and psychology, rather than probing the practical knowledge built into what teachers know how to do. Again technical rationality is the governing assumption.

There is another way of looking at change, which we call the **reflexive** conception, whose fundamental idea is that the way the teachers order their classrooms reflects a reasonable and considered accommodation to the circumstances in which they find themselves. Teacher behavior thus reflects how they accommodate conflicting demands and resolve *dilemmas* inherent in their work (Olson 1980). This is the central point. These dilemmas are manifold and complex, their resolution is sophisticated, and what teachers do cannot be explained adequately by looking for causes in their environment or at the plans of the system. Teachers themselves make plans based on their assessments of their working environment and the problems it poses.

Research based on this conception of change would seek to describe the nature of teacher thinking—the nature of the structure of their thought as it is brought to bear in practice. Methods that ask teachers to reflect on their practice are important—for example, stimulated recall and repertory grid techniques.

School reform within the reflexive perspective can come about in two ways. First, teachers can understand better the knowledge and purposes built into the way they teach. The work of Schon (1983) with various groups of professionals, for example, is aimed at improving professional practice by asking professionals to analyse their beliefs using stimulated recall protocols. Related to this direct analysis of practice is another approach. Experience with new curricula and curriculum materials can be the basis of exploring the nature of one's practice. Curriculum projects can have the often unintended but beneficial effect of asking teachers to reflect upon their practice in a critical way, because, while the materials may have been set up to accomplish certain learning outcomes, working with the materials also affects the way teachers think about their work. We should study those effects of curriculum projects as well as student achievements.

It is the second approach we wish to pursue in this chapter through the close analysis of the work of a group of eight teachers who experimented with the use of microcomputers in their classrooms, and who explored new curriculum possibilities in two ways: the first group tried to define the nature of computers as a curriculum *subject*; and the second group explored the *impact* of computer-based learning on the subjects they were teaching. In both sets of cases it is through our analysis of the routines these teachers use to do their work and how they think about these routines that we have come to understand why they use computers as they do. These cases in turn serve to show how a reflexive conception of curriculum change can both help us understand the relationship between teacher thinking and change, and contribute to improved classroom practice that lies at the heart of school reform.

COMPUTERS AND THE CLASSROOM ORDER

In 1984 we began a 12-month research product, funded by the Ontario Ministry of Education (Olson, 1986), to investigate how teachers were using computers in the classroom. We wanted to understand not only *how* computers were being used but *why* they were being used in these ways. Although the eight case studies we compiled documented several seemingly different computer applications—creative writing, graphics, geographical simulations, remediation in elementary math and language arts, and elementary French—two very distinct patterns of computer use emerged: teaching computer awareness as a new school *subject*, and using the computer as an instructional *tool* to teach existing school subjects. We shall focus on the former here.

As we probed how and why these two distinct uses evolved, we began to understand the many factors which combined to influence the teachers' practice: what we can call their 'espoused theories' of computer use (Argyris and Schon 1974), that is, their theories about what they should be able to accomplish with the technology in the classroom; the contextual factors that influenced what actually happened in the classroom, such as limited training and expertise, limited resources, the expectations of students, school and parents, the absence of school board or Ministry of Education mandates and guidelines, and the rather unique process of innovation in which they were involved; the unanticipated consequences of introducing a new, untried element into existing, well-tried classroom routines; and their underlying concerns with regard to their classroom, their students, and their role as teacher.

Before we analyze these elements in greater depth, a brief word about the background and methodology of our study. The eight case-study schools included elementary, intermediate, and senior schools, all under the jurisdiction of the same metropolitan school board. The board had originally installed a single computer system (keyboard, monochrome and color monitors, disk drive and printer) in each of its schools and then, in 1982, it initiated a pilot project scheme in which teachers interested in having a classroom computer were invited to submit an application to the board, outlining specific objectives to be attained and specific evaluation procedures to judge the outcomes of the classroom computer experience. All of the schools we investigated had been awarded one or more additional computer systems (to a maximum of ten) under this pilot project scheme. The teachers' experience with computers ranged from absolute novice to night-school instructor at a nearby university, but all had one thing in common: they had deliberately sought the opportunity to incorporate computer use into their classroom practice.

Preliminary interviews with the schools' principals to ascertain the background to computer use in each school were followed by a series of interviews with the teachers concerned, in order to understand the factors which they perceived as influential in determining their classroom practice. Videotapes of their students using the computers, analyses of commonly occurring computer-related situations using Kelly's repertory grid technique, in which teachers were asked to categorize the situations and then construe their response (see Olson and Reid 1982), and a Computer Use Journal each teacher was asked to keep for a one-week period, all provided instances of actual classroom practice which became the basis for further analysis and discussion with the teachers.

Computers as subject

Computer awareness or, in the teachers' words, 'doing computers' had become a new, unofficial school subject on the timetables of teachers in four of the eight case-study schools. Of these four, three were elementary schools (grades kindergarten to five or six) and one was an intermediate or middle school (grades six to eight). Although there are no Ministry of Education guidelines for 'computers' as a subject below the grade nine level, these teachers had interpreted their school board's endorsement of computer innovation as a license to experiment with the technology, their timetable, their classroom routines, and the curriculum.

Despite the lack of local and provincial mandates and guidelines for the subject at these grade levels, there was remarkable consensus amongst these teachers as to what 'doing computers' meant. Built into the ways they described this new subject were notions about its purpose, its scope and sequence, ways in which the subject might be learned and/or taught. As a subject it already had its own, shared terminology.

These teachers considered 'computers' as a new school subject in its own right because of the social, cultural, and intellectual value they attributed to being able to use the technology. Living in a part of the country based largely on 'high tech' industry and in a social environment in which computers were increasingly in evidence, they felt that students should know about and be able to use computers. An additional justification for classroom computer activity, and one that was stressed in the early stages of our study but less so as the study progressed, was the enhancement of students' problem-solving capacities through computer use, although they were more than a little uncertain about exactly how this might be achieved.

Their goal was variously termed 'computer awareness' or 'computer literacy', which translated into practice as familiarity with simple computer terminology, knowledge of the parts of the computer and their functions, and the ability to use a variety of software without the teachers' aid. Simple programming, such as plotting graphics, selecting the required features of menu-driven utility programs, simple Basic and LOGO, was considered an advanced stage of 'awareness' but one that, as we shall later see, proved to be problematic.

Computer awareness is, then, essentially a set of skills, considered to be valuable in their own right. According to these teachers the only way to learn these skills is through hands-on experience—actual practice with a computer system and different types of software. This exposure to the machinery, software, and peripherals, such as joysticks, koala pads, mouses and modems, would, they felt, eradicate possible fear and increase students' 'comfort level' until they felt confident in their ability to use this technology.

A new technology with a new place on the timetable, the computer was also new in an instructional sense. Unlike other school subjects, this was one in which the teachers had had no professional training, regardless of how much they knew about or could use computers themselves; they generally had little experience and few resources on which to draw; learning about the computer required students to share access to a very costly and scarce tool, one which might, for many reasons, refuse to work. These 'newness' aspects of the innovation challenged existing classroom practices and the established relationship between teacher and students, and blurred traditional classroom roles. We found that it was these aspects of computer use, not the technological aspects, that concerned the teachers most.

Miss S, a grade three teacher in an elementary school, offers a specific but typical example of this kind of computer use—'doing computers' as a subject. Miss S had successfully applied to the school board for a computer pilot project in creative writing. There were always at least two computers in her room, one of which was her own. If she could book the school's Apple computers, there might be as many as four. The machines were positioned down the sides or at the back of her classroom. During the course of the day, while she was instructing the class in their regular lessons, individual students or pairs of students worked at the computer. The software was teacher-selected but was not usually related to the lesson Miss S was covering with the rest of the class at that time and might not be linked to the grade three curriculum. During the course of our study, for example, Miss S's class was working on low-resolution graphics on the Apple II computers. This activity was intended as an introduction to graphing: its purpose was to teach her students how to plot co-ordinates, although this is not part of the Ministry of Education's grade three math curriculum. The students each drew a picture on squared paper, plotted the co-ordinates and then, when their turn came to use the computer, entered these co-ordinates into the computer using the graphics program. In this way they gradually re-created their picture on the screen. Miss S estimated that the graphics project would take at least one term and, even then, there would be students who would not finish. Students working on the other computers did math and spelling tutorials or used 'Macpaint' to create symmetrical designs.

The computers were on all day, including recess, lunch break, before and after school, and access was determined by a rota: the students worked at the computer for a predetermined length of time, usually 20–40 minutes, and then, when their time was up, gave up their places to the next students on the rota. Although the rota scheme was designed to ensure equal access to the machines for all students, it was tied to the class punishment/reward system: students who misbehaved or who did not complete classwork forfeited their place on the rota. For Miss S, as for the other teachers, this presented a nagging contradiction: she felt that those students who performed poorly in class, for whatever reason, might reap the most benefit from an alternative form of instruction; on the other hand, the immense enjoyment students got from using the computers made curtailment of that privilege an effective and keenly felt punishment.

The main method by which students learned how to program the low-resolution graphics was through trial and error since Miss S felt that this would also develop their thinking skills, by encouraging them to 'problem solve'. Although she had initially gathered the students around a computer and demonstrated the program, and had subsequently taught 'mini-lessons' on the control commands that the majority of students had found difficult, the students were generally left to figure things out for themselves and help each other if necessary, while Miss S instructed the rest of the class.

We labeled this approach, which was common to all four of the computers-as-a-subject cases, the 'teach yourself' approach. This 'teach yourself' approach is not new to most classrooms. Its use in conjunction with computers can be seen as an extension of self-directed seatwork—individual student research projects, for example, where students work independently with library materials. We found its use with a new, complex technology surprising, however, until we understood the demands and difficulties associated with 'doing computers' as these teachers had defined it. As a new school subject at the elementary and intermediate levels, it is so new that there is no place for it on the timetable, already full with authorized, 'official' school subjects. This means that, if it is to run at all, it has to run as an independent but concurrent activity. For the case-study teachers, this meant trying to teach two things at once. Again, teaching two things at once is nothing new for most teachers—they frequently run multiple reading groups, for example—but the computer's newness, the scarcity of machines and the fact that there is usually little relationship between what is going on at the computer and in the class lesson, make it particularly problematic in this instance. The teachers cannot be in two places at once. If they are instructing the class in its regular lessons, they cannot be at the computer teaching computer awareness to individual or small groups of students.

Other factors that contributed to the 'teach yourself' approach to computers included the teachers' own experiences of having to teach themselves the ins and outs of particular programs using accompanying manuals or tutorials on disk, as well as their perception of their students as members of a new, computer-oriented generation predisposed to the technology: if the teachers could learn to use a piece of software or a program by themselves, they tended to assume that it would be a simple step for their students to do the same. This assumption was reinforced by the fact that there were students in each of the classes we investigated who were as adept at using the computer, if not more so, than the teacher. In fact, teachers relied on these computer 'whiz-kids' to assist other students in difficulty at the machine. If the teacher was busy with the class and a student needed assistance at the computer, then an already computer literate student could be called upon to troubleshoot and tutor, without interruption to the class lesson. The teachers even reported that these students tended to keep an eye on those using the computer(s) of their own accord and would slip over to the machines whenever they spotted someone in need of help.

The advantages of this 'teach yourself' approach in conjunction with peer tutoring were perceived by the teachers to be two-fold; they could attend to the class with little interruption, and those students adept at using the computer had an opportunity to shine in front of their peers. That these students were frequently those who rarely excelled in the more traditional classroom activities was an added bonus.

This 'teach yourself' approach had interesting implications for software selection. If students were to work independently, then software that provided maximum student engagement with minimum teacher support was required. In the teachers' words, it had to be 'idiot proof' and 'user friendly'. Given the rather loose definition of computer awareness, any software that met these criteria could be considered suitable, including drill and practice exercises, puzzles, utility programs, word-processing, and simple programming, such as LOGO.

In spite of their efforts to prepare students to use the computer independently—access rotas, friendly software, peer tutoring, 'teach yourself' by manual or trial and error—these teachers reported that classroom computer use was not working out as intended. They had no way of measuring the thinking skills that computer use supposedly developed; software was often time-consuming to locate and appraise, as was keeping up to date with new developments in the field; even simple programs required far more teacher support than they could easily provide in the situation; programming, and LOGO in particular, was not a self-sustaining activity; they were always pressed for time and found themselves caught between trying to teach the class and having to sort out problems at the computer.

Although software was chosen to run with the 'teach yourself' approach, students using the computer frequently required more help than anticipated. Miss S, for example, complained that students did not read instructions on the screen carefully enough and so required help which she had not anticipated they would need. Mr O, a grade eight English teacher in a French immersion program, complained that students did not always want or need to work through all the steps in a computer program, where the process might be broken down into many small component steps. If the students could not advance at their own pace they became frustrated; if the program did allow them to advance, they sometimes omitted necessary steps and were then not able to loop back to them. Both situations required his intervention.

All the teachers reported difficulty with utility programs and software which used the phrase 'syntax error' to indicate student error. The students did not know how to interpret this imprecise feedback and were reluctant to use available manuals to help.

As we explored the teachers' concerns further, we found that 'time' covered a number of other, more specific concerns related to the management of computer activity. Major concerns which emerged from the interview based on the repertory grid, and to which the teachers frequently returned in our discussions, included the problem of monitoring computer activity, and the ambiguity or uncertainty of computer-related situations.

Because the software was not as user friendly as had been hoped, monitoring students' computer activity became a problem. The teachers could not be in two places at once and, since they felt that their main responsibility was to the class, had to rely on the students at the computer to realize when they needed help and to seek it with minimum fuss. If the students could not help themselves, then one of three things might happen: the teacher might put the rest of the class 'on hold' to assist the student(s) at the computer, although they felt such interruption to be disruptive to the classroom atmosphere and the flow of the lesson; an already computer literate student might be called upon to peer tutor; or the student might be left to proceed alone with the program.

Our videotapes revealed, however, that things did not always work out as intended. Peer tutors were more likely to solve the problem themselves than instruct their peers, who remained none the wiser about their difficulties and just as likely to encounter the same problems again. Students did not always realize when they were proceeding incorrectly with a program, and neither did the teachers. Examples of this that we observed included a student who spent an hour incorrectly entering graphics co-ordinates before receiving corrective feedback from the teacher; another student who spent 40 minutes unsuccessfully trying to produce a picture of a dog on the screen by randomly guessing at the co-ordinates because she had left the graph-paper original at home; a student formatting a poem on the screen which she had previously planned on paper but not understanding the function of the return key to indicate the ends of lines, with the result that she did not understand why her print-out bore no resemblance to her original; a peer tutor who spent most of the morning wandering from computer to computer offering assistance when needed or merely watching, but not getting on with the seatwork she was supposed to be doing.

Apart from the practical, management aspects of monitoring, all the teachers reported uncertainty about the best way to proceed with computer-related interruptions, which they considered ambiguous. Instead of relying on the well-practiced, relatively automatic kinds of responses used with familiar classroom situations, they felt that they needed to clarify computer-related episodes before they could respond. Analysis of their repertory grids and the follow-up discussions revealed a number of common dimensions to their concern about these situations. They felt they needed to determine:

- whether the students could be left to resolve a situation or whether teacher intervention was required
- whether the problem was mechanical or student-centred
- whether the situation could be quickly resolved or would require extra time and effort
- whether or not existing classroom rules were adequate
- whether routine responses would suffice or whether complex judgements were required.

What we see in these four case studies are teachers attempting to cope with a modern, unfamiliar technology using familiar, well-tried routines and responses. But the unanticipated elements of the innovation, such as imprecise negative feedback and unpredictable student responses to the material, have meant that the well-tried methods have not always worked.

At issue is the teachers' sense of control in the classroom environment. They are defining for themselves the content and methodology of a new subject and their uncertainty is compounded by their own limited knowledge and experience, the uncertain status of the subject on the timetable, and the risks they are taking to experiment with an innovation which they, and presumably their school board, consider worth while. It is not surprising that, when things do not work out as smoothly as hoped, they are uncertain about how to proceed. In effect, their understanding of the classroom order has changed, with important consequences for their practice. We shall consider this process in the final part of the chapter.

INTERPRETING THE CASES: CHANGE AS A REFLEXIVE PROCESS

The teachers we have been considering experimented informally with new approaches to teaching. The key to their being able to do this was their access to a relatively scarce resource: a complete computer system. Moreover, they have been given access to expensive software, been supported in various ways by their school administration and resource people in pursuit of their own interests, and encouraged to evaluate and share the results of their explorations of microcomputers. The elements of a reflexive process to innovation are here.

Consider these features. The teachers are not required to 'implement' anything other than what they choose to do. It is they who have decided what they will do and what resources they need to do it. None have everything they want; each has a wish list but they all have the essential equipment to pursue their teaching ideas and their fascination with this new technology. They have all 'volunteered' to become involved in what has proven to be a time-consuming and at times frustrating process. Undoubtedly there are many factors that might explain why these teachers became involved in the first place, none of which would be unfamiliar: renewal; career; personal interests; curiosity; and so on. These reasons do not concern us here.

What does concern us are the lessons that can be learned from interpreting these cases. Clearly there can be only tentative conclusions but we hope ones worth testing further. In this section we will look at all of the cases taken together as examples of a reflexive approach to innovation that was intended to provide teachers with initial opportunities to test practice. We shall look at the experiences of these teachers in terms of the pitfalls and opportunities presented to them through their participation in this kind of innovation.

The positive side of the reflexive process of innovation is that one can pose problems relevant to one's situation. These teachers have explored images of how the computer might function in their classroom and although all expressed satisfaction with what they had accomplished they also spoke about not being able to carry out some of the things they had planned, and they felt that having to document their practice in the way they had been asked to do by the board was burdensome. On the other hand, they were left alone to get on with their projects with minimal interference. Some felt that they needed more support from the board but not necessarily in the form of directions about what to do (Lartner et al 1983).

These teachers discovered that there were aspects of what they had wanted to do that could not be done; the software did not exist, or there were not enough machines, or their own expertise was insufficient. By discovering these things, they were able to adjust their activities to what they could manage and test their ideas within a realistic framework. As Miss S said, 'How else can ideas be tested except in the realistic context of the school?'

In talking to these teachers it became clear that they had used their experiences of innovative activity to begin to reflect critically on their practice—to ask questions both about what they normally do and what they were trying to do that was new. After all, they had chosen to alter aspects of their practice, and they had a vested interest in considering carefully what their experience meant for that practice. There are ample examples in these cases to illustrate this outcome of reflexive innovation.

We do think, however, that this process could become more powerful. We found that teachers did not push their critical scrutiny of practice as far as they might have in pursuing the lessons of their experience (see also Bostrom 1982). This process depends on what manner of framework one can bring to the analysis of practice and, of course, it is unrealistic to expect teachers to be able to step back from practice easily; yet if this could be done, the benefits of grassroots innovation could be substantially increased.

Idealization of practice is a constant danger for the reflexive process. The teacher has a vested interest in having things come out well and the temptation to think wishfully about practice is strong. In a job with so many uncertainties, it would be surprising if teachers did not engage in such thinking. We suspect that the constant association of computer activity with the development of problem-solving skill is a form of wishful thinking, but we also think that researchers like us who ask too many questions are going to be managed by our respondents with references to things like problem solving.

Given the effort they have invested in computers, there are lessons to be learned from their experience that would repay teachers' attempts to discover them. Such attempts might form part of an in-service education agenda. For example, those who favor computers as a subject may be overestimating their cultural and social significance and underestimating problems of the whole curriculum at the elementary level, or again they may not—curriculum issues abound here. These points need to be studied. Those who favor computers as a teaching aid are faced with questions about the usefulness of the computer as a teaching aid in comparison with other ways of achieving the same objectives. It is wishful to think that computers by themselves can create improved instructional contexts. Given pedagogical reform that many think is needed to increase the intellectual productivity of school experience (Judd 1983), it is hard to see how computers can be placed at the centre of school renewal. One can imagine how computers might contribute to inquiry, for example, but only in the context of ideas about how schools can foster inquiry, what inquiry is, and what teachers need to know to be able to stimulate inquiry. None the less, many think that computers can help in the process of developing an inquiry orientation to teaching (Simpson 1984; Bostrom 1982).

The point is that there are some quite difficult decisions to be made here that have very complex and far-reaching consequences, which go well beyond simply placing computers in schools. How can these issues be resolved if one thinks only wishfully about the learning and vocational benefits that are supposed to come from computer experience? The need for a well-developed curricular rationale is obvious here—something against which teachers could test their own ideas. If computers are thought to contribute to increased problem-solving capacity, then some sense of what problem-solving capacity is will need to be outlined in school-relevant terms, as will some theory about the relationship between problem solving and, for example, programming. As it stands, it is hard to see the connection. This is a task for curriculum development activity.

What the reflexive approach can contribute is a school context in which these issues can be debated. In the process of curriculum formation, teachers can study what actually goes on as children use various kinds of software. Take for example the reports on LOGO in these cases. This is LOGO 'in the raw'; teachers trying to find a relevant context for LOGO and not being very successful at it. This is not a matter of assigning blame but of learning from experience: what can LOGO offer teachers? How can its benefits be realized in school-relevant terms? Some might want to argue that schools are not ready for LOGO: others may say that LOGO is not ready for schools. The point is that these efforts to use LOGO (and we mention LOGO only by way of example) suggest what sorts of issues need to be discussed when planning in-service activities associated with powerful software.

Challenges to practice

The routine and the novel

These reflexive experiences with innovation teach us something about how teachers cope with innovation. Doing things in new ways is an extremely complex process, which we have not been able to describe very well and for which we lack adequate metaphors. One way of looking at the teachers' behavior in relation to innovative ideas is to think of them as responding to the routine and novel elements of those ideas: parts of the innovation fit easily into existing routines; other parts do not. Table 8.1 indicates the routine and novel elements of these teachers' experience as we have interpreted it.

Table 8.1 *Routine and novel elements in using computers*

Routine	Novel
Rota access to activity	Deciphering error messages
Peer tutoring	Students as experts in subject matter (programming)
Access to activity as a reward	Students demanding teacher support for ambiguous problems
Working in pairs	High level of individual student attention required
Work is guided by printed documents	Use of material only remotely connected to ongoing teaching
Teacher teaches without interruption	Student demand for access to medium of instruction
Students work on their own	Student control of activity
	Development of seatwork materials
	Students unwilling/unable to read printed documents

Now this is a radically oversimplified picture. First of all there is no such thing as 'the' innovation. New ideas, if they are at all interesting, are too complexly perceived to be considered one thing, yet certain common responses by the teachers can usefully be interpreted in terms of the routine and novel elements of innovation. For example, procedures required to launch and sustain drill and practice activity at the computer do not appear to strain existing routines too far, but having to support computer activity parallel to teaching the rest of the class does place strain on the teacher. LOGO is seen as requiring novel responses but not as fitting in with familiar teaching routines. Teachers realize that LOGO is a much favored form of studying computers as a subject but they have trouble seeing it in routine terms and, according to the cases reported here, have not had much success integrating it. Indeed, in three cases, efforts to create routines from it have led to the conclusion that having students learn Basic is preferable to doing LOGO.

Incorporating elements of innovation within the familiar activities of well-established routines is an important issue. Teachers cannot be expected suddenly to abandon their practice in favor of teaching activities quite remote from what they are used to. The experience of innovation cannot be all novelty. There is simply too much at stake, and yet a totally routine approach to innovation is no innovation at all. There has to be enough that is novel to pose a challenge to practice.

For us, the process is not one of substituting one practice for another but of subjecting existing practices to a challenge posed by another well-conceived practice. The effect of the challenge is to provide reasons to modify the existing practice through a process of critical comparison. Of course, things do not always work out this way. For an alternative practice to be understood it needs to be properly experienced. In these cases, it is doubtful if LOGO was experienced in a way that would enable it to act as an effective challenge; perhaps its challenge to practice never became clear, or, if clear, was too novel. Its potential as a challenge appears to have been muted in these cases. By way of contrast, computer simulations in one of the schools studied were an extension of pre-existing work on simulation and were easily assimilated.

These cases can be seen as efforts to use existing routines to cope with the demands of the innovation. Take teaching computers as a subject, for example. Rather than establish a time when all students would study this subject (and thereby render the one machine useless), the teachers adopted a rota system. Access to the computer was incorporated into the rewards and punishment structure of the classroom. Teachers are used to doing more than one thing at once by setting the students work which 'runs itself'. They used this strategy with the computer as far as they could. Nevertheless, as we saw, there were problems here in using this routine with the computer. One of the novel aspects of teaching computers as a subject was the programming activity considered to be part of computer awareness. That, as it turned out, was not something the students could be left alone to do with minimum support. They required much more support than was expected and this created problems for the 'run itself' approach to the subject. A safer approach was to use software for awareness purposes by thinking of familiarity with different types of software as a literacy topic.

A novel aspect of using computers for instruction was the ambiguity of student problems at the computer. Were they due to machine, software or student characteristics? The extra demand on teachers that resulted from having to identify and cope with delay and interruption episodes was another novel aspect of using computers and one not easily handled by existing routines since a wide range of software could yield a wide range of problems: different machines had different operating characteristics for the same software, and the range of students' responses was unknown. Only considerable experience would allow teachers to integrate this aspect of using computers in instruction into their teaching routines. How teachers do this would be useful knowledge for teacher education.

The instrumental and the expressive

Innovation requires extra effort of teachers. What is the pay-off for teachers willing to engage in reflection? A useful way of thinking about how teachers respond to innovation is to look at instrumental and expressive elements of their behavior. Here we are using a distinction developed from the social psychology of Harré (1979), who divides effects of human behavior into practical outcomes that allow one to find shelter and sustenance and 'those directed to ends such as the presentation of self as rational and worthy of respect, as belonging to a certain category of being which I shall call "expressive aspects of activity"' (p. 19). What Harré calls practical we call instrumental. Instrumental behavior, in our case, is directed at producing student learning. Expressive behavior is directed at creating respect for the teacher and liking for the subject, for example. This expressive behavior can have an indirect effect on learning by creating an appropriate climate, and learning outcomes may come to influence how expressive behavior is appraised. A given teaching behavior can have both expressive and instrumental elements in varying degrees. Table 8.2 gives some examples of instrumental and expressive elements of teaching with computers.

Table 8.2 *Instrumental and expressive elements of computer-based teaching*

Instrumental	Expressive
Teaching Basic commands	Students work on modern equipment: teacher is up to date
Promoting problem solving	Students to make their own rules: teacher is flexible
Producing better writers	Students have fun: teacher teaches an interesting subject
Rehearsing math facts	Access available out of school hours: teacher is dedicated
Teaching spelling	Students have one-to-one access to the computer: teacher meets
Tutoring students in basic concepts	individual needs
	Computer-literate students have privileges: teacher is discriminating
	Teacher is familiar with and collects large quantities of software: teacher is highly competent

The usefulness of this distinction lies in the fact that, without it, it is difficult to make sense of a variety of teacher decisions. Indeed, without it teacher decisions can seem contradictory and confused. How is one to make sense of the idea that a teacher does not favor LOGO as a way of learning programming yet is quite happy for students to tutor each other in LOGO, or that a teacher wants to continue an experiment which she considers impossible to do?

From an instrumental point of view, for reasons we have discussed, teaching the class how to program through LOGO is not favored, but from an expressive point of view, by allowing enthusiastic students to teach each other how to use LOGO, the teacher is giving them the opportunity to experience a challenge. In his own eyes, and hopefully in theirs, he is expressing his interest in computer-literate students and displaying his appreciation of the needs of some children for self-directed activity in spite of the fact that he does not consider LOGO useful. Instrumental outcomes are not at issue here. In this way the teacher maintains certain important relationships with these children.

Other examples can be found of expressive behavior taking precedence over instrumental. A teacher finds that students' mathematical skills improve no more through computer activity than through more traditional means yet she wants to continue to investigate this issue. Is the point here to find a better way of teaching routine material or to provide varied experiences for students that enhance their attitude to learning to do routine work with the teacher? By having the computer in the classroom the teacher is able to make a statement about the kind of experiences she is able to provide for her students—about her attitude to them.

How is one to explain that two teachers think that it would be better for students if they were to learn about computers from a specialist teacher in a computer lab, yet insist that they should have a computer in their classroom for that very same purpose? From an instrumental point of view, this does not make much sense, but expressively it does. The decision to have a computer says something about the kind of experiences available in the classroom—about where the teacher is at in relation to 'modern' things like computers.

Do these expressive elements matter? We think that they do because they are part of being the kind of social person a teacher is, they are part of the way teachers make statements about what matters to them and what sort of climate for learning they are trying to create. The way they view their accomplishments as teachers is in no small way related to these personal statements, and we think it is important for teachers to recognize what they mean. This analysis of the symbolic elements of teaching is part of coming to understand what an innovation means in practice. It is an analysis that teachers need to make of their own practice, and is a way of coming to know oneself better as a teacher and thus a benefit of becoming involved in innovation.

Innovations often involve new ways of assigning meaning to practice. Teaching something using the computer means something different in expressive terms from teaching the same material some other way. Teachers are aware of these meanings and their significance, and are engaged in a process of reassigning meanings as they try new practices. Making these processes more explicit is a way of learning from the process of curriculum innovation and could be a valuable part of curriculum evaluation as teachers systematically analyze the pay-off they seek in teaching with and about computers.

Teacher influence

It is customary to think of the teacher's work in terms of instrumental outcomes, usually student achievement. Thus, teaching is often linked directly with learning and defined in terms of learning. However, to understand the actions of the teachers, it is necessary to think that teachers are doing more than acting as instruments of student achievement.

The concept of teacher influence is useful here. In an earlier study it was found that teachers were unwilling to abandon secure routines in the face of a curriculum that demanded many novel responses. Teachers valued these routines for their expressive power. Through specialized activities teachers prepared students to write external examinations, partly by convincing them that the teacher was a reliable guide who 'knew the ropes'. These teachers expressed their 'reliability' in many ways, and by looking at how they exerted their influence through the 'lens' of the expressive concept we could understand how the classroom 'worked' (Olson 1980, 1981).

We think the expressive 'lens' is valuable in the cases we have been looking at here. In the case of computers as a subject, teachers have isolated the computer activities, allowing them to proceed without affecting the ongoing 'official' work of the class. They have used access to the computer as a way of encouraging better behavior and work during 'official' time. At the same time, the teacher maintains a 'modern' posture vis-à-vis certain computer-oriented students, thus increasing his/her influence over the class.

In the case of the computer as teaching tool, the teachers have integrated the computer into familiar teaching routines—they have not risked dramatic changes in teaching style that might undermine their ability to cover the curriculum effectively and in an acceptable way, or to cope with varied demands if they are a learning support person. They have not risked their influence here, so their influence over the core of the work is secure. Meanwhile the students' perceptions of the subject and of the teacher's capacity to use diverse methods are influenced by the use of computers within existing, familiar methods. No radically different methods have been risked; influence over core activity is protected and increased through what using computers expresses about the teacher.

It is quite reasonable that teachers act to protect their influence over core elements of their work, such as covering the curriculum and maintaining their credibility to do this. It is not surprising, for example, that teachers dislike ambiguous classroom situations where existing routines are in doubt and considerable time is required to deal with problems. Nor is it odd that teachers have to be very careful in the way they distribute support to individual students. There is only so much energy and so much time. But these protective strategies for maintaining influence may be used at some cost to the potential of microcomputer-based teaching, which may require that teachers learn to tolerate more ambiguity, increase individual attention, and engage in divergent thinking. All of these create risks for teachers. How are these risks to be managed? Over-protection of these core elements may set a limit on what can be achieved to reform the curriculum through computer-based teaching unless teachers look critically at the way they exercise influence in the classroom. In short, teachers are constantly faced with dilemmas in their practice—having to resolve conflicting interests or perhaps having to cope with not really resolving these dilemmas.

In what we call the reflexive conception of change teachers have a key role to play because it is they who must find a way of making new ideas work; it is through their taking new ideas seriously that the innovators can assess what new ideas mean in practice. Talking to teachers about these new ideas helps us understand what the rational basis of practice is and how the new ideas fit into the overall framework of teacher intention.

Through understanding the existing practice and its relationship to new practice a useful dialectical process is initiated, in which the new practice helps us understand the old as both are evaluated and re-evaluated. In this process important educational values are brought to the surface and critically assessed.

As we pointed out, there are pitfalls in this conception; there are many places where wishful thinking rather than critical thinking might prevail, for example, but the process is worth while because the rightful responsibility for assessing educational value lies with the teacher—the person who most directly confronts the educational tasks of the school.

REFERENCES

Argyris, C. and Schon, D. (1974) *Theory in Practice: Increasing Professional Effectiveness*. San Francisco, CA: Jossey-Bass.

Bostrom, K. (1982) 'An Evaluative Study of the Effects and Effectiveness of Micro-computer Based Teaching in Schools'. Report to the Social Science Research Council, London.

Dreeben, R. (1970) *The Nature of Teaching: School and the Work of Teachers*. Glenview, IL: Scott, Foresman.

Harré, R. (1979) *Social Being*. Oxford: Oxford University Press.

Judd, Wallace (1983) 'Teacher's Place in the Computer Curriculum'. *Phi Delta Kappan*, **65**, 120–2.

Lartner, S. et al. (1983) *The Impact of Microcomputers in Elementary Education*. Toronto: Ministry of Education.

Lortie, D. (1975) *Schoolteacher*. Chicago, IL: University of Chicago Press.

Olson, J. K. (1980) 'Teacher Constructs and Curriculum Change'. *Journal of Curriculum Studies*, **12**, 1–11.

Olson, J. K. (1981) 'Teacher Influence in the Classroom: A Context to Understanding Curriculum Change'. *Instructional Science*, **10**, 259–75.

Olson, J. and Reid, W. A. (1982) 'Studying Innovations in Science Teaching: The Use of Repertory Grid Techniques in Developing a Research Strategy'. *European Journal of Science Education*, **4**, 193–201.

Olson, J. (1986) *Computers in the Classroom: Implications for Curriculum Development and Teacher Education*. Toronto: Ontario Ministry of Education.

Schon, D. (1983) *The Reflective Practitioner*. New York: Basic Books.

Simpson, B. (1984) 'Heading for the Ha-Ha'. *Teacher's College Record*, **85**, 622–30.

9

TEACHER RESPONSES TO CURRICULUM POLICY: BEYOND THE 'DELIVERY' METAPHOR

John Reynolds and Murray Saunders

INTRODUCTION

Our approach to teachers' thinking has been through the study of the development and implementation of curriculum policy. During our involvement with teachers in the processes of negotiating and implementing the curriculum, we came to feel that there had to be better ways of helping head teachers and co-ordinators to guide these processes than through the generalized models of collaborative planning and group problem-solving proffered in the literature on curriculum change. In particular, it had been our experience that most curriculum planning, however interactive, fluid, and deliberative, proceeded without explicit consideration of how the rationales and plans produced were to be used by teachers, or of just what situation they were for. Teachers' own planning of the curriculum did not seem to involve them in deliberating about the situations for which the planning was intended.

While working with a group of teachers who had been asked to prepare curriculum guidelines for colleagues, we had noticed how frequently but fleetingly individual teachers voiced doubts about the ways in which particular curriculum statements were likely to be regarded or disregarded by their fellows. Generally, these interpolations were rapidly overridden and superseded by sustained argument amongst the whole group which shifted attention back to the form and wording of the guidelines themselves. The flow of discussion consistently moved away from the rehearsal of teachers' likely thinking to rehearsal of justifications of the curriculum text itself. We wondered how to interpret this tendency. Were the majority of the teachers' group *unwilling* to envisage and think through the situational use of the guidelines? Or were they *unable* to do so? Or, within the given group situation, had they *accorded priority* to the curriculum acceptability of the guidelines rather than their practicality?

Informal questioning of the teachers about what underlay this tendency suggested that all three interpretations might apply. For example, the teachers could be said to be unwilling to think through the use of the curriculum text in so far as they believed that it should stand on an ideal, rather than try to pre-empt teacher interpretations. But the group could also be said to be unable to envisage how the guidelines might be used in so far as they could not foresee all the circumstances of the guidelines' use, and, anyhow, different teachers would react differently. In addition, the group could be said to give working priority to the 'curriculum acceptability' of the guidelines in so far as that seemed to be what was expected of them as a teachers' group: it seemed most relevant to the group's job-in-hand. Consequently, we inferred that what we had initially suspected could be an example of a crucial conceptual blockage in teachers' thinking could perhaps be more sensibly interpreted as evidence of the fluid, situation-responsive character of teachers' commonsense thinking. In fact, members of the group were slightly puzzled why we should think the problem was worth pursuing. Perhaps, after all, we should rest satisfied with the generalized, managerially oriented models of curriculum planning that currently prevail.

The research findings on curriculum change then available seemed to support this judgement. The broader import of the widely quoted 1975 Rand Study of government-sponsored innovation in education (for a summary, see McLaughlin 1976) was being disseminated and is now gaining currency amongst local authority advisers and the better-informed head teachers in the UK. Thus it is becoming accepted that the implementation of curriculum innovation, as distinct from its nominal adoption in official pronouncements, confronts teachers with the need to make complex modifications to their ways of working; and that, as a result, both the envisaged new curriculum and pre-existing teacher practices have to be rethought and materially adapted in relation to *local* circumstances. At the same time, it is increasingly recognized that, if effective (therefore situationally attuned) change is to ensue, there has to be genuine collaboration and reciprocal interaction between the initiators of change and the local agents of change, such as head teachers and teacher co-ordinators (see Fullan 1981; Lehming and Kane 1981, for elaboration of these generalizations). Also, it is becoming acknowledged that these local change-agents need to undergo a lengthy learning process to develop their commitment and their general problem-solving and managerial capability (Williams 1980).

Our conceptual unease persisted, however. Colleagues in the curriculum field, though increasingly conscious of the organizational implications of this 'mutual adaptation/management-learning' view of curriculum implementation, seemed to see nothing problematic about what it was that teachers had to rethink and adapt as teachers, rather than as curriculum planners. In as much as that was seen as a problem, it was seen as a matter of instituting the procedures to make school-based curriculum development an effective ideal (Skilbeck 1984). What teachers have to think about as they transmute curriculum plans into courses of action seemed either a non-problem or a narrower question of teaching method.

True, several finer-grained studies of teacher reactions to innovation were available (Doyle and Ponder 1977; Brown and McIntyre 1982; Olson 1980), which brought out more specific characteristics of teacher appraisals of curriculum outlines. Olson, for example, had shown how teachers construe the meaning of the overt content of curriculum proposals selectively, in terms of their situational import. That is, they 'read' curriculum texts in the context of the particular in-school negotiating, lesson-preparing, marking, and classroom-managing demands that seem likely to be made upon them. Although teachers may not verbalize these appraisals, they interpret curriculum change in terms of anticipated side-effects, especially side-effects that complicate or destabilize their relations with pupils and colleagues. Olson implied that this was because there were no reliable techniques available to teachers for handling the practical dilemmas entailed; and thus that they adhered to ways of thinking that, in their individual experience, had led to dependable teaching method and content. The implication of such analysis (see also Leithwood 1982) is that the tenor and detail of curriculum proposals should be attuned to the beliefs, anxieties, and operational needs of teachers, and that strenuous clarification and exemplification of practical implications are essential.

However, it had been our experience that teachers who found themselves in curriculum management and leadership roles did not see compelling significance in the above conclusions, partly of course because they felt that they 'already knew it'. It may be that to capitalize on those conclusions we need to get clearer why teachers in those roles still defer to the conventions of formal curriculum discourse in their exposition of policy and programmes, why they draw upon projections of the educationally desirable ('curriculum aims'), rather than indicate preconditional doings and transactions. In other words, even those with long experience of curriculum negotiation and implementation adopt the vocabulary and tenor of the curriculum prospectus or sales brochure, rather than that of practical situational advice. It is only in informal face-to-face discussion that teachers shift to the idiom and tone of what Doyle and Ponder called the 'practicality ethic'.

We formed the view that there was a curious incompatibility between curriculum discourse and teachers' 'natural' tendencies in thinking about their work, an incompatibility that was not attributable simply to the shifts of role between planning and teaching. This incompatibility seemed curious because (although we do not press the comparison) there seems no parallel incompatibility between the conventions of directive employed by, say, dramatists, and the mental processes of those who produce their plays; or between those of composers and the musicians who render their scores. Thus it seemed to us that the question that earlier research had not recognized was why there was a disjunction between curriculum proposals and teacher practices *in the first place*. Why is there a *dissociation* between the conventions followed in addressing curriculum matters and the tendencies in teachers' applied thinking that have been demonstrated?

More materially, what effect does this dissociation have on curriculum negotiation and development? Might it confound the relationship between teachers' pre-active and interactive thinking? Or might the dissociation be inevitable, given the usual separation of planning and pedagogic roles? Perhaps it was a constraint to be lived with; or one to be minimized by frequent evaluation of whether curriculum ideals were being achieved.

BACKGROUND TO THE RESEARCH

At this uncomfortable stage in our consideration of teachers' thinking, we might have consigned the problem to conceptual footnotes and reimmersed ourselves in the staple business of curriculum evaluation. Fortuitously, a reactivation of government interest in curriculum policy brought the practicalities of implementation into official salience, offering us an opportunity to re-interrogate such conceptual issues within the broader and now better-funded context of policy management.

The 1981 Education Act had required schools to implement curriculum principles within and across working practices, rather than simply to append new curriculum components piecemeal, within the English tradition of ad hoc educational reform. As it bears on this chapter, the *substance* of government policy could be summarized as the redevelopment of the school curriculum so that it meets principles of relevance, breadth, balance, and challenge to all pupils. The *approach* being used to implement these principles is the requirement of government that individual local education authorities (LEAs), and individual schools within them, devise effective curriculum policies based on the above principles, manifest in statements of aims; and that they establish procedures to monitor how the curriculum they provide matches these aims. However, articulation of the intervening practical tasks entailed by these requirements had been limited to their pointed delegation to LEAs and schools, via terse reference to the responsibility of schools for 'delivery' of an appropriate curriculum.

'Delivery' is an appealingly business-like metaphor whose rapid incorporation into the vocabularies of Department of Education and Science officials, Her Majesty's Inspectorate (HMI) and LEA advisers showed how serviceable a term it was for those in managerial positions. In so far as their job was to see that teachers 'delivered the goods', then certainly the metaphor directed attention to those upon whom blame for non-implementation of policy might be laid. But we suspected that the metaphor of delivery oversimplified and undervalued the disparate negotiations and adaptations that teachers had to undertake in responding to policy in the face of other demands. We argued that, if the teacher capabilities required to meet curriculum principles and procedures were to be appreciated and adequately conceptualized, they had to be investigated within a range of school conditions over substantial time spans; and that different types of problem and negotiation might be involved at different stages.

Government curriculum policy had been strongly influenced by earlier reports by Her Majesty's Inspectorate (DES 1978). HMI stated that the breadth and quality of children's learning in primary schools could be improved if the teachers assigned special responsibility for areas of the curriculum were required to execute that responsibility more effectively. These teachers should design schemes of work, give colleagues guidance and support, assist them in teaching, procure resources, and develop means for evaluating such curriculum development. Our research strategy took its particular form from recognition of an opportunity to monitor how teachers in local primary schools were responding to the incorporation of these HMI recommendations into national and local curriculum policy. Thus we conceived our research questions at two levels of interest. At the level of *curriculum policy evaluation*, the questions were: how are LEA advisers and teachers responding to this tightening of curriculum responsibilities and principles? how are they implementing particular curriculum guidelines? At the level of *conceptual enquiry*, our questions were: how do changed curriculum requirements influence the situations that teachers have to handle? how can the capabilities that teachers need to articulate and handle these situations be conceptualized?

The local situation at the time that our research questions were crystallizing was as follows. The LEA we studied was already dissatisfied with the variable coverage and quality of the curriculum in its then 700 primary schools and was using HMI recommendations to strengthen in-school curriculum planning. In 1979/80 separate working parties produced five documents to guide primary head teachers and curriculum co-ordinators: job specifications for co-ordinators, suggestions on the curriculum aims and structures of language teaching, of mathematics, and of history/geography; also a self-appraisal schedule for head teachers. We made a pilot study in 1981 into schools' initial reception of those earlier guidelines. Between 1980 and 1982 additional curriculum guidelines—for science, for art, for physical education, and for literature—were similarly produced and distributed. Then, after a review of recent implementation research, we obtained funding for a two-year research project on what was happening in local primary schools in response to the input of guidelines.

Our first step in developing a researchable conception of these responses was to differentiate the situations of role, time, and knowledge within which the various users of policy texts and requirements have to work. Adapting a model used much earlier by Leithwood et al (1974) in their studies of curriculum change in Ontario, we located the main policy-users along what we call the policy implementation staircase. Thus Figure 9.1 is an idealized representation of the process by which HMI and government statements become transmuted into LEA and in-school curriculum guidelines and teacher practices at different levels of that staircase. Of course, in reality there is much interaction between agents on different steps of the staircase. Moreover, policy messages are not transmitted and received in a one-off process. As Berman (1981) and our own data illustrate, the overall process of curriculum policy passes through very differerent phases—for example, of policy image development, of support generation, and of classroom adaptation and implementation (or of assimilation or rejection). Despite these limitations, the staircase model is useful in explaining our presentation of findings. It locates how the conduct of the various agents took into account that of those above and below them, illustrating the basis from which we subsequently emphasized the concept of teachers' strategic conduct and curriculum competence.

To collect evidence on policy-users' practices the project's research fellow made regular visits to nine primary schools. At each visit the head teacher and curriculum co-ordinators of that particular school were debriefed on what action (if any) they had taken in relation to guidelines, what problems they had encountered, how their scales of priority were shifting, etc. More general patterns of response across the LEA were established by two questionnaire surveys before and after the above case study approach.

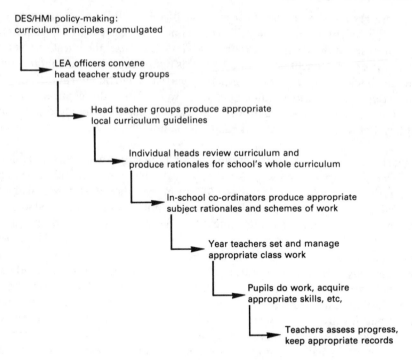

DES/HMI policy-making:
curriculum principles promulgated

LEA officers convene
head teacher study groups

Head teacher groups produce appropriate
local curriculum guidelines

Individual heads review curriculum and
produce rationales for school's whole curriculum

In-school co-ordinators produce appropriate
subject rationales and schemes of work

Year teachers set and manage
appropriate class work

Pupils do work, acquire
appropriate skills, etc,

Teachers assess progress,
keep appropriate records

Figure 9.1 *The implementation staircase.*

RESPONSES TO POLICY IN ONE LOCAL AUTHORITY

LEA adviser responses

Our LEA had four advisers with specific concern for education in its 700 primary schools. As in other LEAs, their influence on the curriculum had been diffuse, having been constrained by their thinness on the ground, the breadth of their roles, and the complex factors bearing on the work of individual schools. Thus HMI's general recommendations on primary education provided the advisers with the external authority and incentive to convert their own diagnoses of lack of continuity, balance, and progression in primary curricula into concerted rather than piecemeal action.

The advisers were in the situation of having to respond to HMI recommendations via their structurally ambiguous relationship with head teachers, who have effective responsibility for each school curriculum. The advisers' strategic response was to use an annual series of LEA-sponsored conferences to introduce, incidentally, a special system of study groups, composed of head teachers, with a brief to produce curriculum guidelines for all local schools on major areas of the curriculum and its management. By emphasizing that the guidelines to be produced were 'discussion documents', the advisers avoided confronting the tradition of head teacher autonomy in curriculum. They cultivated a vocabulary that avoided any suggestion of LEA direction or control, and, by encouraging head teacher participation, fostered a feeling of local self-help and commitment. Thus, by responding to central government through the medium of study groups, the advisers provided forums for negotiation and promoted curriculum consensus. However, through an emphasis on appeals to local head teachers' dissatisfaction with lack of comparability and continuity amongst curricula in the county, the advisers secured the heads' tacit acquiescence to what was actually a local accentuation of HMI recommendations.

At the same time, head teachers, both inside and outside the study groups, perceived that the emergent guidelines were not just 'for discussion'. They recognized their strategic implications, medium and long term. That is, they saw them as intimations of how the advisers expected them to provide written justification, several months on, of their responsibility for the curriculum. These intimations were not threatening because these justifications were to be in abstract, idealized terms with which it was hard to disagree. Secondly, the head teachers recognized the probable use of the guidelines, several years on, in the advisers' monitoring of, for example, the implementation of new emphases on experimentation in science and higher-order skills in writing; but they saw that as a bridge to be crossed if and when reached. It seemed that the advisers' strategy worked because both they and the head teachers understood each others' strategic stance in relation to the time scale involved.

At the adviser/head teacher meetings that we attended we noted how the advisers used jokes and irony to activate the participants' taken-for-granted background knowledge of the practicalities of curriculum change. Although there was no direct reference to such practicalities these jokes and innuendos served as what sociologists call 'contextualization cues' (Gumperz 1982). Hence despite, or even because of, the participants' mutual wariness, both the study groups and the later dissemination meetings between head teachers seemed to promote a complicitous understanding amongst those present. This complicity appeared to be significant not least because it enabled participants to pick up indirect cues in relation to the use of policy statements. Subsequent interviews with individual heads supported this interpretation. For example, a member of one of the groups observed:

> Heads know that the conferences were a strategy, but there was tacit agreement or acceptance that manipulation of this sort was occurring: we do need authority-wide help and initiatives. Heads respond to other heads: there is a need to break down ill-will, resentment. So using the conference was useful and necessary.

Similarly, a head teacher outside the study groups gave this sketch of the dissemination meetings, at which other heads from the groups took the lead:

> A head teacher spokesman for each document gave a résumé: it was only a guide, not a 'you will do' ... heads like to talk to each other. When they talk to an adviser, they have their tongue in their cheek. With heads presenting the documents, we are more willing to listen. Heads are more honest to each other, they really say what they think, but not always to an adviser. They cover up. It boils down to the fact that heads know it is easy to get a scheme and present it to teachers; but it's very different when you put it into practice in individual schools, with different circumstances.

So this head teacher went along with the 'for discussion' status of the guidelines, though sceptical about their impact upon staff in his school.

All the head teacher groups needed many days out of school to discuss and draft the guidelines. The most protracted gestation of guidelines kept a group of some 20 head teachers out of their schools for up to 25 half-days, over five terms, before they eventually negotiated acceptable co-ordination between record-keeping and guidance on specific subject areas. Crucial to the senior adviser's approach of nudging, rather than directing, the group was his strategic overview of how curriculum principles of constructive feedback might be pursued in the situation of ambivalent relationships between advisers, head teachers, and other teachers. Thus he was able to combine, on the one hand, implicit appeals to head teachers' appreciation of the managerial utility of a record-keeping system in supervising, indirectly, teachers' work in their schools, with, on the other hand, explicit appeals to the pedagogic ideal of sensitive assessment of pupils' work across the curriculum.

In short, the LEA advisers were able to use government policy to negotiate an accommodation of interests at the level of adviser and head teacher statuses and responsibilities. However, that accommodation depended as much on what was left unstated as on what was made explicit. It depended on what had been made mutually manifest in face-to-face meetings but which was not overtly communicated at those meetings, still less communicated in the guidelines themselves.

Head teacher responses to policy

Most of the primary head teachers in the LEA had been appointed in the 1960s and early 1970s, a period in the UK of educational expansion and optimism, and, not unrelatedly, of non-explicit, permissive curriculum policy. The heads had had little, if any, induction into curriculum management and formalized curriculum vocabularies. From the late 1970s they had had to cope with falling rolls and financial stringency, compounded from 1980 onwards by their periodic reception of the nine sets of LEA guidelines referred to earlier. Each school had to initiate a curriculum review process, oriented to production of an overall policy, which was to be backed up by specific aims and content for each curriculum area. The size, circumstances, and staffing situation of schools varied very considerably, with the smaller, more rural schools known to lack teachers with the subject expertise to make policy principles of curriculum breadth and balance readily achievable.

A preliminary questionnaire survey established that head teachers in general had, none the less, responded positively to the first five guidelines, even though individual heads were aggrieved about their schools' limited resources. As our study progressed, we built up detailed case material on ways in which the internal circumstances of schools—such as head teachers' teaching loads, number of posts on higher salary scales, staff qualifications, school buildings layout, etc.—exerted a material influence on the process of policy review and implementation. Our second and main questionnaire survey confirmed that head teachers of small schools (under 120 pupils) were most likely to experience difficulty, with such factors as those just mentioned being mutually compounding. The survey data also confirmed what the case material had suggested: the schools in which there was the most active response to the guidelines tended to be those in which head teachers had low teaching loads, in which there was a modicum of staffing 'slack', and in which at least three or four scale posts (on higher salaries) were available. Without these conditions, head teachers were more likely to adopt a passive stance, with their priorities lying with routine work associated with school 'tick over'.

However, it was also very apparent that the presence or absence of such conditions was insufficient to explain the range of variation between head teacher responses to policy. Might that variation be attributed to differences in head teachers' understanding of the relation between curriculum principles and courses of action? Might it be attributed to variable degrees of 'curriculum competence'? As we mulled over transcripts of our debriefing interviews with head teachers and questionnaire data, we developed a plausible interpretation of the material. The first, hardly original step in this synthesis is as follows. All head teachers had to evolve a broad strategy for accommodating both external demands upon them, in particular the LEA policy requirements, and the internal demands of the day-to-day running of the school and their face-to-face relations with colleagues. The external demands had to be met periodically only, through the medium of formalized discourse, whereas the internal demands were continuous, requiring intuitive improvisation rather than considered statements. Therefore head teachers tended towards a general strategy of using LEA guidelines retrospectively rather than prospectively, more as a vehicle for (external) *justification* than a conceptual map for in-school curriculum *explication*.

The following transcript extracts illustrate the sense of this distinction:

I think very often [the guidelines] have been very useful—not exactly starting points, but referral-back documents—to see if our thinking on certain aspects of curriculum is the same as or coincides with the County documents or is terribly different ... they were useful but not as it were something that we took over—sort of retrospective, making comparisons with what we had got. (School C)

We will have a complete reappraisal, starting with a staff meeting. I would have initiated the change, irrespective of the documents. Moreover, they will become an important part of the appraisal. If schemes are incompatible with the documents, then we shall think again. (School B)

It is important from time to time to go back and look at the guidelines to remind yourself of where you really ought to be going. (School K)

I think they clarify everything that we have been thinking of in the past. I'm sure we've been on the right lines but it's really given us confidence and it clarified everything, and if we have any hesitation on anything we look at the guidelines and say, 'Well, we have been doing the right thing in the past'. (School A)

It seemed that head teachers used curriculum guidelines as a way of 'checking' (their word in several interviews) that the practices of the school for which they were responsible would be seen as officially acceptable outside the school. Yet it would be an oversimplification to characterize this strategy as no more than one of legitimating what they had done within the here-and-now of working conditions. It was our impression that head teacher thinking oscillated between forward-thinking and rationalization of past actions. Thus their use of policy in checking school practices should probably be seen as part of a more general strategy for orchestrating past, present, and future within the distinctive temporality of school life. For example, distant curriculum goals had to be considered in relation to shorter-term non-curriculum goals, such as minimizing staff stress, some of these goals being not only interdependent but conflicting. In other words, head teacher action upon curriculum policy was dependent on their wider evaluation of what was at stake—in relation to an *emergent* balance of considerations. Thus their thinking about how to handle policy had to respond to the simultaneities of the *present*, whilst taking cognizance of *future* relations with LEA advisers and school governors, *and* the nature and intensity of patterns of *previous* interactions with colleagues.

Up to this point, our interpretation may seem to amount to an elaboration of the view that teachers' thinking reflects their dependence on coping strategies (Westbury 1973; Hargreaves 1978), extending the idea of coping to include head teachers' strategic use of justificatory discourse. However, our material gives a basis for clarifying the extent to which the 'more active' head teachers did much more than cope with policy requirements, as compared with the 'more passive' heads. At the level of surface generalization, the former were more confident and more reflective. They were confident in as much as they could work out the effective implications of the guidelines, in relation to what the LEA would hold them responsible for; and they were reflective in as much as they had an idea of 'the curriculum' as 'the total intended learning experience' rather than a collection of syllabuses. They could thus rehearse the impact of colleagues' practices on curriculum breadth and balance.

The 'more active' heads used the guidelines to check the curriculum in two different senses: they checked both the intended ('ought-to-do') curriculum and the operative curriculum as constituted by teachers' working practices. On the other hand, the 'more passive' heads dissociated the intended and the operative curriculum, concentrating their response to LEA requirements on the production of acceptable curriculum documentation, rather than reflection upon colleagues' practices and their lack of match with policy principles. The more contact that heads had with other heads, the less anxious they seemed about document presentation and vocabulary. The head teachers who were most anxious about the shop-window function of their own curriculum documents tended to cull 'appropriate' statements of curriculum aims from others.

Overall, the general emphasis in head teachers' use of LEA guidelines was to exert leverage upon staff to make their curriculum planning more explicit and systematic. But the particular leverage that they exerted usually coincided with *previously* identified curriculum dissatisfactions, for example weaknesses or discontinuity in maths teaching. Indeed, apart from their use as a means of public justification and shop window, head teachers seemed to incorporate the guidelines into their existing strategies for handling their schools' internal and external relations.

Though our data were not full enough to generalize other than tentatively about head teachers' curriculum competence, the material suggested that the concept might be useful. For example, 'curriculum competence' directs attention to the teacher's ability to deal simultaneously with a range of considerations, to bring about a satisfactory state of affairs, rather than to pursue discrete curriculum goals. Yet as part of their strategy for ensuring an acceptable state of affairs, heads needed to subscribe to what they informally acknowledged was the idealized (goal-oriented) convention of curriculum discourse. 'Curriculum competence' seemed to require that they had the extra edge of consciousness to distinguish what was shared convention ('complicity') from valid representation of what their colleagues were about. Lacking that consciousness, the more passive heads seemed to dissociate their day-to-day improvisations and negotiations from problems of curriculum planning and implementation. Even if this tendency was compounded by the head teachers' unfamiliarity at this stage of policy development with the idea of curriculum management, it suggests that head teacher abilities to connect formalized discursive practices with their day-to-day non-discursive practices in getting things done is a key competence, one that helps to explain the wide variation in head teacher responses to policy requirements.

Curriculum co-ordinator responses to policy

The curriculum co-ordinators in the study were teachers with several years of primary school experience who had been assigned specific responsibility for areas of the curriculum. Because of falling rolls and the small size of many schools, the additional allowances payable to teachers with such responsibilities were not available in many schools, with the result that in those schools subject areas such as history/geography, science, and music were not formally co-ordinated. Hence most of the co-ordinators whose responses were analysed were mathematics or (English) language co-ordinators, holding Scale 2 or Scale 3 appointments. It was only in a few larger primary schools (300 pupils), that they had relaxation of their otherwise continuous classroom contact to facilitate their implementation of policy requirements.

Co-ordinators initially used the curriculum guidelines in ways similar to head teachers. For example, they drew upon them as statements of an 'approved' curricular orientation, especially in deriving correct terminology for internal policy statements, rather than as a practical help in thinking ahead about the operative curriculum. They drew upon them to frame justifications to colleagues for schemes intended to develop continuity and progression in subject areas. As did head teachers, co-ordinators used policy to 'check on' and, in some cases, to pressurize colleagues to change existing practices. Thus for active co-ordinators the guidelines helped to structure discussion with colleagues, acting as a 'platform' or approved framework for initial change. They also used them in the sifting and selection of commercially published schemes.

The evidence was that co-ordinator impact on other staff is long term, eventual, or intermittent. It was striking that curriculum discussion, policy formulation, and action had to be 'fitted into' routine classroom and school commitments, resulting in long periods of inaction, with short bursts of activity, as these extracts illustrate:

> ... I can't insist at this stage that certain things are done because of purely and simply lack of time. It would take time to make things if you are going to do a lot of discovery, enquiry, investigation work—it requires quite a lot of equipment if you have got big classes and a lot of it can't be bought either. If it's tailor-made for an area or something. Other than that, and the fact that we haven't any record keeping in it, other than those two facts then ... I am happy with the way things have been for the last two years. I think that long-term plans are going to scale.

> What has caused me more anxiety than anything else—the fact that I am the science co-ordinator and the games organizer and that pressure is difficult. I've never been good at keeping three balls in the air at once and one of the three is crashing down. It's got to be a certain amount of patience as regards my job.

> Another thing, from my own point of view, is a lot of other things that I am involved in because I am also responsible for games and if you get in five or six tournaments a term that takes up a lot of time. That Open University project was another thing—it was a pilot one aimed to try and test out ways you could successfully get staff going, and it had quite powerful negative effects. It would be twelve months certainly before I could start on anything again. That was a couple of years ago, so really this year there is no reason why we can't get anything going.

Most co-ordinators had to mediate between the guidelines and the rest of the staff, in the sense of explaining terminology and the operational significance of general recommendations. As one co-ordinator put it,

> ... the language document had to have a lot of explanation. It wasn't easy to read and even when you had read it there was a lot of waffle in it, a great deal.

Major factors that limited co-ordinators' impact on colleagues were (1) their own subject expertise (for example, in English language teaching), (2) their status and authority in the school, (3) time for monitoring the effects of discussions and schemes of work. The necessity for co-ordinators to accommodate these factors led them to make resource management their main priority, rather than the development of teaching strategies and curriculum content for use by colleagues. Resource management (recording books, moving or centralizing resources, etc.) was an effective means of being 'visibly busy' and 'servicing' colleagues so as to win their support and co-operation. One co-ordinator referred to this process as the 'grafting syndrome'. These extracts illustrate these key tendencies:

> I think it has certainly helped that I have done a lot of donkey work. I've made it easier for the staff doing SMP [School Mathematics Project] and will carry on to do so. It has meant a lot of sewing for me and a lot of faffing about but having the equipment ready for them—now if I left them to get their own equipment then it just wouldn't be done as well. They would be moaning about it because it is a job collecting the equipment. It's a life's work really. I thought O.K. I'll collect all the equipment and if they want I'll even go and set it up for them and put labels on it. We'll do it between us. We'll fit it in in the right places on shelves in cupboards, and short of doing the lessons myself—I think this has helped really. Nobody has taken it as interference. I do consider it my job really, except that I hate the sewing.

> I think people are most receptive to personal example in every case. I think you can sit and talk to them about things for days and get nowhere, but by going out and actually doing it, or expecting them to do it having shown you are prepared to do it yourself, is the most receptive ... We're at the stage now where if I say we are going to have a 'science fair' and I am going to do all the work, then people will muck in: if I say we are going to do a science topic and I've organized it and they can see it's organized, or we are going to have a discussion about curriculum documents or whatever. People will look at it to see that I've done the ground work. We're not at the stage where I could go and say 'I want to introduce new ways of teaching energy. Which of these particular ways of teaching energy do you like?'

> Unlike the maths in the school we are not using one scheme. We are with reading but in general language work we aren't, as everybody seems to have slightly different perspectives in language. So I feel we have to start off with the practical things and then move into the ambiguous areas which are likely to be more controversial. There are going to be a few. We've done some already with the remedial scheme and it has got everybody thinking ...

Curriculum co-ordinators seemed to need skills more of curriculum *design* than of formal planning: in other words, how to translate curriculum aims and content into interesting, adaptable, feasible activities for children. This seemed to involve a consciousness more of feasible medium-term aims, those realizable within a term's or a month's work, rather than of specific objectives or abstract long-term ideals. Most significantly, in transforming such aims into concrete modifications to existing teacher and pupil practices, co-ordinators constantly redeployed curriculum means and *re*interpreted curriculum ends.

Co-ordinator impact on school practice was enhanced by the following group of factors:

- frequent informal discussion of planning with colleagues;
- demonstration of teaching strategies ('change by example'), often in the co-ordinator's own classroom;
- offering curriculum content and materials;
- 'high profile' head teacher support, especially in juggling time allocations or providing resources, and in expressing public approval; and, not least,
- 'grafting' and generally, 'putting oneself about' in a non-interfering way.

Probably the most important feature of this list of factors is their essentially operational rather than 'rationally planned' character. There was no mention, for example, of 'getting aims and objectives right'. However, it is fair to say that effective co-ordinators did have a definite sense of the curriculum direction in which they wished staff practices to develop.

The difficulties of translating general discussion into policy statements that could influence actual change of practice led to a tendency towards diminishing activity in the movement over time from discussion to policy implementation. The rate of diminishing activity depended not only on the availability of scale posts, knowledgeable post-holders, and scope for manoeuvre in time allocations. It also depended upon the self-confidence and commitment of co-ordinators, and upon co-ordinators' sensitivity to the tendency towards dissociation of the 'approved' curricula embodied in the guidelines and actual working practices.

Summary interpretation of responses to policy

In setting up the research we had two aims in mind: to provide feedback to the LEA on how its policy guidelines were being handled, and to improve conceptualization of what teachers had to think and do in the process. In the event, we had some methodological difficulty in reconciling the need, in pursuing the first aim, for time-extended, cross-sectional material with the need, in pursuing the second aim, for detailed (hence early) recall by teachers of what they had thought and done. It was not acceptable to teachers or feasible for us to visit particular schools and debrief staff more often than every three to four weeks, by which time their recollection of deliberations and operational priorities could have faded. However, in our view, what might be criticized as an empirical weakness was, rather, a necessary sacrifice: a practical trade-off that enabled us to share and understand a reality inherent in school working conditions and practices.

Our point here is that, for all heads and curriculum co-ordinators, their making a response to policy requirements was only one amongst many other pressing concerns, such as regulating pupil behaviour, marking books, etc. For that reason significant descriptions of what teachers thought and did about curriculum policy involved recognizing their shifting and precarious scales of priority over time. We needed to appreciate the distinctive temporality of work within a school system. Thus the empirical limitation of our strategy of periodic debriefing probably helped us to recognize two complementary tendencies in teachers' response to policy. The first tendency was for it to be conditional, intermittent, and eventual. That is, discussion and subsequent adjustments to practice had to be in phase with the tempo and shifting circumstances of school life, and attuned to the interactive norms between heads, teachers and pupils through which those temporalities were mediated. Our visits and questions had to be similarly phased and attuned. The second tendency was that, as policy requirements became opportunely and selectively incorporated into the flow of day-to-day transactions, teachers' actions and thoughts about them receded in their memory. They were not forgotten but could be activated only via appropriate questions. For example, it was soon evident that productive debriefing questions were never of the kind 'What changes in your teaching have you considered over the past several weeks?' or even 'What curriculum problems have you had?' Instead, lines of questioning that generated animated, concrete answers were of the kind 'What are you dealing with at the moment? ... What did you have to do (about X)? ... Why was that? ... Was the situation similar last week/month/term?' Of course, this is to confirm that most teachers find it easier to verbalize the here-and-now of their work, their ways of coping with the 'task environment'. Equally, the point is that the very effort of engaging teachers in medium-term retrospective thinking brought out the sharpness of their knowledge of the particular school ethos and environment. In no sense had they 'forgotten' how they handled their particular situation, or come to take it for granted. However, their answers brought out, albeit indirectly, that they saw curriculum guidelines as but one (recently additional) part of their total work situation, seldom as *the* way to define or context that situation.

Hence the central question for us was, given the 'softness' of our case material and the low-key emergent nature of the policy implementation process, what interpretation might defamiliarize what those involved already regarded as an inherently indeterminate and tiresome business? What interpretive generalizations would be suggestive but empirically defensible? To have confined ourselves to inferences that could be demonstrably substantiated by the data would have drawn us in either of two dissatisfying directions: either towards the more general, officially recognized aspects of the process, which were over-familiar through managerial models of curriculum planning, or towards the specificities of personal and local considerations. As intimated in the introduction, we had found that such managerial and localistic perspectives screened out what was more difficult but educationally significant in policy implementation; that is, how teachers transmuted curriculum principles into working practices.

In order to articulate this capability, we judged that we had to go some way beyond the case material that we had built up. In doing so, we draw upon the distinction illustrated in Figure 9.2 between the mainstream managerial vocabulary of policy 'delivery' and 'compromising' description of unacknowledged teacher skills. Thus the diagram embodies our main interpretive claim from the case material: that what head teachers and co-ordinators had actually to bring about in making acceptable responses to LEA guidelines bears richer articulation than it gets in official discourse. There is a gap between the skills of making acceptable responses to policy and acceptable ways of describing them.

For example, the figure brings into relief cognitive and interactive processes for which the formal guidelines for teachers and job specifications provided no frame of reference. In making an active response to policy requirements, heads and co-

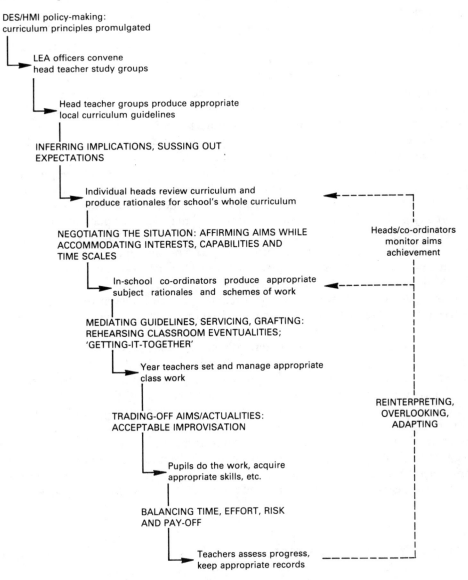

Figure 9.2 *Unacknowledged operations on the implementation staircase: situational competence highlighted.*

ordinators had to suss out the situation both outside and inside the school, and find some accommodation between internal and external interests and trends. (Not that these mental processes were in the form of deductions from explicit assumptions—what Sperber and Wilson 1985 term 'non-demonstrative inferences'.) Then, to get things moving, they had to negotiate unobtrusively with colleagues over interpretations of requirements, which, for example, 'had teeth'. Most of this negotiation was informal, with its effectiveness bound up with the extent to which the parties were sensitive to their respective degrees of confidence and capability. In following up heads' initial mobilizing of staff on the whole curriculum, co-ordinators had to be able to show rather than tell colleagues what was expected in their subject areas. In effect, they serviced colleagues' needs as they arose, rather than proffered advice.

It was evident, however, that these 'human relations skills' were only part of a wider competence needed. Heads and co-ordinators had to be knowledgeable enough about the import of policy documents to mediate them in relation to colleagues' differing 'stages of concern' (Hall and Loucks, 1978). But again this capability was insufficient in itself. Given colleagues' scope to find excuses for deferring action, heads and co-ordinators had to avoid initiatives that could justify a sense of 'overload'. Hence, in getting new schemes of work actually implemented, older texts had to be phased out while the use of fresh material was phased in. In short, the ability to manage time and collaborative effort was central. Not surprisingly, teachers found it difficult to articulate this ability in detail, encompassing as it did the management of pupil attention spans within school time slots, at one end of the scale, to the bearing in mind, at the other end, of long cycles of staff commitment, turnover and school governance. To think in detail about how to handle policy could be said to involve the artful orchestration of disparate time scales and tempos of teacher response.

Our argument here, we shall emphasize, is more in criticism of orthodoxies in curriculum discourse than a grounded assertion about teachers' thinking while planning. In answer to our questions about what steps they had taken, and then about what considerations they had in mind in so doing, heads and co-ordinators frequently emphasized timing and anticipation of colleagues' and pupils' reactions. The point seems trite but bears on the convention that planning curriculum is a distinctive process in which courses of action are inferred from educational goals. Our data showed what informal planning of change had in common with everyday inference and imagination. In thinking about the implementation of policy, teachers were envisaging contingencies and mentally rehearsing particular interactions with particular colleagues or groups of pupils. 'Skills of planning' seemed to involve judgements about what curriculum principles it was reasonable to sacrifice, given anticipated states of affairs. But there was no official vocabulary available to respect and promote such skills of judgement.

COMPLICITY OR COMPETENCE?

Now of course the move that we have made in distilling our case material and in incorporating it into a managerial diagram (as in Figure 9.2) needs explaining. We do so in terms of communicative intention, then of its convergence with a theory of institutional tendencies in schools.

The idea behind the diagram is to expand the discursive repertoires of those involved in curriculum development. Thus it does not disown the managerially serviceable view that curriculum planning and implementation can be conceptualized as a goal-driven, problem-solving cycle. At the same time, it superimposes a complementary conceptualization of the *unacknowledged* processes. By highlighting these, it indicates (1) that the 'cycle' can also be characterized in terms of non-official processes and understandings, which may transform predetermined goals; but (2) that the unacknowledged processes, if they are acknowledged, can be harnessed in the service of policy goals.

For example, our data showed how and why teachers' concern about policy was initially directed towards ascertaining what counted as an acceptable response, and was subsequently conditional, intermittent, and eventual in character. But to appreciate these tendencies need not detract from the value in development work of conceiving the long-term policy process as having *potential* goal-directedness and continuity; of thinking of teachers' thinking as being *purposive* rather than *purposeful*—of being oriented to satisfactory states of affairs or intentionalities, rather than to prior goals or discrete intentions.

Our material indicated that advisers, heads and co-ordinators all meet a similar problem: colleagues at the next step down in the implementation staircase are more concerned to pick up justificatory vocabularies than to analyse the planning and implementation skills that they need. But those vocabularies do scant justice to the complexity and disjointedness of the processes involved. It is for this reason that we suggest that, despite its association with a gritty managerial frame of mind, curriculum and policy discourse promote complicity rather than competence. That is, they draw teachers into deceptive *justification* of their practices at the expense of their franker *explication*—for example, of the interpretive appraisals, negotiations, and trade-offs that are necessary. Recognition of these skills is a prerequisite in the articulation of the wider competence that teachers need in responding constructively to external requirements.

This is not to say that teachers are accomplices in deception (or self-deception) in a pejorative sense. Complicity is not only a crucial ingredient in good manners, for example in sparing embarrassment to those we interact with. It is the means by which we establish cultural conventions—of which language is of course the most important—and sustain social relations, hierarchy, and institutional norms. Complicity in the use of descriptive conventions is readily understandable. Indeed, the conceptual point here is that our propensity to share understandings through adoption of descriptive conventions can be *too* effortless and spontaneous in some circumstances. Thus in most everyday interactions we move *unreflectively* in and out of descriptive conventions, without being able to articulate the ground rules for the application of those conventions. In most social life we depend more on direct inference about the conventions that the situation demands, rather than on our reflexive capacity to monitor those conventions.

It is because of this immediate 'situational intelligence' that dissociation between ways of talking/writing about what we do (discursive practice) and joint idioms of practical action (non-discursive practice) can develop (Giddens 1979). As a result, what is inferred to be acceptable to say in one social setting (for example, a formal curriculum planning group) may seem unacceptable in another setting (of relaxed conversation and humour). Thus there is often a fundamental difference between the descriptions used in what Goffman (1959) called the 'front' and the 'back regions' of institutional life. To draw upon the descriptions used in the latter within the social settings of the former will seem to compromise those involved. In the case of policy implementation, for a head teacher to acknowledge to an adviser or school governor that he thought about policy in terms of an accommodation of internal and external interests would compromise their professional relationship.

THE LOOSE-COUPLING PERSPECTIVE

If the tendency towards avoidance of compromising description and towards dissociation of discourse and practical conduct is so universal, why should it be a particular problem in the education system? We suggest that its special significance in curriculum policy can be freshly explored from the standpoint of 'loose-coupling theory' (Meyer and Rowan 1978). The shift of analytic viewpoint involved here originated in organization theory, but, paradoxically, derives its cogency from suggesting why practices in school are unlike those of most other organizations. Most other organizations have measurable ends and proven means, so practices are 'tightly coupled'. Loose-coupling theory claims to show why in schools there is an endemic discrepancy between what teachers claim they are doing when addressing those outside the school, and what teachers and pupils actually experience and have to do inside the school, as conditioned by its 'hidden' or 'operative curriculum'. This discrepancy develops because teachers find themselves espousing goals that are ambitious, broad, and often mutually conflicting, while having poorly articulated, poorly understood means for achieving those goals. Moreover, because in practice individual teachers interpret these broad goals very differently, school staff have to evolve working practices in which administrator, teacher and pupil activities are to be only loosely linked and infrequently monitored. Thus schools are unlike 'rational' work systems, which have interlocking activities and rapid feedback on goal achievement, such as factories, hospitals, the armed services. In the case of schools it is impracticable to assume, for example, close connection between the activities of (1) the production of plans for a course, (2) individual teacher use of plans in classroom circumstances, and (3) individual pupil response to individual teacher use of recommended aims. As a result teachers have to invest more time and effort than most other workers in coping with the lack of mesh and the chronic tensions that inevitably develop between such loosely coupled activities, since each has its situation-specific, means–end adjustments.

At the same time, teachers are expected to give business-like accounts of what they are about to outsiders. Thus the generalized, optimistic tenor of curriculum discourse helps teachers to build and sustain norms of confidence, convenient to both insiders and outsiders, in what schools are doing. However, school staff recognize that to advertise the practical difficulty of, for example, realizing their more ambitious publicly declared aims would impair professional mystique; and it could prompt interference damaging to the stability, continuity, and flexibility that the educational process needs. This relationship simultaneously creates 'discretionary space' in curriculum practice for the exercise of avoidance, putting-off, disowning and overlooking, as well as for the exercise of initiative, improvisation, and creative deviation. Users of curriculum discourse are drawn into a complicitous relationship that helps to buffer teachers from insecurity and acrimony.

CONCLUSION

The loose-coupling viewpoint enables us to recognize the basic problem of dissociation between curriculum discourse and curriculum practice: the lack of mesh between, on the one hand, the (planning-derived) protocols of procedure and vocabulary by means of which curricular matters are formally addressed, and, on the other hand, the idioms of everyday conduct through which the teachers of particular schools reconcile their own satisfactions, capabilities, and circumstances with external requirements and support. To understand this dissociation is to appreciate how the conventions that underlie curriculum writing and debate can be well adapted to public justification and course administration but segregated from the tacit norms that teachers draw upon in evolving working practices between themselves, administrators, their pupils, and the situations that they recurrently experience. This dissociation makes it difficult to articulate curriculum competence: the inevitable trade-offs between aims and actualities—by skilled rearrangement of constraints and opportunities and through juggling of time, energy, and resources—that teachers have to bring about. Such trade-offs, which become routinized and 'accepted', structure and characterize the operative (rather than espoused) curriculum of individual schools. It is the operative rather than documented curriculum of the school that most needs perceptive analysis and management, and that depends on developing a capacity for reflexive negotiation of practices.

In recognizing the kinds of interpretive judgements and adaptations that teachers have to make in using curriculum policy, we can see why the metaphor of curriculum 'delivery' inhibits sensitivity to what is really involved. That metaphor's connotation of efficient, replicable transmission of X to Y does no justice to the arts of interpreting abstract curriculum principles so as to make them usable within given school conditions and without subverting the mutual understandings and habits that constitute an operative curriculum.

We are not implying that the advisers, head teachers and co-ordinators who helped us in our research were 'trapped' in the complicitous conventions of curriculum and managerial discourse. As our material showed, they frequently moved in and out of these conventions via jokes, irony, and informal asides. But spasmodic movement between passing insight into one's total situation and discounting that insight by inserting one's thoughts into another frame of reference is no basis for articulating curriculum competence. This concept needs official recognition and expression as the capability that enables teachers to appraise situations, mentally rehearse interactions, influence colleagues, and design classroom activities; and, overall, to make adaptations and negotiate accommodations that have an educational direction.

REFERENCES

Berman, P. (1981) 'Educational Change: An Implementation Paradigm'. In Lehming and Kane (eds).

Brown, S. and McIntyre, D. (1982) 'Costs and Rewards of Innovation'. In Olson, J. (ed.) *Innovation in the Science Curriculum*. London: Croom Helm.

Department of Education and Science (DES) (1978) *Primary education in England*. London: HMSO.

Doyle, W. and Ponder, G. (1977) 'The practicality ethic in teacher decision-making'. *Interchange*, **8**(3), 1–12.

Fullan, M. (1981) *The Meaning of Educational Change*. Toronto: Ontario Institute for Studies in Education.

Giddens, A. (1979) *Central Problems of Social Theory*. London: Macmillan.

Goffman, E. (1959) *The Presentation of Self in Everyday Life*. New York: Doubleday.

Gumperz, J. J. (1982) *Discourse Strategies*. Cambridge: Cambridge University Press.

Hall, G. and Loucks, S. (1978) 'Teacher Concerns and Staff Development'. *Teachers College Record*, **80**(1), 36–53.

Hargreaves, A. (1978) 'The Significance of Classroom Coping Strategies'. In Barton, L. and Meighan, R. (eds) *Sociological Interpretation of Schooling and Classrooms*. Driffield, Yorks: Nafferton Press.

Lehming, R. and Kane, M. (eds) (1981) *Improving Schools: Using What We Know*. Beverley Hills, CA: Sage.

Leithwood, K. A., Russell, H. H., Clipsham, J. S., and Robinson, F. G. (1974) 'School Change: Stages, Constructs and Research Methodology'. *Interchange*, **5**(1), 33–48.

Leithwood, K. A. (ed.) (1982) *Studies in Curriculum Decision-Making*, Toronto: Ontario Institute for Studies in Education.

McLaughlin, M. W. (1976) 'Implementation as Mutual Adaptation: Change in Classroom Organisation'. *Teachers College Record*, **77**(3), 339–51.

Meyer, John W. and Rowan, B. (1978) 'The Structure of Educational Organisations'. In Meyer, M. W. (ed.) *Environments and Organizations*, San Francisco, CA: Jossey-Bass.

Olson, John (1980) 'Teacher Constructs and Curriculum Change'. *Journal of Curriculum Studies*, **12**, 1–12.

Skilbeck, M. (1984) *School-Based Curriculum Development*. London: Harper and Row.

Sperber, D. and Wilson, D. (1985) *Relevance: Communication and Cognition*. Oxford: Blackwell.

Westbury, I. (1973) 'Conventional Classrooms, Open Classrooms and the Technology of Teaching'. *Journal of Curriculum Studies*, **5**, 99–121.

Williams, Walter (1980) *The Implementation Perspective*. Berkeley, CA: University of California.

NAME INDEX

Abelson, R. P. 149
Ackoff, R. 97
Ade, W. 37
Amarel, M. 22–4, 108
Anderson, L. M. 22, 87, 156
Angus, M. J. 108, 111
Apple, M. 30, 54
Argyris, C. 98, 181
Atkinson, P. 31

Baker, E. L. 91
Ball, S. 30
Bartholomew, W. J. 26–7
Bateson, G. 162, 166
Baumrind, D. 28
Baxter, J. 110
Becher, R. 37
Becker, H. 22, 32
Ben-Peretz, M. 88
Bereiter, L. 139–40
Berlak, A. 23
Berlak, H. 23
Berliner, D. C. 7–8, 62, 69, 78, 151
Berman, P. 199
Biddle, B. J. 106
Bidwell, C. 53
Bloom, B. 72–3
Bohm, D. 163, 177
Bostrom, K. 187–8
Bransford, J. D. 130, 149
Bromme, R. 10, 127, 131, 138, 142
Brophy, J. E. 28, 126, 138
Brousseau, G. 140
Brown, O. 112
Brown, S. 197
Brück, H. 162
Bryan, W. 73
Buchmann, M. 115
Buckley, P. 87
Bussis, A. 22–4
Byrne, C. J. 107, 110

Calderhead, J. 15, 64, 130, 136
Carew, J. 30, 52
Carnahan, R. S. 95

Carpenter, T. P. 139
Carter, K. 10–11, 148, 150–4
Carter, V. L. 162
Chi, M. T. H. 62
Chittenden, E. 22–4, 108
Clandinin, D. J. 108
Clark, C. M. 8–9, 21–2, 87–97, 107, 127, 142–3, 147, 150
Clift, R. T. 111
Coates, T. J. 161
Connell, R. W. 27–31
Conners, R. D. 22
Cooper, H. M. 126
Cooper, J. M. 87
Copeland, W. 26, 29
Cushing, K. 62

Dahllof, U. 85
Dale, R. 26, 29–30
Davis, R. B. 139, 156
de Groot, A. D. 69
Delamont, S. 31
Denham, L. 140
Denscombe, M. 29–30
Densmore, M. 6–7
DES 198
Dewey, J. 99–100, 106, 110
Dobslaw, G. 127
Dornbusch, S. M. 126
Doyle, W. 2, 10–11, 28–9, 138–9, 148–56, 197
Dreeben, R. 29, 180
Dreitzel, H. P. 28
Duda, R. O. 79
Duffy, G. 22–3
Dunkin, M. J. 106

Eaton, J. F. 140, 156
Eaton, S. 12–13
Eddy, E. 29
Edgar, D. 30–1
Edwards, R. 52, 54
Eisner, E. W. 90
Elbaz, F. 22, 108
Ellis, A. 162, 165, 168
Elmore, J. L. 87–8, 93
Ericcson, K. A. 149

Erickson, F. 148
Erlwanger, S. H. 156
Etzioni, A. 52
Evertson, C. 28, 87, 126

Feiman-Nemsor, S. 22–6, 30, 115
Fenstermacher, G. 29, 106
Ferraro, C. O. 162
Floden, R. 22–3, 26, 30
Florio, S. 87
Fogarty, J. 127
Franks, J. J. 130, 149
Freud, A. 162
Fullan, M. 196
Fuller, F. F. 112

Gardner, H. 109
Gaskill, P. 37
Gauthier, D. P. 98
Gendlin, E. T. 163, 175
Geoffrey, W. 72
Gibson, R. 52
Giddens, A. 211
Ginsburg, M. 27
Giroux, H. 27, 30
Gitlin, A. 29–30, 54
Glaser, R. 62, 77
Goffman, E. 211
Goodlad, J. I. 91
Goodson, I. 30
Gracey, H. 24
Grant, C. 25–6, 29, 38
Green, A. 22, 29
Green, T. 106
Greene, M. 100
Greeno, J. G. 62, 72
Greenway, P. 22, 31
Grice, H. P. 130
Griffey, D. C. 62, 76
Griffin, G. 27
Grossman, P. 110, 114, 118
Gudmundsdottir, S. 110
Gump, P. V. 150
Gumperz, J. J. 201

Hackman, J. R. 138

Hage, K. 140
Hall, G. 210
Haller, E. 28
Hammersley, M. 23, 29, 52
Hargreaves, A. 204
Hargreaves, D. H. 3
Harnischfeger, A. 140
Harootunian, B. 91
Harré, R. 190–1
Harter, N. 73
Hashweh, M. Z. 109, 121
Hill, J. 95
Hodges, C. 26
Hofer, M. 126
Hofstädter, D. 162
Hogben, D. 25
Hömberg, E. 143
Hopf, D. 140
Housner, L. D. 62, 76
Hoy, W. 29, 37, 52
Huberman, M. 77

Ingvarson, L. 22, 31

Jackson, P. W. 8, 80, 85, 162
Janesick, V. 22
Joyce, B. R. 87, 91, 127
Judd, W. 188
Juhl, K. 127

Kane, M. 196
Katz, L. 26
Kearney, G. 161
Keddie, N. 22
Kerr, D. H. 98
Klein, M. F. 91
Kolodner, J. 75
Korthagen, F. A. J. 18

Lacey, C. 31, 37, 49–50
Lampert, M. 22
Larkin, R. 29
Lartner, S. 187
Lawson, M. 25
Lazarus, R. S. 162
Lehming, R. 196
Leinhardt, G. 62, 72, 108–9, 126, 143
Leithwood, K. A. 197, 199
Lesgold, A. M. 79
Liebermann, A. 140
Lightfoot, S. L. 30, 52
Little, J. W. 30
Lortie, D. C. 3, 24–5, 80, 180
Loucks, S. 210
Lundgren, U. P. 85

McArthur, J. 29
McCutcheon, G. 88
McIntyre, D. 197
McIntyre, D. J. 27
McLaughlan, M. W. 196
McLeod, M. A. 93
McNair, K. 127
McPherson, G. 29
Maddox, H. 25

Mahoney, M. J. 162
Mardle, G. 25
Marland, P. W. 22
Marton, F. 109
Meichenbaum, D. 162
Metz, M. 24, 30, 52
Meyer, J. W. 212
Miller, G. A. 161–2, 167
Möbius, E. 162
Morine-Dershimer, G. 15, 87, 91, 126
Munby, H. 24

Natriello, G. 126
NEA 162
Newberry, J. 30
Newell, A. 87
NIE 5, 85–6
Nietzche, F. 166
Norman, D. A. 109

Ohlsson, S. 79
Oldenbürger, H. 126
Olson, J. K. 12–13, 180–2, 192, 197
Ortony, A. 139

Peck, L. 162
Pedulla, J. J. 126
Peterson, P. L. 21–2, 91, 94, 97, 107, 127, 142–3, 147
Petty, M. 25
Pollard, A. 28, 31
Ponder, G. 29, 197
Popham, J. W. 91
Popkewitz, T. 27, 31
Post, T. A. 79
Powell, M. 162
Pylypiw, J. 93

Raether, W. 162
Raths, J. 26
Rees, W. 37
Reid, W. A. 98, 182
Resnick, L. B. 109
Reynolds, J. 13–14
Richert, A. R. 9, 110, 114
Robbins, D. 95
Romberg, T. A. 139
Ross, R. P. 151
Rowan, B. 212
Rumelhart, D. E. 139, 149

Sabers, D. 62
Sarason, S. 26
Saunders, M. 13–14
Schank, R. C. 149
Scheffler, I. 106
Schon, D. A. 3, 80, 96, 98, 100, 118, 179–81
Schultz, J. 87, 148
Schwab, J. J. 111, 113
Schwille, J. 52
Sendelbach, N. B. 89, 93
Sharp, R. 22, 29
Shavelson, R. J. 72, 97, 108, 142

Shortliffe, E. H. 79
Shroyer, J. C. 128, 136
Shulman, L. S. 9, 78, 108, 110, 114
Simon, H. A. 87, 98, 149
Simpson, B. 188
Sinclair, K. E. 161
Sirotnik, K. 24
Skilbeck, M. 196
Smith, B. O. 106
Smith, D. A. 108–9
Smith, E. L. 89, 93
Smith, L. C. 72
Sperber, D. 209
Stein, P. 62
Steinberg, R. 110
Steinbring, H. 142
Stephens, J. 25
Stern, P. 97, 108, 142
Sykes, G. 118

Tabachnick, B. R. 6–7, 21–5, 27, 30–1, 38
Taylor, P. H. 90
Teitelbaum, K. 38
Thoreson, C. E. 161
Thorndyke, P. W. 131
Tikunoff, W. J. 87
Trabasso, T. 149
Travers, R. 23
Tuska, S. 25
Tyler, R. W. 89

Uttendorfer-Marek, I. 172

Vallance, E. 87, 91
Voigt, J. 140
Voss, J. F. 79

Wagner, A. C. 11–12
Walker, M. 25
Wang, M. C. 126
Ward, B. A. 87
Warren, R. 30–1
Watzlawick, P. 162, 166
Weick, K. 53
Weidenmann, B. 162
Westbury, I. 29, 204
Whiteside, M. T. 25
Wiggins, D. 100–1
Wiley, D. E. 140
Williams, W. 196
Wilson, D. 209
Wilson, S. M. 9, 118
Winkel, R. 162
Wise, A. 30, 54
Wright, B. 25

Yinger, R. J. 8–9, 15, 87–8, 92, 95, 97, 150
Young, R. E. 22

Zahorik, J. A. 90–1, 94
Zeichner, K. 6–7, 21–31, 38, 158

SUBJECT INDEX

Academic work 10, 148, 152
Accountability
  see Teacher
Activities 87, 90, 156
Activity structures 72, 151
Automaticity 73

Behaviour
  expressive 190–2
  instrumental 190–2
Behavioural objectives 90

Classroom
  ecology 2, 10, 29, 138, 179
  learning 18, 106–7, 139–40, 157
  management 11, 74, 150
Cognitive psychology 5, 8, 15, 81, 105, 110,
    139–40, 149
Computers 12, 181–6
Criterion referenced tests 44
Curriculum
  guidelines 13
  implementation 16, 153, 195–213
  innovation 4, 12, 14, 17, 179–93
  planning 90, 195–213
  studies 5

Diagnosis 9, 96
Dilemmas 11, 34, 39, 180
Double binds 167

Expert systems 79–80
Expertise 61, 69

'Framing' 8, 99

'Grooving' 72

Hidden curriculum
  in teacher education 26–7
HMI 198–9

Implicit theories 6, 15, 22
Innovation
  see Curriculum
Institutional control 52–5
Instructional flow 10, 143, 153
Internalized adjustment 50–1

'Knots' 11–12
  model of 168
  resolution of 171–5
  types of 162–5
Knowledge
  acquisition 139
  bases 105, 113, 118
  craft knowledge 21–31
  pedagogical content 9, 16, 114, 118
  practical 108, 125
  professional 6, 15, 106
  of pupils 7, 10, 16, 64–9, 125–44
  structures 147, 149
  of subject matter 4, 9, 104–22, 127, 141
  typificatory 7, 63–4
Knowledge-in-action 3, 9, 80

LEA policy 14, 198
LOGO 182, 184–5, 188–91
Loose-coupling 53, 212

Metacognitive skills 61
Methodology
  see Research methodology

NIE 5, 85–6

Parents 1, 42, 48
Pedagogical laboratories 8, 78
Pedagogical reasoning, 9, 118–21
Performance Based Education 44, 46
Practical problems 98
Practical reasoning 100–1
  see also Knowledge
Professions
  decision-making in 1–3, 80, 84, 99
  research on 98
Protocol analysis 5
Psychoanalysis 11, 15
Pupils'
  conceptions 18
  misconceptions 10, 156–7
  problem-solving 12–13, 44
  understanding 9, 11, 125–43

Reflective teaching
  see Teaching

Research methodology 5, 15, 33, 62–3, 111, 130–1, 149–50
Reward system 10, 154–7

SCIS 89
Socialization, theories of 24–5
Sociology of education 5
Steering group 85
Stimulated recall 5, 18, 130–1
Strategic redefinition 50–1
Subject co-ordinators 4, 14, 199, 205–7
Subject matter
    see Knowledge
Symbolic interaction 6, 15, 21
Systematic observation 5

Task demands 138, 147–8, 150
Teacher(s)
    accountability 4
    affect 161–2
    anxiety 12
    beliefs 21–2, 39
    constraints on 7, 10, 21, 24, 28, 37, 42, 53–5, 141, 184, 206, 213
    cultures 23, 24, 29–31, 52
    decision-making 1, 84, 108, 114, 127, 147, 156
    expert 7, 61–81
    ideology 5

judgements 108, 126
knowledge, *see* Knowledge
language for 4, 81
novice 7, 61–81, 104, 112
perspectives 21–2, 32, 36
postulant 7, 62–81
professional development 17–18, 26, 28
routines 7, 16, 71–2, 77, 92, 141, 179, 190
schema 8, 61, 77, 109, 126, 149
scripts 72, 77
socialization 24–55
training 17, 75–9, 158, 175–6
values 21
Teaching
    authoritarian 43, 176
    difficulties in 78
    expertise in 60, 76, 109
    flexibility in 94
    interactive 8
    metaphors of 1–3, 96, 213
    pre-active 8
    progressive 23
    quality 137
    reflection in 12, 18, 81, 99–101, 120, 187
    student teaching 32–49
    traditional 23
Technical control 53–4
Technical rationality 96–7, 179